1u

Fueling Freedom

FUELING FREEDOM

EXPOSING
THE MAD WAR ON
ENERGY

STEPHEN MOORE AND KATHLEEN HARTNETT WHITE

REGNERY
PUBLISHING
A Division of Salem Media Group

Regnery® is a registered trademark of Salem Communications Holding Corporation

Cataloging-in-Publication data on file with the Library of Congress

ISBN 978-1-62157-409-5

Published in the United States by
Regnery Publishing
A Division of Salem Media Group
300 New Jersey Ave NW
Washington, DC 20001
www.Regnery.com

Manufactured in the United States of America

10 9 8 7 6 5 4 3 2 1

Books are available in quantity for promotional or premium use. For information on discounts and terms, please visit our website: www.Regnery.com.

Distributed to the trade by
Perseus Distribution
250 West 57th Street
New York, NY 10107

To my new wife, Anne, who is my
personal unrelenting source of energy.
—Stephen Moore

In honor of and in appreciation for my late parents,
Mary Clare and Andrew Stone Hartnett.
—Kathleen Hartnett White

CONTENTS

PROLOGUE

I n this book, you will learn why most of what you think you know about energy—and what our kids are being taught about energy—is flat-out wrong. In one of the great ironies of history, a frantic global movement to eliminate fossil fuels—the foundation of modern life—has achieved comprehensive power throughout the developed world at the very moment when the supply of those resources, especially in the United States, has exploded. Here are some of the astonishing facts about America's bountiful energy future:

America has more recoverable energy supplies than any nation—by far. We have more oil and natural gas than Saudi Arabia, Iran, Russia, China, and all of the OPEC nations *combined*.

Thanks to the shale oil and gas revolution, America will never run out of energy. We have hundreds of years' worth of oil, natural gas, and coal—with existing technologies.

The revolutionary drilling technologies pioneered here in America—including horizontal drilling and hydraulic fracturing—have more than doubled recoverable U.S. energy supplies. Contrary to false reports in the media, virtually no documented environmental problems have been associated with fracking—ever.

By the year 2020 the United States can be energy independent for the first time in half a century. With the pro-America energy policy outlined in this book, America will be the dominant energy producer in the world, and OPEC will be brought to its knees.

At least fifty trillion dollars' worth of recoverable energy—the greatest storehouse of treasure in history—lies beneath federal lands and federal water. Drilling for these resources will create millions of new American jobs and could increase the growth rate of GDP from 2 percent to 4 percent or more.

The federal government will collect three to ten trillion dollars in royalties from oil, natural gas, and coal resources over the next thirty years. Producing American energy is the single best means of balancing the federal budget, eliminating our trade deficit, and retiring our nineteen-trillion-dollar national debt.

Wind and solar power—so-called "green energy"—are niche energy sources that meet less than 3 percent of our needs, even with hundreds of billions of dollars in taxpayer subsidies. President Obama's own Energy Department admits that even if we continue those enormous subsidies, less than 10 percent of our energy will come from wind and solar by 2030. We will be highly reliant on fossil fuels for at least the next several decades.

INTRODUCTION

Power Up

A powerful summer storm swept through Northern Virginia a few years ago, leaving more than a million homes without electric power for days. One of those homes belonged to the Moore family. The sweltering July temperature hovered around a hundred degrees, and it was so humid you felt like you needed gills to breathe.

"Sure, we're miserable," Steve joked to his three children, "but look at the bright side. Think how much we've reduced our carbon footprint! Consider it a life lesson in what it means to live green." They saw no humor in that. Without Facebook, ESPN, and air conditioning, they felt like they had surrendered their basic human rights.

One night the family all sat on the couch, sweating and talking. At first, it had been a rustic adventure. Grilling their food on the barbecue. Reading by candlelight. Playing flashlight tag inside the house. But the novelty wore off quickly. "What did people do before the age of electricity?" one of the kids asked. "I would have killed myself," he moaned, only half joking.

Electrical power is the central nervous system of our modern economy and our twenty-first-century lifestyles, and living without it for a few days is a reminder of how vulnerable we are to being sent back to a pre-industrial age. Yet every initiative of the so-called green movement is intended to reduce our access to electrical power—although they never admit that explicitly.

The power outage that gave the Moore family a new appreciation for the electricity that powers our lives was caused by Mother Nature. But we are convinced that rolling brownouts are coming—especially in states like California, which are trying to rely on unreliable green energy sources—thanks to the radical environmentalists who have achieved a choke-hold on our politics.

Green groups, for example, have declared war on coal, which still produces nearly 40 percent of our electricity. The Obama administration is listening and has slammed the brakes on coal production. Technological progress is making this cheap and domestically abundant energy source cleaner all the time. Yet the global-warming alarmist James Hansen, a scientist at NASA, has compared the railroad cars carrying coal across our country to the "death trains" that transported Jews to Nazi concentration camps.

Natural gas is our second major source of electrical energy. The technological miracle of hydraulic fracturing—"fracking"—has given us hundreds of years' worth of this clean-burning fuel that reduces greenhouse gas emissions. But the Sierra Club is vowing to shut down natural gas too. Regulations by the Environmental Protection Agency against methane (natural gas) could seriously impair our use of natural gas. The anti-fracking movement spreads (groundless) fear about contaminated water, but as the Moore family discovered, when you lose electricity you often lose access to potable water.

Of course, Big Green hates oil and nuclear power too. That's why we're not drilling for oil in many parts of Alaska or on other energy-rich federal lands and waters and why we're not building the Keystone XL pipeline. This is public policy that is not just anti-growth but dangerous to our health and safety.

Sadly, schoolchildren are the target of propaganda about "saving the planet" with alternative energy sources. If global warming is a threat, we will be saved not by building windmills or riding our bicycles to work, but by applying advanced technology and *electrical power* to find ways to keep the planet cool. That isn't going to happen because of regulatory dictates from the United Nations or the White House.

Many Americans believe the green fairy tale that things were better in the past than they are now. Sure, the economy has been weak for many years now—poverty is too high, wages are stagnant. But seventy-two hours without air conditioning, TV, a dishwasher, a hair dryer, and Google taught the Moores how much progress has been made in the past twenty, thirty, and fifty years. Today the percentage of people below the poverty line who have air conditioning is higher than the percentage of middle-class families who had it in 1960.

Anyone who thinks that we can get the power we need for our modern society from "clean, renewable" sources like wind and solar power is living in a world of make-believe. After tens of billions of dollars in subsidies, these sources provide 4.3 percent of our electricity. Most of the rest comes from fossil fuels. A rapid rush to renewables in Germany has led to retail electric prices three times the average U.S. rate. You can't power a $15-trillion economy with wind and solar power.

The Master Resource

The story of human advancement is the story of the discovery of cheap, plentiful, and versatile energy. Fossil fuels are the ignition switch to modern life. Almost all other inventions—the steam engine, the printing press, life-saving medicines, the microchip, the iPhone, you name it—are derivatives of electric power. Where electricity is in wide use, there is prosperity. Where electricity is lacking, poverty and deprivation are the norm.

For many centuries mankind relied on what is now called "renewable energy"—windmills, wood, water, and the sun. The notion that green energy is "in its infancy" is laughable. These sources of energy go back thousands of years. And the data recently gathered by economic historians surveyed in this book show that wind and water wheels never provided much power. It wasn't until man harnessed fossil fuels—predominantly oil, gas, and coal—that industrialization achieved unprecedented productivity.

Fossil fuels proved to be abundant sources of energy, scalable and reliable in a way that many forms of renewable energy are not. Christopher Horner of the Competitive Enterprise Institute likes to say that you can build windmills with steel, but you can't build steel with windmills. The great steel works of Pittsburgh could not have built America's industrial framework if their power had come from windmills. Detroit's automobiles could not have replaced horses (and horse manure) if they had run on solar power.

Energy, in short, is the wellspring of mankind's greatest advances.

With this book we aim to document and explain the extent to which fossil fuels have vastly improved human life across the world, releasing whole populations from abject poverty. Virtually everything needed to sustain the life of a human being—food, heat, clothing, shelter—depends upon access to and conversion of energy. The productivity fueled by hydrocarbon energy sources, coupled with economic freedom, allowed the emergence of an enduring middle class for the first time in history.

Today, hundreds of years after the Industrial Revolution began, most of the human population is dependent on fossil fuels for 80 to 90 percent of its energy supply. That will surely be the case at least for many decades. The long-held superstition that America is running out of oil and gas has been disproved with the latest shale oil and gas revolution.

Throughout history, elites, of course, have enjoyed comfortable wealth. They were rich; they could afford expensive energy. They weren't the ones who did without light or heat or transportation or enough food and leisure time. Someone else did the back-breaking and time-consuming work for them. The women and children would spend hours every day fetching the water from the river. But for all but the very wealthy, life before fossil fuels was grindingly difficult. Cheap energy narrowed that quality-of-life gap as no one could have imagined.

But now that energy is more abundant than ever, it has come under severe and unrelenting assault. The unprecedented stakes in today's contentious energy policy debates about carbon are not just economic but moral. Europe has started deindustrializing. The governments of many of the most developed countries in the world have mandated as rapid a transition as possible from carbon-rich energy to zero-carbon energy like wind, solar, and biomass. The inherent limitations of wind and solar are physically intractable. We are facing a regression to the limited energy horizons of pre-industrial societies.

Never before have the rulers of a society intentionally driven it backward to scarcer, more expensive, and less efficient energy. Every previous energy transition has made electric power and transportation fuels cheaper and more efficient. What goes by the name of a green energy revolution will for the first time in modern times disrupt energy reliability and raise prices for financially-strapped families. And these people call themselves "progressives"!

Green energy policies assume centralized control of the sources, production, and consumption of energy, and that means centralized control over all economic activity and consumer choice. Name a product that doesn't depend on affordable and reliable energy. United Nations bureaucrats talk about "wisely planned [energy] austerity," guided by apparently omniscient "planetary managers." Not only is our material prosperity in peril; freedom itself is at stake.

Please read on and make up your own mind. We have two energy paths to choose from. With the facts before you, we're confident the right choice will be obvious.

ENERGY AT A CROSSROADS
Doomslayers vs. Doomsayers[1]

Planet of the Powerless

In the blockbuster movie *Dawn of the Planet of the Apes*, the bands of humans resisting a global government of super-intelligent apes have been deprived of electricity, making their struggle nearly impossible. They are rendered powerless—literally. The apes understand that depriving the humans of electricity will keep them in a state of submission. In the film's climax, men heroically reopen a power plant in San Francisco, bringing electricity back to the whole city. Now they can resume industrial production and fight back.

The not so subtle and perhaps inadvertent message from that Hollywood film is that without abundant energy, we return to the Stone Age. The harnessing of electricity transformed human life, homes, and work. The enterprising, inventive man who literally vanquished darkness, Thomas Edison, deserves a position high on the list of humanity's greatest doomslayers. A versatile, convenient, and clean source of heat, light, and power, electricity is now the nervous system of civilization. Without it, we are helpless.

Dawn of the Planet of the Apes is an entertaining reminder of the vulnerability of the power on which prosperous societies depend. Before we submit without a whimper to climate policies that would supplant the carbon-rich energy on which we rely with weak and parasitic renewable energy, we should look carefully at the many services that abundant, affordable energy contributes to our lives.

The agenda of the so-called green movement, one of the most influential political forces in America today, does not end with carbon-based energy. It is a war on free-market economics. In the summer of 2015, major environmental groups gathered in Venezuela to solve leading ecological problems like global warming, concluding, "The structural causes of climate change are linked to the current capitalist hegemonic system." Their anti-industrialism would send us to a Planet of the Apes future where energy is rationed—though elites could opt out by buying paper carbon credits to avoid the austerity imposed on the rest of us. This agenda, history has shown, is a recipe for killing economic growth, stifling innovation, and harshly authoritarian government.[2]

Why would anyone choose such a grim future with so much success behind us and with such energy promise at hand?

The Great Facts of the Great Energy Enrichment

Our book begins by recognizing the "Great Fact" of human progress depicted in Figure 1.1 on page 5. Something monumental happened around 1800, something that had never happened before. For millennia, the average human life was short and lived at subsistence level. The growth of the human population was slower than a crawl. But in the nineteenth century, there began a substantial and sustained improvement in the fundamental measures of human well-being.

Economists and historians are familiar with the historic effects of the Industrial Revolution. But few people appreciate that this spectacular

Wisdom from *The Rational Optimist*

In his book *The Rational Optimist*, Matt Ridley makes a lively case for how profound human progress has been:

> Since 1800, the population of the world has more than doubled and real incomes have risen more than nine times. Taking a shorter perspective, in 2005, compared to 1955, the average human being on Planet Earth earned nearly three times as much money (corrected for inflation), ate one-third more calories of food, buried one-third as many of her children and could expect to live one-third longer. She was less likely to die as a result of war, murder, childbirth, accidents, tornadoes, flooding, famine, whooping cough, tuberculosis, malaria, diphtheria, typhus, typhoid, measles, small pox, scurvy, or polio. She was less likely, at any given age, to get cancer, heart disease, or stroke. She was more likely to be literate and to have finished school. She was more likely to own a telephone, a flush-toilet, a refrigerator, and a bicycle. All this during a half century when the world population more than doubled, so that far from being rationed by population pressure, the goods and services available to the people of the world have expanded. It is, by any standard, an astonishing human achievement.[3]

Almost none of this progress would have been possible without the kind of energy in fossil fuels.

improvement in the human condition is really a story of the fossil fuels revolution. The world moved away from inefficient and limited "green" energy like the medieval windmill to coal and other modern forms of energy that could be adopted on an industrial scale. Fossil fuels were a necessary condition of the Industrial Revolution's unprecedented improvements.

Despite all the doomsday predictions of recent history—famine, peak oil, overpopulation, and global warming—look at the staggering record of sustained material advance and economic growth since 1800. And the marvel of it all is that these advances have most benefited the poor! A little more than a century ago, it was common for mothers helplessly to watch their infants die from what we would consider a common cold. The average person today lives more than three times longer than our ancestors did in 1800.

The graph of global progress on page 5 charts four basic measures of human welfare over the past two thousand years—life expectancy, real income per capita, population, and energy consumption. Emissions of carbon dioxide resulting from human activity are here used as a surrogate for consumption of energy derived from fossil fuels. Before the Industrial Revolution, man-made emissions of carbon dioxide were marginal. The United States now uses about two hundred times more energy than in 1800, and almost all of it comes from fossil fuels.

Is it not startling that most of humanity had been stuck with a real average income of $1–7 per day until the past two centuries?[4] Throughout history, a small group of privileged persons, of course, could afford expensive energy. They weren't the ones who would do without light or heat or transportation or enough food and leisure time. Someone else would do the back-breaking and time-consuming work for them. But for everyone else before the age of fossil fuels, life was indeed "poor, nasty, brutish, and short," in the memorable words of Thomas Hobbes.[5]

The almost vertical trajectory of our graph that begins around 1800 coincides with the beginning of the English Industrial Revolution. Some would vilify this breakthrough as nothing more than a bunch of steel cathedrals, assembly lines, and dark plumes of pollution—the infrastructure for what critics consider now excessive consumption. Such emblems, however, mask the physical dynamics of the great change—an energy enrichment that spawned phenomenal economic productivity and dramatic improvements in human living conditions.

What textbooks call the Industrial Revolution might be better described as mankind's Great Energy Enrichment—a massive increase in the availability of versatile energy. As the historian Carlo Cibolla explains, "the Industrial Revolution can be defined as the process by which a society acquired control over vast sources of inanimate energy."[6] Those sources were fossil fuels, first coal in England, soon followed by natural gas, and then crude oil in the early twentieth century.

Average real income per capita—on a global basis—is now ten to twenty times higher than at the beginning of the Industrial Revolution. The classical economists writing in the early days of industrialization—Adam

FIGURE 1.1

Global Progress, 1 AD–2009 AD

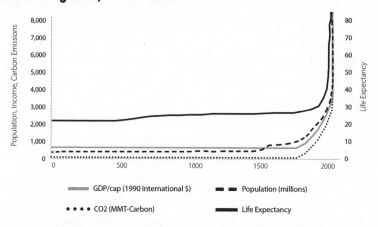

Sources: Updated from Indur Goklany, "Have Increases in Population, Affluence and Technology Worsened Human and Environmental Well-being?" Electronic Journal of Sustainable Development 1, no. 3 (2009); based on Bruce W. Frier (2001). "More is worse: some observations on the population of the Roman empire", in Walter Scheidel, Debating Roman Demography, URL = https://books.google.com/books?id=vh3pmAodawEC&pg=PA144#v=onepage&q&f=false; Angus Maddison, Statistics on World Population, GDP and Per Capita GDP, 1-2008 AD, University of Groningen, 2010, http://www.ggdc.net/MADDISON/Historical_Statistics/vertical-file_02-2010.xls; World Bank, World Development Indicators 2015, http://databank.worldbank.org/; T.A. Boden, R. J. Andres, Global CO2 Emissions from Fossil-Fuel Burning, Cement Manufacture, and Gas Flaring, 1751-2011, at http://cdiac.ornl.gov/ftp/ndp030/global.1751_2011.ems, visited December 15, 2015; CDIAC, Preliminary 2011 and 2012 Global & National Estimates, at http://cdiac.ornl.gov/ftp/trends/co2_emis/Preliminary_CO2_emissions_2012.xlsx, visited February 2, 2016. Notes: Data are sporadic until 1960. This figure assumes that trends between adjacent data points are linear. Life expectancy is a surrogate for human well-being; living standards are depicted by affluence, or GDP per capita; and CO2 is a proxy for fossil-fuel usage.

Smith, David Ricardo, Thomas Malthus, and John Stuart Mill—assumed that wages would *decrease* as the population grew, a reasonable assumption before the great energy enrichment, when the three factors in production were land, labor, and capital. A continually growing population would eventually outstrip the agricultural capacity of a finite amount of land. The classical economists did not foresee that man-made energies would replace land and labor as production factors. As we shall see in later chapters, man-made energies vastly amplified the economic fruits of land and the productivity of labor, operating as a form of (energy) capital.

In our graph of human progress, population barely increases over the first millennium AD. Between the years 1000 and 1750, the global population increases substantially, tripling to 760 million. But from 1750 to 2009, population rises eightfold, to almost seven billion human beings—a decisive departure from all previous epochs. The many predictions, from Malthus in the 1790s to Paul Ehrlich in the 1970s, that a rapidly increasing population would lead to catastrophic famine were completely wrong. Indeed, "Never in human history," writes Indur Goklany, "had indicators of human well-being advanced so rapidly."[7]

Never before has mankind been better nourished. As we shall show, you can thank fossil fuels for a global food supply that exceeds the demand of more than seven billion mouths. Access to food may be limited by geography or political corruption, but the supply itself is sufficient to meet the nutritional needs of all humanity. In America, we produce three times as much food as we did a century ago, in one-third fewer manhours, on one-third fewer acres, and at one-third the cost. In the past, more than half of Americans were employed in agriculture, and food was still relatively scarce and expensive. Now about 3 percent of the population produces all the food that three hundred million Americans consume. We even often have to pay farmers to stop growing so much food.

The same graph also depicts the unprecedented economic growth driven by industrialization. The economic historian Deirdre McCloskey puts it in perspective: "The scientific fact established over the past fifty years by the labors of economists and economic historians is that modern economic growth has been astounding, unprecedented, unexpected, the greatest surprise in economic history."[8]

Economic growth and increased energy consumption were tightly connected over the past century. In 2000, the correlation between energy consumption and income per capita measured across sixty-three countries was an extremely close 96 percent.[9] "Each variable shows an advance of approximately sixteenfold in one hundred years, with energy consumption rising from about 22 to 355 EJ [exajoules], and the world economic product increasing from $2 to $32 trillion."[10] The rise of the gross world product from $2 to $32 trillion within a century is nothing less than astonishing.

While almost no one questions the magnitude of the economic growth that accompanied the Industrial Revolution, little is said about the energy enrichment that is still fueling modern economic growth. All the talk about decarbonizing ignores the ongoing role of energy in producing the economic growth that has released billions from intractable poverty for the first time in human history.

As Michael Kelly, a fellow of the Royal Society, reminds us, "A decarbonized global economy is going to have to outperform the achievement of fossil fuels. If not, mankind's progress will have to go into reverse in terms of aggregate standard of living. We should be honest and upfront about the sheer scale and enormity of the challenge implied by decarbonization."[11]

As revealing as our graph of human progress is, it doesn't convey one of the greatest benefits of the modern world's energy-driven economic growth. Those who have gained the most from that growth have not been the wealthiest but the poorest. With the Industrial Revolution, McCloskey points out, "[f]or the first time the economy performed for the People instead of mainly for the Privileged."[12] From the beginning, it was not the aristocracy, clerisy, warrior class, or industrial titans who gained the most but the average worker and the most impoverished. No longer was intractable poverty the common lot of mankind. An enduring middle class emerged. The historian Robert Fogel concludes that "the average real income of the bottom fifth of the [American] population has multiplied some twenty-fold [over the twentieth century], several times more than the gain realized by the rest of the population."[13]

The United States has long been envied as the nation with the highest standard of living. Just what might that standard mean? In 1875, the average American family spent 74 percent of its income on food, clothing, and shelter, not unlike the rest of the world. In 1995, the same American family spent 13 percent of its income for these fundamental necessities.[14] Discretionary income fuels freedom and material progress!

Many traditional economists downplay the importance of energy for economic growth or subsume the energy factor among others, such as the division of labor, economic freedom, innovative technology, or commercial ethics. Yet without the exponential increase in power, harnessed in innovative mechanical devices, the productivity distinguishing the Industrial Revolution and its aftermath would have been impossible.

Matt Ridley captures the importance of the energy factor: "By 1870, the burning of coal in Britain was generating as many calories as would have been expended by 850 million laborers. It was as if each worker had twenty servants at his beck and call. The capacity of the country's steam engines alone was equivalent to six million horses.... That is how much energy had been harnessed to the application of the division of labor. That is how impossible the task of the British nineteenth-century miracle would have been without fossil fuels."[15]

Fossil fuel was one of several conditions for modern growth, but it was a necessary condition, especially for the sustained economic growth that followed the industrial breakthrough. Coal, oil, and natural gas offered far more than pre-industrial energy sources like wind and wood could—a vast store of concentrated, versatile, reliable, controllable, portable energy.

Climate Policies and the Assault on Prosperity

Most green energy policies undermine human progress. They are regressive, disproportionately hurting low- and middle-income families by driving energy prices higher, thus eroding their standard of living.

As the Obama administration was drawing to a close, the lower end of middle-class income in the United States appeared to be sliding toward the poverty level. Numbers released by the Social Security Administration in the fall of 2015 revealed that 51 percent of all U.S. workers were making less than $30,000 a year—only twenty-five hundred a month after taxes. Income for middle-class families declined by 3 percent on Obama's watch, and the average worker went ten years without a raise.[16] In such an economic environment, is it conceivable that our leaders would push even harder in pursuit of their green dreams?

For the Obama White House, it has been full speed ahead with this destructive agenda. Although Congress has repeatedly declined to give the Environmental Protection Agency the authority to regulate carbon dioxide, the EPA has arrogated this power to itself with its so-called Clean Power Plan, a two-thousand-page set of regulations that is already threatening the nation's vast and intricate system of electric power.

The plan is futile—all pain and no gain. By EPA's own admission, the mandated carbon cuts will not meaningfully reduce predicted warming. Gina McCarthy, the administrator of EPA, justifies it as a gesture of sacrifice by the wealthiest country in the world. Americans should embrace economic decline for its symbolic value? Even before the Clean Power Plan took effect, many coal-fired power plants had closed and major coal companies had declared bankruptcy, at a cost of thousands of jobs. In response, President Obama, by executive action, froze coal production on federal lands, where 40 percent of total U.S. production is located.[17]

The Left's strategy is to make American coal so expensive that the industry can't survive in global markets. The environmentalists want an utterly debilitating "production tax" of as much as $40 a ton. Colin Marshall, the chairman of Cloud Peak Energy, a major U.S. coal producer, didn't mince words when he said that Obama "has chosen to pander to special-interest groups whose stated goal is to shut down the U.S. coal industry"—and the economies of our coal-producing states— Illinois, Ohio, Kentucky, Pennsylvania, West Virginia, Wyoming, and Montana—be damned.

In addition to killing Americans jobs and raising utility bills by hundreds and perhaps thousands of dollars a year per family, shutting down the U.S. coal industry will actually harm the environment. Clean coal technologies have sharply reduced emissions of lead, sulphur, soot, and carbon monoxide. The air we breathe today is much cleaner than in previous decades. More importantly, U.S. coal is much cleaner than Chinese coal and that produced in other nations. The Clean Power Plan will reduce consumption of clean coal and increase the burning of dirty coal.

President Obama and some leaders of the wealthiest countries in the world are adamant about phasing out fossil fuels when there are *no alternative energy sources* capable of providing the countless goods and services that fossil fuels make possible. Modern societies remain utterly dependent on fossil fuels. See Figure 1.2. The climate crusade is indeed a mad war on human welfare.

FIGURE 1.2

Global Energy Consumption (2013)

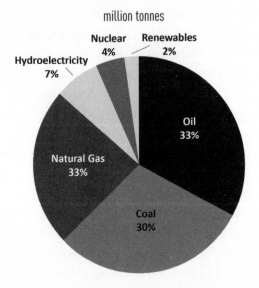

million tonnes

Nuclear 4%   Renewables 2%

Hydroelectricity 7%

Oil 33%

Natural Gas 33%

Coal 30%

Source: BP Statistical Review of World Energy 2014, www.bp.com/statisticalreview

The Choice: Economic Growth or Decline?

Two powerful but conflicting forces are contending for the future of the American economy and indeed of our very way of life. On one side is the shale revolution, which has unlocked a vast store of oil and natural gas, refuting those who insist that we are running out of energy. In less than six years, the United States has laid claim to a globally dominating supply of oil and natural gas. In a development that was unimaginable only a few years ago, America had become the largest energy producer in the world by 2013. This "shale gale" is the achievement of optimistic, determined people operating in a competitive market. These gutsy entrepreneurs slew the boogeymen of "peak oil" and "sustainability" without grandiose government plans or subsidies.

On the other side are climate mandates formulated and imposed by government functionaries—mandates rejected by our elected representatives in Congress. The goal of climate policies is to eliminate the coal, oil, and natural gas on which the world relies for 80 to 90 percent of its energy. In a glaring contrast to the shale revolution, the climate crusade is driven by activists, politicians, bureacrats, and "experts" whose only means of realizing their dream is government power. Climate policies all assume the centralized governance of energy production and consumption, unavoidably constraining economic growth and personal liberty.

The contrast between these two forces is stark and simple. The shale energy boom increased the economic pie. Taxpayer-subsidized green energy shrinks the economic pie. The kind of economic growth we take for granted in the modern world would have been impossible if we had been limited to sources of energy that depend on taxpayer subsidies. Climate policies to decarbonize human society augur energy scarcity, exponentially higher prices for basic goods, loss of personal freedoms, and an end to the prosperity achieved in the twentieth century that has lifted billions out of grinding poverty.

The Clean Power Plan is not merely another heavy-handed, expensive environmental regulation. It is nothing less than a federal take over of our nation's entire electric sector.[18] Most people don't recognize the stakes of the global warming crusade. Current climate policies do not aim for a modest reduction of carbon emissions. Their goal is to "decarbonize" human society. And for what? Even the architects of these schemes admit that the green plans don't work. According to the calculations of the UN's Intergovernmental Panel on Climate Change (IPCC), the so-called national pledges at the heart of the Paris climate agreement of December 2015 don't add up to enough reduction of carbon dioxide to control warming. Climate policies have been futile but highly damaging.

The shale revolution, on the other hand, offers economic growth, employment, national security, and even global stability. On New Year's Day, 2016, the first tanker in more than forty years carrying oil produced in the United States left a Texas port headed for Europe. Other tankers filled with U.S. oil followed within a week. Liquefied natural gas produced in America will be next. With access to global markets, the United States can operate as the energy superpower it has become. Thanks to domestic oil and natural gas, we are far less vulnerable to adversarial powers and the chaos in the Middle East.

In a speech to the United Nations General Assembly in 2015, President Obama warned of "dangerous risks pulling us back into a darker, more disordered world."[19] He was referring, of course, to the increasing turmoil in the Middle East, but his own climate policies merit inclusion among those "dangerous risks." If actually enforced, the UN's climate plan, enthusiastically promoted by Obama, would make the world darker as electricity prices soared, "disordering" a global economy still wholly reliant on fossil-fueled production and transport.

Amid the Gloom, It's Still Getting Better

For a more optimistic view of mankind's fate than the doomsayers', consider that our children still enjoy, or have good reason to hope for, a level of prosperity, income, health, comfort, mobility, education, and liberty unimaginable to our recent ancestors. And while Western nations have substantially higher living standards than those of developing countries, the improvements of the past century are global in their reach.

The doomsayers—or "doomsters," as the late economist Julian Simon called them—misunderstand the human factor. Human beings can solve problems, generate abundance, and slay the dark forces that would subjugate humanity. When free and well-fed, human beings typically innovate to improve their lot, and those innovations benefit everyone. When scarcity arises, history shows that human beings figure out how to increase the supply or substitute one resource for another. Free human beings are problem-solvers and creators who so far have overcome the impasses that the pessimists have at every turn declared hopeless. The biggest threats to human flourishing are government dictates to save us from ourselves because they deny human liberty—the wellspring of innovation.

The collapse of oil prices in late 2015 disrupted the shale revolution but by no means ended it. The industry, remarkably enough, keeps finding ways to reduce the cost of drilling. In many places, fracking is profitable at a price of $40 per barrel, and in most places it is profitable at $50 per barrel. In a few years, the cost of fracking will be cut in half again. Cheap energy is here to stay as long as government doesn't outlaw it.

The presence of large deposits of carbon-rich energy is not a guarantee of rising per-capita income, as autocratic Russia and the members of OPEC demonstrate. It takes economic freedom, property rights, and respect for the dignity of the human person to lift all boats. Cheap energy is the springboard to growth. It isn't the source of growth itself.

Who knows what forms of energy superior to fossil fuels will be developed in the future by creative human minds? While we are highly skeptical about the potential of wind energy, solar could emerge in the decades ahead as a competitor to fossil fuels. But right now, solar ventures are massive money-losers, staying afloat only with cascades of government subsidies. The Malthusian belief that the cost of fossil fuels must rise over time explains the seemingly invincible faith in the economic feasibility of green energy. But in reality the cost of fossil fuels is rapidly falling. The price of natural gas has fallen by more than two-thirds, and green energy can't possibly compete with $2 natural gas. Nuclear energy has enormous potential, but it too is having a hard time competing with cheap fossil fuels. For the foreseeable future, there are no reasonable or cost-effective alternatives to fossil fuels. A new study in the *Journal of Economic Perspectives* finds that the oil price would have to rise to above $300 a barrel (from $40 now) for electric cars to be financially viable.

Are Greens the New Reds?

We are worried that government climate policies could arrest or unravel the unquestionable gains in human welfare that have flowed from modern economic growth. There were astonishing advances in material living standards and human freedom during the twentieth century, but in that same century some 170 million persons perished at the hands of brutal totalitarian regimes—four times the number of persons killed in the century's wars. The march of progress is not steady or inevitable.

Many cultural historians contend that "environmentalism" is the ideological successor to failed Marxist and socialist ideologies. The historian Paul Johnson, for one, comes out swinging: "The idea that human beings have changed and are changing the basic climate system of the Earth through their industrial activities and burning of fossil fuels—the essence of the Greens' theory of global warming—has about as much basis in science as Marxism and Freudianism. Global Warming, like Marxism, is a political theory of actions, demanding compliance with its rules."[20]

Every policy prescription for addressing climate change is a call for more government control. Would the Left embrace the green agenda if it meant more individual freedom and more capitalism, not less? History suggests that if climate change becomes a threat to civilization in the future—and who knows what catastrophes Mother Nature might fling at us, including changes in the intensity of solar rays—man's ability to alter the climate will be immeasurably enhanced by economic growth and technological advance. The climate change agenda will undermine that ability.

Ideological environmentalism and legitimate environmental protection are now entangled in the multi-purpose notion of climate change. Vaclav Klaus, late president of the Czech Republic, warned lovers of freedom about the deceptive power of global warming theory back in 2007: "The hypothesis of man-caused global warming and the role of humanity in that process is the last, and to this day, the most powerful embodiment of the environmental [political] ideology."[21] When the EPA asserted power over carbon dioxide—a benign natural gas and ubiquitous byproduct of human activity—the executive agency seized "the commanding heights of the economy and society," writes Charles Krauthammer. "Global warming...is a creed, a faith, a dogma that has little to do with science."[22]

The climate ideologues of today are simply reformulating the misanthropic pessimism of the 1970s. The theory of man-made global warming or climate change revives the globalists' long-promoted but tired call for sustainability. As Rupert Darwall amusingly said, anthropogenic global warming provided a "killer ap" for the ho-hum notion of sustainability.[23]

Robert Zubrin's excellent book *Merchants of Despair* explains the logical kinship between these two pessimisms: "[T]he global warming argument recasts the basic Malthusian line in a novel form, but with the equivalent end result. Instead of claiming that human activity must be limited because there are not enough resources, it is said that what is limited is not resources but the right to use those resources..., therefore human aspirations must be crushed, and authorities must be constituted that are capable of doing the crushing."[24] Whether promoted as planned austerity or more glaringly as international governance without nation states, the activists and political leaders of the climate crusade imagine "planetary management." This is all evidenced by the green movement's latest mantra on fossil fuels: "keep them in the ground."

Doomsday Revisited

Doomsday predictions about running out of food, water, energy, and other resources necessary for human survival are a regular feature of human history, and in its alarmist form, the theory of man-made global warming seems to be just another one. Yet the infiltration by this latest scare of our cultural, financial, academic, media, legal, and religious institutions is unprecedented. All the other predicted global catastrophes either never took place or were averted by human problem-solving. The agricultural revolution in the second half of the previous century, for instance, repudiated the predictions of worldwide famine, the most famous of which was Paul Ehrlich's. The shale revolution likewise repudiated the many "peak oil" theories. Energy prices have been steadily falling, not rising, over the last hundred years, which is evidence we are not running out. See Figure 1.3 below.

The *Wall Street Journal* responded to the UN Paris climate accord with the reminder, "It pays to be skeptical of politicians who claim to be saving the planet."[25] Doomsday fear plays into the hands of politicians out to expand their power. In the past fifty years, the vague but multi-purpose concepts of resource exhaustion, sustainable development, and

FIGURE 1.3

Energy Prices Relative to Wages

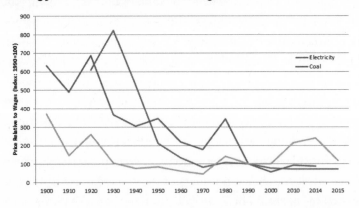

overpopulation have been successfully invoked to justify more intrusive and centralized government, seen as the only way to avert mankind's self-destruction.

The Bet: Doomsaying Ehrlich vs. Doomslaying Simon

The doomslaying economist Julian Simon (1932–1998) argued that mankind will never run out of natural resources. Human beings, he posited, are the ultimate resource because human intellect and imagination will always find more resources, come up with substitutes, or develop new technology. "There is no physical or economic reason why human resourcefulness and enterprise cannot forever continue to respond to impending shortages and existing problems with new expedients that, after an adjustment period, leaves us better off than before the problem arose."[26]

In the most famous wager in the history of economics, Simon challenged the preeminent doomsayer of his time, Paul "Population Bomb" Ehrlich, to a bet on the future scarcity of five commodity metals (selected by Ehrlich): copper, chrome, nickel, tin, and tungsten. If after ten years (1990), the inflation-adjusted prices of the metals had risen, Simon would pay Ehrlich a sum based on the price changes. If the prices fell, Ehrlich would pay Simon.[27] Over the ensuing decade, the population of the world grew by 850 million, but Simon won the bet handily (and Ehrlich paid under the agreed terms). Simon offered another wager at double the stakes, but Ehrlich turned him down.[28]

Paul Ehrlich deserves credit for his willingness to put his theories to the test. Today's global warming alarmists, however, hide behind the slogan of "settled science"—no debates, no questions answered, no contrary evidence acknowledged. When the actually observed global mean temperature became cooler than the IPCC models had predicted, the topic changed from "global warming" to "climate change." And now any weather deemed extreme or unusual—hot or cold, wet or dry—is declared evidence of the theory.

This approach fails the test of a genuinely scientific theory formulated by Karl Popper, the great twentieth-century philosopher of science. A credible scientific theory, he said, must be precisely stated and falsifiable by empirical evidence. When contrary evidence emerged, the alarmists merely recalibrated models and enlarged the scope of corroborating evidence for the theory. And they did so incoherently! Now ice storms, hot spells, floods, droughts, and any odd weather all "prove the theory" of climate change and man-made global warming. And the media parrot this incoherence without a question.

Winding Down the Fossil-Fuel Era—and Modern Civilization with It

Shrinking man's "carbon footprint" is now widely assumed as a moral good. Yet our carbon footprint is the necessary result of living longer, healthier, and freer lives than our ancestors did only a century ago. And on a closer look, high consumption of fossil fuels has allowed prosperous countries to shrink man's physical footprint on the natural world. "Decarbonizing" is a delusional concept. Our bodies are built of carbon. It is the chemical basis of life on earth.

A front-page article in the *Wall Street Journal* in late 2015 nonchalantly described the Paris climate agreement as a "broad, new international effort to *wind down the fossil-fuel era*" (emphasis added).[29] How have these reporters overlooked the fact that civilization depends on fossil fuels for as much as 90 percent of its energy? Indeed, the defining characteristic of modern civilization is reliance on fossil fuels to provide countless energy services throughout an intricate, multi-trillion-dollar infrastructure refined over the past century. Politicians and environmentalists may have been chattering for decades about nixing fossil fuels, but there are still no alternatives capable of providing the diverse, affordable energy services that flow through every corner of human society. With fossil fuels cheaper than ever, green energy is becoming financially less feasible over time.

Just which countries are actually "winding down the fossil-fuel era"? China, India, and several other developing countries are building or have plans to build over two thousand new coal-fired power plants. These developing countries may have "pledged" to reduce their output of carbon dioxide but on the condition that their pledge not complicate economic development. India's negotiator at Paris, Jairam Ramesh, was refreshingly candid, noting, "It would be suicidal...to give up on our coal for the next fifteen to twenty years at least, given the need."[30] And who will count on Russia and the countries of the Middle East to cooperate in the diminution of the market for fossil fuels?

The Misanthropes among Us

Most of the doomsaying elites are candid about their contempt for the value of human life and about their political endgame. All-powerful, centralized governance, preferably on a global scale, is necessary, they affirm, to save the planet and to establish an equitable distribution of the world's financial and physical resources.

The IPCC chief, Christina Figueres, has called communism the optimal system for avoiding dangerous global warming.[31] In other settings, she has acknowledged that the UN's climate program has provided the political and organizational wherewithal to replace the economic system that made modern economic growth possible. As she nonchalantly comments, "This is the first time in the history of mankind that we are setting ourselves the task of intentionally within a defined period of time, to change the economic development model that has been reigning for at least 150 years, since the Industrial Revolution."[32] That's a frighteningly arrogant statement if we ever heard one. It takes a central planner with frightening arrogance, an uncompromising faith in the power of government, and no sense of history to articulate such a wrong-headed vision of the future.

The economic development model that the UN climate czar consigns to the dustbin of history allowed a middle class to flourish and, by the

UN's own admission, has released more human beings from abject poverty than any other economic system in history.[33] The hallmarks of that model are economic freedom, private property rights, and competitive markets. Under this economic system, the government's fundamental role is to protect, not arrest, individual freedom. And the dynamic of that growth remains intertwined with the availability and creative conversions of fossil fuels.

In the 1970s, when political environmentalism was emerging, the Club of Rome[34] became a remarkably influential purveyor of gloomy scenarios spelling the end of economic growth and requiring centrally controlled economies. Its manifesto *Limits to Growth* sold more than nine million copies and was translated into more than three hundred languages—and all the while, economic growth continued.[35] In its 1991 publication *The First Global Revolution*, the organization unashamedly revealed the misanthropic worldview behind its political objectives: "The common enemy of humanity is man. In searching for a new enemy to unite us, we came up with the idea that pollution, the threat of global warming, water shortages, famine and the like would fit the bill."[36] This was the "scientific consensus" of the time. Not to be outdone in misanthropy, Paul Ehrlich wrote, "Giving society cheap, abundant energy would be the equivalent of giving an idiot child a machine gun."[37]

The Marxist founder of the United Nations Environment Program (UNEP), the late Maurice Strong, contended that "the only hope for the planet" is the collapse of industrialized civilizations. The "planetary management" advocated by these alarmists is to be carried out by experts, managers, and technocrats acting under the supposed authority of science rather than by the democratically expressed consent of the people.

Few Americans on either end of the political spectrum appear to be aware of this dark side of the global warming issue, and few public officials seem willing to risk the wrath that the mainstream media reserve for climate heretics. Yet opinion polls consistently show that a strong majority of U.S. citizens abhor the idea of global governance. Europeans may have become accustomed to their governments' social engineering, but we doubt that a critical mass of Americans are willing to surrender to green mandates that would limit the number of miles a person is authorized to drive per week. If our democratic form of government is to endure, energy policies of this national consequence must be under the authority of Congress and not merely the policy preference of the president.

A Declaration of War against Fossil Fuels

Rupert Darwall has identified what he calls the global warming policy paradox: anti-carbon policies tend to aggravate the very problems they are intended to avoid.[38] The IPCC, whose pronouncements most countries treat as authoritative, concludes that carbon dioxide emissions must be cut by more than 80 percent to "avoid dangerous interference with the climate." High on the list of predicted horrors if we don't heed this warning is food scarcity. Yet a reduction of carbon dioxide emissions of this magnitude would mean curtailing the use of the carbon-rich fertilizers that have fed the world since the 1950s, putting the developing world at risk of famine. Increased atmospheric carbon dioxide, moreover, is increasing the agricultural yield of cereal grains. Satellite imagery shows the earth is becoming greener. Meanwhile, biofuels, claiming more and more productive crop land, are already making food more expensive. Making farmland less productive by restricting the use of natural gas–derived fertilizer while dedicating millions of acres of prime farmland to biofuels is a sure way to reduce the food supply.

Given the weakening evidence for severe global warming and the counterproductive consequences of climate policies, surely increased economic growth offers the better bet for adaptation to whatever change in our climate may lie ahead. In other words, America's future may not offer a climate any different from today's, but the future that the alarmists propose is a regression toward the pre-industrial era devoid of the freedoms and prosperity afforded by plentiful energy.

The greens assume we can rapidly shift to renewable energy with few problems other than a slight increase in cost. But it's not so simple. States with onerous renewable-energy standards such as Colorado and California are still relying heavily on coal to fill in the gaps. Backup generation necessary to avoid grid meltdown when wind or sunshine fluctuates may be the largest component of cost. Yet the climate alarmists—the very people who dismiss their opponents as "science deniers"—are in denial about the fundamental physical realities that make renewable energy inherently limited.

Having made substantial progress in their effort to kill coal, the environmentalists are turning to natural gas as the next victim. We have to move "beyond natural gas," says the Sierra Club, even though natural gas is reducing carbon emissions. In fact, they don't seem to like any other feasible source of electricity, such as nuclear and hydro. We get about 90 percent of our power from sources that the environmental Left is trying to shut down. Four percent at most comes from wind and solar power. If we try to rely on wind turbines and solar panels, prices will skyrocket and the power supply will dwindle.

Who knows what fuels and energy systems may replace hydrocarbon in the future, but right now there are no alternatives that can compare in cost and versatility to fossil fuels. For the better part of two hundred years, "experts" have predicted that the end is nigh for fossil fuels. And as recently as 2011, at the beginning of the shale revolution, President Obama warned that "we are running out of oil."

As we write, the price of oil has fallen to between $30 and $40 a barrel from $105 in 2014. This lower price is a sign of greater availability. If we look at the long-term trend of the price of oil, coal, and electricity, we see the continuing decline in price. The Malthusians have been wrong for many decades. There is no shortage of oil, gas, or food; they are getting more plentiful all the time. Technological progress always moves faster than the use of the resource—so instead of being finite, for all intents and purposes, our energy resources are limitless. As Mark P. Mills and Peter Huber put it, "What lies at the bottom of the bottomless well isn't oil, it's logic."[39] The doomster prognosticators misunderstand the master resource that is energy and the ultimate resource that is the human person, capable of endless creativity if free to innovate and prosper by that innovation.

So President Obama and the Malthusians were flat-out wrong. We are not running out of oil and gas, America is running into it. We are not degrading our environment but improving it. We have learned how to produce and consume energy with extraordinary environmental sensitivity. That is very good news for us and our children. America is one of the most fossil-fuel rich nations on the planet. In addition to its newly reclaimed position as the globally dominating producer of oil and natural gas, this country also holds the world's largest reserves of coal—perhaps a five-hundred-year supply. From an economic competitive standpoint, for the United States to stop producing fossil fuels would be like Iowa's giving up corn or Columbia's giving up coffee.

Energy Abundance: A Gateway to Health and Wealth

The pivotal physical breakthroughs in mankind's history all can be viewed as energy revolutions. The first was the Neolithic agricultural revolution, when men shifted from hunting to farming. The Industrial Revolution's creative applications of fossil fuels holds second place among mankind's energy revolutions. And electricity—a new form of energy providing limitless services including vanquishing darkness—is yet another transformative energy enrichment. Even the recent digital revolution in communication and information technology can be viewed as another epochal energy advance. Now photons—light itself—transmit knowledge at great speed. And the shale revolution is another worthy candidate for mankind's energy hall of fame. Achieved by creative refinements of technology, the shale revolution secured access to the source rock of fossil fuels—the world's mother lode of hydrocarbons thought forever locked in shale.

Each of these revolutions achieved more power, light, services, and information at greater efficiency, higher speeds, and with smaller, more compact infrastructure. We doubt that the green energy revolution will

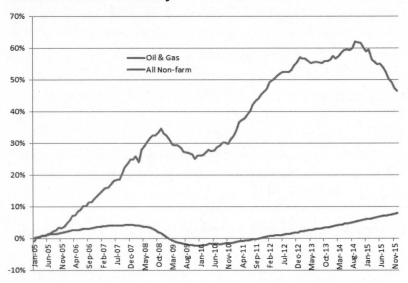

FIGURE 1.4

Growth in Oil and Gas Employment Outpaces the Rest of the Economy

become a lasting member of those energy revolutions that so amplified our lives—at least not anytime soon.

The recent breakthroughs in fracking and horizontal drilling, access to shale oil and gas, improvements in deep-sea drilling, and production of Canada's oil sands have opened a new era of abundant energy, which no one would have predicted at the turn of the millennium. It is critical that policy makers understand the magnificent potential of this new era of fossil fuels and reject attempts to disrupt this bountiful future.

If we get our energy policies right in America—which is simply to keep the government from picking winners and losers and letting energy sources compete in the free enterprise system—America is set not just to be energy independent, but energy dominant. The price of energy will continue to fall in the twenty-first century. We will produce millions of new jobs in the energy sector, and become the primary energy source of the world, just as we are already the breadbasket of the world. The shale boom has already been responsible for all net new jobs in America from 2007–2012. See Figure 1.4.

Yet much of humanity has not yet had access to the energy enrichment that has so amplified and eased our lives. Although the benefits of cheap and abundant energy from fossil fuels have improved living conditions across the world, over a billion human beings still have no access to electricity, and green policies are thwarting access to affordable electricity to those still living in energy scarcity. International financial institutions like the World Bank and the International Monetary Fund mandate expensive, unreliable green energy and will not finance energy projects using fossil fuels. Rather than suppressing access to the most efficient and affordable electric generation from fossil fuels, the practical and humane course would be to enable use of affordable fossil fuels in an environmentally responsible manner.

Superabundant, made-in-America energy will help reduce income inequality because cheap energy is vital for the poor. And as energy costs fall around the world thanks to the breakthrough in drilling and mining technologies, the world will get richer too. The world's poor, many of whom now lack basic power, will be liberated by this cheap energy revolution and will benefit the most. While the plunge in the price of oil challenged the industry which drove the shale revolution, the decline in oil prices and gasoline prices at the pump saved American consumers an estimated $150 billion per year, or at least $750 per family. Low energy prices are a massive economic stimulus. Because energy is an ingredient of everything that is produced, lower energy costs lower the price of everything.

The shale oil and gas revolution will make us safer. It is one of the greatest national security trump cards America holds in the war against terrorism. Until a few years ago, most of the proved oil reserves were in the hands of nationally-owned oil companies in some of the most autocratic countries of the world: Saudi Arabia, Iran, Russia, Venezuela, Libya. If our government allows America to become an energy-exporting power, the influence of these countries and their allies will wane.

If we sell oil to our allies rather than buy oil from our antagonists, the axis of geopolitical power will tilt in our favor. Shale oil and gas have defanged OPEC, which disrupted the world economy for more than forty years. The oil sheiks who have ruled energy policy for all these decades are in a state of panic, and only the green movement in America can save them.

Fossil fuels are wonder fuels. If we want a just, prosperous, healthy, and safe world that respects the rights and dignity of the individual, we have a moral imperative to use them in a responsible and productive way. As we shall show later, there is an estimated 1.5 trillion barrels of recoverable oil on federal lands. Even at $30 or $40 a barrel, that's worth roughly $50 trillion. The greatest blunder that America could make for this generation and those to follow would be to leave this treasure chest of energy resources in the ground.

HOW THE SHALE REVOLUTION
IS CHANGING EVERYTHING

The American Energy Revolution

As recently as the 1970s and early 1980s, major oil and gas companies and large independents dominated the domestic energy landscape. The "majors" or "Big Oil," as they are called, subsequently abandoned the domestic basins in search of larger finds internationally.[1] In their absence, individual oilmen in small and mid-sized U.S. companies launched an energy revolution that has changed the world in less than a decade.

After decades of declining production and dependence on imports for almost 70 percent of its oil and natural gas, the United States surpassed Saudi Arabia and Russia to become the world's number one energy producer (measured in barrels-of-oil equivalent) in 2013 and remains so today.[2] Imports of petroleum to the United States decreased almost 60 percent from 2007 to 2013.[3] Domestic oil production rose from five million barrels a day in 2007 to 8.6 million barrels a day in

2014—a 40 percent increase in seven years. In May 2015, production reached 9.6 million barrels a day even with a plunge in the price of crude oil. Russia and Saudi Arabia lead us in crude oil production by little more than a million barrels per day, a negligible amount. See Figure 2.1. The United States has also doubled its export of petroleum products to a hefty one billion barrels per year.[4] This historic upsurge, achieved in less than a decade, owes almost nothing to federal energy policy (in fact federal energy policy has tried to slow down domestic oil production) or the majors, and few Americans are even aware that this colossal energy breakthrough has taken place.

Determined, creative, courageous men and women competing in a free market achieved what seven presidents promised but failed to achieve—making the United States the world's energy superpower, no

FIGURE 2.1

Growth in Output of Major Oil Producers

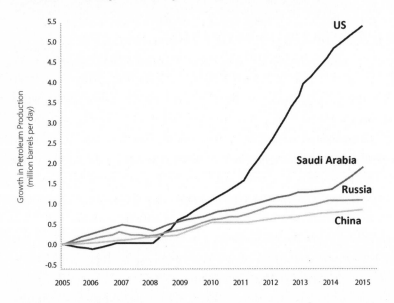

Source: U.S. Energy Information Administration

longer unavoidably dependent on oil imports from countries hostile to our fundamental values of individual liberty and economic freedom.

Strangely enough, the energy bonanza has coincided with the presidency of a man hell-bent on eliminating fossil fuels to avert alleged global warming. If Barack Obama has an energy policy, it is to "decarbonize" our economy and "lead the world" to a global agreement to "save the planet" by ditching the use of the hydrocarbon bounty of American energy. Our geopolitical foes in Russia, the Middle East, and South America derive most of their revenue from the sale of oil and natural gas. Yet after more than eighteen years without warming global temperatures, the president seeks to increase our dependence on these thuggish regimes and declares that global warming is a greater threat than ISIS.

The cause of the extraordinary rise in U.S. energy production has been the shale boom, an American technological revolution that has unlocked oceans of previously inaccessible oil and natural gas, combined with competitive markets, economic freedom, and property rights. A mix of innovative technologies developed by dogged engineers and adventurous investors has released vast volumes of oil and natural gas trapped in hard shale rock. Through hydraulic fracturing, horizontal drilling, seismic imaging, and deep-data geophysical analytics, U.S. producers cracked the shale energy code and are transforming the world's energy markets.

The shale boom has enlarged the economic pie, offering prosperity to every American. It kept the Great Recession from becoming the Great Depression 2.0 and turned multitudes of small, rural mineral-rights owners into millionaires. Local, state, and federal government have seen revenues soar. Hundreds of related industries are expanding or opening new plants, creating good new jobs. Recent studies estimate that more than $100 billion has already been invested in new chemical, plastic, and fertilizer plants and related manufacturing in the United States.[5]

Low energy prices give American manufacturing plants a powerful advantage over foreign competitors that must cope with energy prices two to four times higher than in America. And low energy prices may have increased disposable income by an average of $1,200 per household in 2014.[6]

America's energy endowment is even more impressive when you take coal into account. Called the Saudi Arabia of coal, the United States holds 481 billion tons of coal reserves—the largest in the world. The lower forty-eight states have enough coal to meet current demand for 520 years. Alaska has even larger reserves that have not yet been tapped.[7]

These natural resources are an incalculable blessing to America. Wise use and free trade of our abundant energy could eliminate our reliance on corrupt and dangerous countries for oil. Among the top ten energy-producing countries, only the United States and Canada are constitutionally committed to the dignity of the human person (see Figure 2.2). By contrast, several of the biggest oil producers use their revenue from oil sales to fund terrorism.

FIGURE 2.2

Ten Top Oil-Producing Countries in 2014
(EIA International Energy Statistics)

1. United States	13,973,000
2. Saudi Arabia	11,624,000
3. Russia	10, 853,000
4. China	4,572,000
5. Canada	4,383,000
6. United Arab Emirates	3,471,000
7. Iran	3,375,000
8. Iraq	3,371,000
9. Brazil	2,950,000
10. Mexico	2,812,000

Measure: Total Petroleum and Other Liquids in Million Barrels per Day

The Canadian journalist Ezra Levant has written provocatively about the ethical issues surrounding the development of Canada's oil sands[8]— issues debated within Canada and across the world.[9] The "real test of ethical oil," he argues, is not "comparing oil sands to some impossible, ideal standard but comparing it to its real competitors." American and Canadian oil is produced with far higher environmental sensitivity by countries that are "more peaceful, more democratic and more fair" than the other major oil-producing nations.

If the North American energy revolution had occurred thirty years earlier or if the federal government had not shackled domestic energy production, we might have avoided today's protracted, fractious, and deadly entanglements with the Middle East. And the United States could, right now, be exporting oil, natural gas, and coal to our free-world allies held hostage to high-priced Russian energy. We know that ISIS terrorist networks are funded to the tune of $1 million a day through oil dollars.

In late 2015 Congress finally repealed the outdated ban on exporting domestically produced oil, promising a tremendous boost to the American energy industry. Congress created the export ban in 1973 when the Arab Oil Embargo drove gasoline prices sky high and created temporary scarcity at filling stations across the country. Since then we have gone from scarcity to glut. Multiple federal studies conclude domestic exports will not increase consumer prices and will likely have the opposite effect.[10] Other studies find that this policy change alone will increase domestic oil and gas output by at least $100 billion a year.

The shale boom should renew our faith in free enterprise. This country's thousands of small and mid-sized energy companies—the independent, successful, and peaceful army of the U.S. shale revolution—have proved that the American dream is still alive.

Before taking a closer look at the shale boom and the opportunities this energy bonanza creates for our country, consider the human faces of America's colossal energy resurgence.

Economic Heroes of the Century: The American Energy Entrepreneurs

George Mitchell

Although many contributed to the shale boom, George Mitchell of Galveston, Texas, is widely regarded as the "Father of Fracking." Born in 1919 to Greek immigrants (his father changed the family surname, Paraskevopoulus, to Mitchell), he and his family lived above their shoeshine parlor and laundry.

Mitchell worked his way through Texas A&M University and graduated first in his class in petroleum engineering. The classic independent Texas oilman, he won big, lost big, and then won big again, drilling perhaps ten thousand wells before selling Mitchell Energy to Devon Energy not long before his death at ninety-four in 2013.

As early as the 1950s, Mitchell was focused—his colleagues might say "fixated"—on the natural gas in the geological formation now known as the Barnett Shale, underneath the Dallas–Fort Worth region. He realized that his conventional drilling was extracting only a minute portion of the gas he sensed was trapped in hard rock. Mitchell vertically fracked the first well in the Barnett Shale in June 1982, but the output was slim and the drilling cost high. Convinced that vast reserves of natural gas were down there, he continued to frack a few wells every year with different techniques. Most people who knew him thought he was obsessed with an irresolvable, extremely expensive puzzle.

The technology of "fracking"—making small fissures in hard rock to allow the release of oil and natural gas—goes back seven decades. Floyd Farris of Stanolin Energy received a patent in 1948 for a technique he called "HydraFrac." After years of expensive trial and error, Mitchell Energy cracked the Barnett Shale with a similar but yet decisively refined fracking technology in 1998. Instead of fracturing a well with heavy gelatinous fluids and loads of chemicals, Mitchell used lots of water under extremely high pressure and then used sand to prop open the fissures. Mitchell Energy had figured out how to release the natural gas held in shale rock, and the United States now sat atop a massive store of accessible energy.

In 2002, Devon Energy drilled its first horizontal well into the Barnett Shale, producing seven times more natural gas than conventional drilling techniques. In the early days of the boom, the effectiveness of the technology was a shock even to longtime insiders of the oil and gas business. Many oil men and their engineers shook their heads when they heard of Devon's success. Shale rock, in contrast to softer, more porous sandstone, was so hard that it was thought to be impermeable. Reaching the oil and gas trapped in shale, a seasoned engineer noted, was "just as startling as saying that ice doesn't freeze anymore."[11]

By 2012 the majority of wells in the United States were horizontal, and production in the shale fields had increased dramatically. The early wells were extremely expensive, and even today many horizontal wells are considerably more expensive than traditional vertical wells. Yet nimble independent energy companies are rapidly cutting the cost of production while increasing the output.

Bud Brigham

"The Bakken boom in North Dakota more than doubled in size on September 7, 2008, the day the U.S. housing market crashed and a deep economic recession began."[12] That was the day Brigham Exploration, founded and run by Bud Brigham, began fracking in the Bakken shale fields of North Dakota. Brigham was the first to drill a much longer horizontal well bore, extending the lateral scope of a well from one to two miles. In principle, this should almost double the productivity of a single well.

In a daring move, Brigham then deployed a new tool, developed by the independent oil company EOG, called swell packers. This technology was enormously expensive—it required Brigham to take on considerable debt at a moment when Wall Street was crashing—but promised to double the length of prior wells and thus dramatically improve the economics in the play. The technologies Brigham applied would set a record for the number of sections of the well that could be fractured. He was gambling $8 million on the well, with considerable debt, at a moment when substantial portions of Wall Street were crashing. Brigham's well was successful and dramatically amplified the amount of oil and natural gas extractable from a single well, eventually doubling the geographic extent of the Bakken field.

Harold Hamm

The founder and CEO of Continental Resources, the fourteenth-largest oil company in the country, Harold Hamm owns more oil and natural gas reserves in America than anyone else in the industry. The youngest of thirteen children and "the son of [Oklahoma] sharecroppers who never owned land," he headed straight to the oil fields after high school.

Harold Hamm is credited with discovering the magnitude of the Bakken shale fields. One of the first players in the Bakken, as early as in 2002, he gathered up a substantial majority of the region's prime oil leases. His application of various fracking technologies to many wells allowed innovation that increased productivity and cut costs.

Through several boom and bust cycles, Hamm made billions of dollars during the boom years 2006–2014, when oil prices were $80 to $100 a barrel. But even with oil below $50 a barrel, he is still making money. Everywhere he drills, Harold Hamm finds more oil.

Jim Henry

Another trailblazer in the improbable shale revolution is Jim Henry from Midland, Texas. Humble, gracious, and generous, he is revered throughout the upstream oil and gas business and within his community. He is also an extraordinarily savvy and dynamic oilman. A forty-five-year veteran of the oil business and owner of a succession of small, independent companies, Henry led the vigorous and sustained revival of the historically prolific but long moribund Permian Basin oil fields of west Texas.

Observing the increasing success of Mitchell's fracking technologies with natural gas in the Barnett Shale region, several big oil companies

experimented with these technologies in the Wolfcamp geological formation in the Permian in the late 1990s. Production there was difficult and
the results were modest, and they departed by 2000. Henry was able to
take over some of their oil leases, and he applied a version of Mitchell's
drilling techniques near the area where the bigger companies previously
had drilled. In 2003, Henry's Kaitlin 2801 well was successful. He then
moved seventeen miles south and succeeded again. At that point he knew
he had discovered a huge field where many more wells could be drilled,
and he quietly gathered up oil leases on three hundred thousand acres in
the Wolfcamp formation.

Since the first producing well in 1920, the Permian has produced 28.9
billion barrels of oil and eighteen trillion cubic feet of gas.[13] Because of
Henry's breakthroughs, those numbers likely represent only a small portion of the oil and natural gas now recoverable in a field previously
thought to have peaked in 1973.

Henry emphasizes that vertical fracking in the Permian recovered
only about 3 percent of the oil "in place," that is, remaining within the
geological formation. Horizontal drilling increases recovery to about 7
percent of the oil in place. The Permian Basin may have doubled its oil
output within the past several years, but 93 percent of the mother lode
of oil in the Permian is still in the ground. Increased production merely
awaits another of the drilling innovations that distinguish the shale
revolution. Sustainable oil, anyone?

Henry himself was once persuaded by the "peak oil" theories of
irreversible and near-term depletion of oil resources. But that theory
"went out the window," as he puts it, when George Mitchell's hydraulic
fracturing "did the impossible" and successfully drilled through apparently impermeable shale to release the oil and natural gas from the source
rock itself.[14] (See Sidebar on page 37, "The Shale Energy Transformation.") Never say never, Henry learned. Through fracking, the energy
output from the Permian Basin rose from 850,000 barrels per day in
2007 to over two million barrels per day in July 2015.[15]

The history of U.S. oil production is marked by booms and busts,
but the increase in oil production from shale is unlike previous,

temporary booms caused by favorable economics. The shale upsurge is a true revolution driven by new drilling technology, imaging, and data access on a scale and at a speed that are dizzying to insiders.

The revived Permian Basin accounts for two-thirds of all oil produced in Texas and more than 18 percent of total U.S. production. Output there continues to soar in spite of the plunge in oil prices and a steep drop in the number of drilling rigs in the fields. During a period of low oil prices, more output from fewer rigs indicates the increasing productivity and the declining cost of production in select wells.[16]

The shale revolution, Henry points out, was a far more collaborative project than were previous booms. Producers shared information and techniques that increased productivity and decreased drilling costs rather than rushing to get patents. Company owners, employees, geologists, engineers, drillers, and the many service companies essential to upstream oil and gas "feel that we are in this together," says Henry, and there is enough potential growth for all participants in the industry to thrive.

Who would have predicted that the resurgence of domestic oil production—and especially the revitalization of the mighty Permian fields— would be the result of risky, complex innovations of small oil companies? Henry's workforce peaked at around 120 at the height of his Wolfcamp activity, but most of the time his staff has not exceeded forty. Exxon-Mobil, by contrast, has 83,600 employees. There is nothing wrong with huge corporations operating on a global scale. Small companies, however, are often the source of innovation and motivation that are difficult to replicate on a giant scale. Jim Henry's story shows what small businesses, economic freedom, property rights, financial incentive, and innovation can achieve. And the legal institutions and culture of the United States are unmatched in fostering this powerful and creative engine of economic growth.

The shale revolution was the work of small to medium-sized companies operating on private and state lands. The United States is fortunate not to have a nationally owned oil company, as do the members of the Organization of the Petroleum Exporting Countries. But production on

The Shale Energy Transformation

The oil and gas extracted in the shale fields began as small aquatic organisms in an ancient inland sea covering the central region of North America from the Great Plains to what we now call Pennsylvania. And by an ancient inland sea, we mean *ancient*—formed sixty million years ago, during the Cretaceous Period. Historical geologists conclude that the sea was formed when a collision of the earth's tectonic plates gave rise to the Rocky Mountains in the west and the Appalachians in the east. When the marine creatures living in the inland sea died, they settled to the seabed and over time formed layers of organic material. Rocks eventually covered this material. The pressure from the rocks generated heat for millions of years, transforming the organic sludge into hydrocarbons otherwise known as crude oil and natural gas. The shale of the shale revolution is what petroleum geologists call the "source rock" of oil and gas, a kind of cradle in which the hydrocarbons are generated and stored in rock.

Today's refined fracking technologies speed up this natural geological process by millions of years. The minerals extracted in conventional vertically drilled wells are the hydrocarbons that eventually seeped from source rocks over millions of years and collected in pools. When vertically drilled, natural geological pressure helps move the contents of that reservoir to the surface. Geologists have known for decades that natural pressure may produce far less than 10 percent of the oil or natural gas in the particular geological formation that created the pool. The shale boom aims at the remaining 90 percent.

federally owned land has remained anemic—not for lack of recoverable energy underground but because of regulatory interference.

These men and many others did far more than Barack Obama or any politician or economist in Washington to bring about the 2009–2015 economic recovery. The $830 billion federal spending, borrowing, and subsidizing binge known as the American Recovery and Reinvestment Act of 2009 had nothing to do with it. The real economic stimulus has been the risk-taking oil and gas companies that launched and drove the shale revolution.

The New Energy Superpower

The shale revolution received a blow when oil prices began a plunge in June 2014. A year later half the drilling rigs had left the shale fields and over a hundred thousand jobs had disappeared. Yet the prodigious productivity—more than 9.5 million barrels a day in March 2016—and increasing global influence of U.S. oil survived.

The domestic shale industry has been a victim of its own success: producing so much oil that it glutted global markets just as China's economy began to sag. When the surplus recedes, the price of oil is likely to stabilize now that the outdated ban on exports of crude oil has been lifted. Great Britain and Japan already have indicated an interest in importing oil from the United States. Meanwhile, critical masses of shale drillers are rapidly reducing the cost of production while increasing their output.

"OPEC's Clout Hits New Low," the *Wall Street Journal* reported in the summer of 2015.[17] The cartel's market share had declined from more than half of global production to roughly one-third of global production.[18] The bulk of OPEC's loss of market share is attributable to American shale oil, which accounts for 75 percent of the growth of the global supply of oil.[19]

For the first time in more than fifty years, the world oil market revolves around the United States rather than OPEC—a sixty-five-year-old cartel of state-owned oil companies, the majority of which are unstable and inimical to U.S. interests. Saudi Arabia, determined to reclaim its lost market share, has ceded to America its monopolistic role as the world's only swing producer. Instead of reducing production in response to low prices, the Saudis are maintaining and probably increasing their production. The Saudis' increasing domestic demand for energy is checking the amount of oil available for export. This is a major new dilemma for a country that derives roughly 90 percent of its revenue from the sale of crude oil. Unlike most of the world, the Saudis generate their electricity from oil. As the *Wall Street Journal* noted in July 2015, "in a country where subsidized crude oil still powers most homes and businesses, and where a gallon of gasoline costs less than a bottle of water, Saudi Arabia's ravenous energy appetite is starting to strain the kingdom's oil infrastructure and hamper its ability to throttle up exports."[20]

If the United States, with its wide-open and decentralized oil industry, can act as the swing producer, the global oil market can function as a genuinely competitive market. Fortunately, the United States does not have a minister of oil setting production levels. Our domestic energy market consists of four thousand small and mid-size companies competing in a relatively free market. Could Adam Smith's "invisible hand" now replace the autocratic bullies of OPEC?

The shale revolution is entering its second stage as producers consolidate, innovate to cut costs, and absorb the accumulated data from thousands of fracked wells over the last decade. Mark Mills, a physicist and venture capitalist in the information and communications technology world and fellow of the Manhattan Institute, persuasively argues that the next stage of the shale revolution, "Shale 2.0," can double production and reduce costs by half, enabling the United States to continue and expand its international energy ascendency. The first stage of the shale revolution, Mills reminds us, "was not sparked by high oil prices.... [I]t began when prices were at today's low levels—but by the invention of new technologies. Now, the skeptics' forecasts are likely to be as flawed as their history."[21]

The shale gale, as the energy guru Daniel Yergin calls the boom, has already achieved what not long ago was considered impossible. It was made possible not by government planning or "public investment" but by technological advances in the private sector, financial capital, and the entrepreneurial spirit, ingenuity, and grit of men like Harold Hamm, George Mitchell, Jim Henry, and Bud Brigham.

The implications of the shale revolution for international stability are enormous. Two million barrels per day of American oil would reduce the European Union's dependence on Russian imports by half. U.S. natural gas exports are already reducing Vladimir Putin's energy stranglehold over our NATO allies.

How Much U.S. Energy Are We Talking About?

The United States is blessed with vast and continually underestimated energy resources. America has more oil, coal, and natural gas than any other country in the world.

The official estimates of the U.S. Geological Survey (USGS) are notoriously low. In 2000, the USGS estimated that the Bakken shale field in North Dakota held between four and five billion barrels of shale oil. Harold Hamm concluded that oil deposits there were almost five times more than the government experts calculated. In 2012 he said, "We estimate that the entire field, fully developed in the Bakken is 24 billion barrels."[22] He was right, and this single oilfield doubled America's proved reserves overnight.

The Bakken oil field is larger than the state of Delaware. In July 2014, North Dakota reached record production of one million barrels of oil per day. In 2007, North Dakota produced only two hundred thousand barrels per day. Not all states have shale fields, and some that do have prohibited hydraulic fracturing—most notoriously New York and California. Texas dominates the shale revolution, producing three times more oil than North Dakota, the second-highest producing state. Texas and North Dakota together provide nearly half of all crude oil in the United States.[23]

Those regions where shale resources are under development see the boom all around them. In addition to North Dakota and Texas, fracking is also underway in the Marcellus Shale and the Utica Shale in Ohio, Pennsylvania, and West Virginia, as well as the Haynesville and Fayetteville shale plays in Louisiana, Arkansas, and East Texas. Geologists may have long known that the oil and natural gas in shale rock were there, but they underestimated how much there was. This energy was never considered "technologically recoverable" because there was no known method to extract the energy at anywhere near affordable costs. Now we have those methods and they are getting cheaper to employ every year.

No country has been as efficient, innovative, or environmentally sensitive in the extraction of oil and gas as the United States, and no country has done it as profitably. Competition and reasonable regulation are part of the reason for our success, but there is another factor, distinctively American phenomenon. This is the only country in the world where mineral rights can be privately owned. In all other countries, the state owns the oil, natural gas, and other subsurface minerals. The incentive of private property rights in fungible resources propels the U.S. oil and gas business as nowhere else in the world. Nevertheless, federal policy is stifling our potential.

Ninety-six percent of the production in the shale revolution has occurred on private and state lands, over which the federal government has far less regulatory jurisdiction than on federally owned lands. President Obama occasionally takes credit for the shale boom when it serves his purpose, but under his administration production on federal lands— which hold plenty of shale resources—has declined substantially. In 2013, the Obama administration leased the fewest acres for oil and natural gas production on record.[24] The federal government owns seven hundred million acres of our country's land—almost 30 percent of the total land area of the United States.[25] Only 5 percent of that seven hundred million acres is leased for oil and natural gas development.

Alaska has huge untapped mineral resources, but the federal ownership of almost 70 percent of the state's land prevents their efficient development. Intrusive regulation, endlessly delayed permits, and outright bans on oil and gas development continue to limit production. Declining production from Alaska's North Slope imperils the structural integrity of the Trans-Alaska pipeline, an engineering marvel that carries oil eight hundred miles from the remote North Slope to the port of Valdez, where it is shipped on tankers to refineries in California and other western states. Built at great cost in 1977, the pipeline was designed to move six hundred thousand barrels per day. Federal obstruction of new drilling has substantially reduced the volume of oil flowing through the pipeline, causing it to deteriorate. The loss of this strategic energy asset would be a disaster.

Oil and gas development on a minuscule portion of the remote Arctic National Wildlife Refuge (ANWR)—two thousand of the refuge's nineteen million acres—has been blocked for decades. Yet, oil and gas production would occur on only 0.01 percent of the Refuge's nineteen million acres![26] Original concerns about the effect of drilling on the caribou population are no longer valid. In 1968, there were six thousand Caribou in the ANWR. By 2009, the population approached sixty-seven thousand, and the animals were thriving amidst energy development in nearby areas.[27] The USGS estimates that this tiny portion of ANWR contains over ten billion barrels of oil and could yield one million barrels per day,[28] but President Obama is threatening to put ANWR permanently off limits to energy development.

And then there is the American mother lode of hydrocarbon resources found in three western states—*oil shale*. This resource is to be distinguished from *shale oil*. The distinction between oil shale and shale oil can be confusing, but oil shale derives from a solid known as kerogen. When heated, the kerogen produces petroleum-like liquids and natural gas. According to the USGS, the United States sits atop 2.6 trillion barrels of oil shale.[29] Roughly half of this resource—four times the amount of Saudi Arabia's proved oil reserves—is now technologically and economically recoverable. The United States is not running out of oil.

Offshore Resources

American taxpayers own the more than 1.7 billion acres of the submerged land of the Outer Continental Shelf (OCS) off our coasts.[30] According to the Bureau of Ocean Energy Management, the OCS holds eighty-six billion barrels of oil and 420 trillion cubic feet of natural gas—all of that technically recoverable—but the federal government has leased only 2 percent of the OCS for energy development.[31] Even as the nation was becoming increasingly dependent on imports of oil from countries hostile to U.S. interests, Congress enacted a prohibition on oil and gas development on most of the OCS in 1982, making the United States the only developed country in the world to prohibit oil and gas production off its coasts.

When the ban was finally lifted in the fall of 2008, President George W. Bush issued a plan for development of the OCS, which the Obama administration quickly rescinded in 2009. And in response to the 2010 oil spill from BP's Deepwater Horizon well, the administration issued a six-month moratorium on both deep and much safer shallow offshore wells. During the ensuing "permitorium," when the government obstructed the issuance of necessary permits, at least ten of the huge drilling rigs used in deep-water drilling moved to other parts of the globe.[32]

Greens vs. Growth

Since the early 1970s, policies driven by an entrenched environmental establishment have blocked or restricted development of domestic oil and natural gas. This effort has not reduced consumption of these fuels but has sent U.S. dollars to purchase oil from other countries—countries that oppose the foundational values of our nation. As many as 150 federal laws suppress the development of key domestic energy sources—oil, natural gas, coal, and uranium—enabling environmental activists to block projects planned for federal lands. One presidential signature can deprive Americans of critical natural resources. In 1996, for example, President Bill Clinton designated 1.7 million acres of land in Utah's Grand Staircase Escalante as a national monument, putting the largest store of low-sulfur coal in the country off limits.[33] This is the least polluting form of coal and in the highest demand.

Environmentalists allege that fracking contaminates community water supplies, putting residents at risk of cancer and other illnesses. The propaganda film *Gaslands* is famous for its depiction of a West Virginia homeowner igniting methane-laden tap water with a match. But that phenomenon has nothing to do with modern fracking. It is almost always due to naturally occurring methane migrating into shallow aquifers far above the areas that are fracked. After vigorous review by the federal and state governments, the Environmental Protection Agency reported that it knows of no incidents of water contamination directly caused by fracking anywhere in the country.[34]

Legitimate questions remain about the volume of water used in the fracking process, wastewater disposal, and the importance of recycling fracking water. The same industry, however, that created the technologies that made the shale revolution successful is rapidly developing technologies to minimize water use and to recycle waste water.

From an environmental point of view, the shale revolution has come at a promising time. Over the last four decades, American industries have dramatically reduced air and water pollution. The most important "criteria pollutants" listed in the federal Clean Air Act have declined by 60 to 70 percent. The accumulated technology, science, and practical know-how can make the shale boom the most environmentally sensitive engine

FIGURE 2.3

Change in CO^2 Emissions by Country, 2006–2012

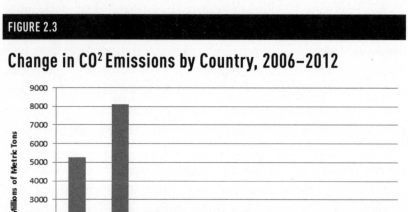

of growth in our nation's history. Increased use of natural gas now abundant from shale is already cutting greenhouse gas emissions. In fact, the U.S. has reduced its carbon emissions more than any other major country—thanks to shale gas. See Figure 2.3.

The shale revolution has also calmed fears of "peak oil." Doomsday predictions about "using up" the food, water, energy, and other resources necessary for human survival are a regular feature of history. In the third century AD, for example, a dour Saint Cyprian wrote, "The world has grown old and does not remain in its former vigor. It bears witness to its own decline; the rainfall and the sun's warmth are both diminishing; the metals are nearly exhausted; the husbandman is failing in the fields; the sailor on the seas...."[35] More recently, the Club of Rome issued its infamous *Limits to Growth* in 1972,[36] a Chicken Little report as groundless as Cyprian's lament.

History again and again reveals the human capacity to overcome temporary scarcity by finding new resources or substitutes. The shale revolution is the most recent and powerful example of this elasticity of natural resources. It is now clear that oil and natural gas are much more sustainable resources than we realized only a few decades ago. This is an achievement of the "ultimate natural resource"—the human mind—which will adjust, adapt, and create unless political powers suppress the freedom to innovate.

"Climate change" has supplanted "peak oil" as the anxiety du jour, and it poses the greatest regulatory threat yet to fossil fuel energy sources. With a president who declares the increasingly gauzy concept of climate change a greater threat to civilization than ISIS, the headwinds facing the shale revolution may be daunting.

What makes today's popular doomsday predictions about climate change disturbing is the degree to which they have become institutionalized in the media, entertainment, academia, law, and the regulatory state. The notion of shrinking mankind's "carbon footprint" has become a cultural norm. Yet our carbon footprint is the means by which we live longer, healthier, and freer lives than our ancestors did only a century ago. Show me someone who uses very little carbon, and I will show you someone who is likely very poor (or very, very rich). And on a closer look, high consumption of fossil fuels has allowed prosperous countries to shrink man's physical footprint on the natural world. "Decarbonizing" is a delusional concept. Our bodies are built of carbon. It is the chemical basis of life on earth.

In his important book *The Age of Global Warming*,[37] Rupert Darwall notes that policies intended to avoid the climatic dangers of fossil fuels lead to unintended results. The wind and solar farms required to supply power for large urban areas would destroy millions of acres of natural biodiversity. Imagine how many tens of thousands of acres would have to be paved over to provide electricity for Manhattan if it were all done with windmills. To power the entire nation with windmills would lead to the industrialization of the wilderness of America. How is that green?

Eliminating fertilizer made from natural gas would reduce the food supply—increasing the chronic hunger now suffered by five hundred million human beings. Germany's rush to renewables has increased the use of coal-fired electric generation just to keep the electric grid from melting, and wood—the preindustrial dirty fuel—now accounts for roughly 50 percent of the European Union's renewable portfolio.

The pedigree of today's doomsday prophets goes back two centuries to the English cleric and economist Thomas Malthus, who speculated that the earth's carrying capacity sets ironclad limits on the size of the human population. We will address Malthusian theories at greater length in subsequent chapters, but we observe here that Malthus and his disciples have—to date—always been wrong. Nevertheless, they have often done a lot of damage along the way.

Malthusian energy policies forecasting "peak oil" have regularly recurred since the middle of the nineteenth century when Edwin Drake drilled what history regards as the first commercial oil well. Only months before the shale revolution made itself felt, concern about peak oil and increasing oil imports produced the Energy Policy Act of 2007. Among other follies, that law imposed the Renewable Fuel Standard for corn ethanol and advanced biofuels, providing generous subsidies for ethanol

Two Energy Models and Two Economic Models: Solyndra v. Mitchell

Solyndra Model: Venture Socialism

- Hundreds of billions of dollars of taxpayer subsidy to "jump start" unprofitable renewable energy.
- Government picks winners and losers; subsidized winners undergo bankruptcy.
- Tax and regulate fossil fuels to create scarcity and increased price.
- Average cost per green job from stimulus subsidies: $10 million.
- Economic pie contracts—weak economic recovery from recession.

Mitchell Model: Private Capital in Competitive Free Markets

- Risk-taking entrepreneurs invest in innovative technology in competitive private market.
- Shale revolution creates thousands of new high-paying jobs within a few years.
- Continuous innovation reduces cost and increases output of production.
- The economic pie grows and everyone benefits.

makers. The ethanol mandate has achieved none of its objectives—reducing oil imports, displacing gasoline, improving air quality, and reducing carbon dioxide. The advanced biofuels that the law sought to promote are still non-existent in commercial quantity), though the EPA has fined refiners millions of dollars for their failure to blend gasoline with those nonexistent biofuels.

What the ethanol mandate did accomplish was reduction of the global food supply in what is still the basic source of calories for much of the world population—grains. A year after the law was enacted, corn prices increased from $2 per bushel to $8. Food shortages occurred in many developing countries as the price of corn also increased the price of all food grains. In 2015, the ethanol mandate absorbed 40 percent of the U.S. corn crop. Multiple studies now conclude the production of ethanol is a net energy loss and increases genuine pollution and carbon dioxide. Ethanol policy is a prime example of counterproductive, outdated, and ethically offensive federal energy policy.

Green Energy: The Wrong Bet

There are so many reasons to be optimistic about the shale revolution, but the chief obstacle to this extraordinary energy opportunity remains the federal government. As Harold Hamm reminds us, the U.S. is on its way to becoming "energy dominant in the world" before the end of this decade. Private markets can chart the course; we don't need grand federal plans.

We can't take full advantage of America's energy opportunity if we keep pouring tax dollars into inferior "green energy" sources like wind and solar. That's the wrong bet. After decades of lavish subsidies and mandates, let the renewables industry find its own place in the competitive market of diverse fuels without any taxpayer subsidies.

Our national leadership needs to promote drilling in North America. We should not be hesitant or embarrassed to responsibly develop our energy bounty. Reducing the pollution once associated with oil, natural gas, and coal is one of the major public policy success stories of the second half of the twentieth century, but nobody talks about it. However disappointing to some who have pledged their careers to politicized climate science, carbon dioxide is not a genuine pollutant capable of harming human health. Fossil fuels—abundant, affordable, concentrated and versatile—are superior to other energy sources at this time.

The "green energy" lobby is on a never-ending quest for taxpayer handouts for an industry that supplies less than 3 percent of our nation's energy needs. In the first eight months of 2015, wind produced 1.7 percent of all energy consumed and 4.3 percent of our electricity. Solar power produced 0.6 percent of all energy consumed.[38]

The shale industry, by contrast, does not need or seek government funds. (Oil and natural gas producers take advantage of tax deductions available to all businesses, but they don't use taxpayer-funded subsidies.) The shale industry creates new value and thus enlarges the economic pie. Subsidizing renewable energy merely distributes a static or shrinking pie. All the government needs to do to encourage the great American oil and gas renaissance is to get out of the way. That's a message that only the Saudis and the Iranians could hate. Unfortunately, getting out of the way doesn't come naturally for politicians and federal regulators.

Paying Down the National Debt

One issue to consider in the debate over national energy policy is this: how much could the federal government raise in royalties, drilling fees, and income taxes if it allowed a drilling on federal lands? We have examined the latest geological inventories made by the U.S. Energy Information Administration, the USGS, and private think tanks like RAND to get a rough estimate of how much energy there is and what it is worth.

With the aid of Jack Coleman, a former Interior Department engery expert, we found that the untapped resources in states like Alaska, California, Colorado, Texas, and Utah and under the Outer Continental Shelf are so bountiful that the recoverable totals of oil with existing technology are more than 1.5 trillion barrels. And there is approximately three quadrillion cubic feet of natural gas. The value of this energy is at least $50 trillion, and at least fifty times annual U.S. consumption. This estimate is almost certainly low, because drilling technologies are improving so rapidly that Uncle Sam is continually raising the inventory of what is "technically recoverable."

By allowing drilling on federal lands, the United States could increase output by nine hundred thousand barrels of oil per day for twenty years, which would increase production by 150 percent through 2037. There could be a corresponding 80 percent increase in natural gas output (0.9 Tcf/year increase for twenty years). If those figures seem implausible, consider that U.S. oil and gas output are already up about 75 percent since just 2007.

If President Obama's successor allowed drilling on federal lands and pursued what the government calls a "high-production" strategy over the next twenty years, we estimate that royalties would bring in $1.1 trillion, with an added $0.15 trillion from natural gas. Another $1.25 trillion in direct federal income taxes would be collected on the oil and gas industry. Lease payments would raise approximately $210 billion, bringing total revenues over twenty years to just over $2.7 trillion.

The total passes $3 trillion when including federal income taxes on suppliers and other contractors involved in these production activities, plus federal income taxes on the million or more new, highly paid employees of the exploration and production companies, their suppliers and contractors. State income, property, severance, and other taxes could raise another trillion dollars or more for states and localities. That's more revenue than just about any bipartisan deficit-reduction plan could ever deliver. In short, the oil and gas under our federal lands and waters is the fiscal equivalent to a cure for cancer.

Imagine how foolish it would have been if the Saudis had decided forty years ago not to drill for their oil. When President Obama absurdly argued after the 2015 Paris Climate Change Conference that we must keep these resources "in the ground," did he remotely understand that he would deprive Americans of millions of high-paying jobs and the nation of $50 trillion of added output over the next two decades? This could be the greatest act of national economic self-mutilation in world history.

To be clear: we are not talking about drilling in Yosemite or Yellowstone, or as President Obama once jibed, on the National Mall next to the Washington Monument. Instead we are urging an all-out national commitment to drilling on non-environmentally-sensitive lands, from the Arctic to New Mexico and offshore.

This national energy strategy would secure America's economic leadership for decades to come and would strengthen our national security by ensuring that the world is never again held hostage by OPEC or other unfriendly interests. It is the game-changer America has been waiting for. All that is required is the kind of visionary leadership that was shown by John F. Kennedy who told the American people we were going to the moon.

The shale revolution, which has unlocked vast new reserves of American energy, could be one of the most important developments in modern history. It offers more promise for prosperity and stability—not only in this country but around the world—than any economic or diplomatic plan that politicians and bureaucrats have yet dreamed up. And yet it's the progressives in the Western world who are standing athwart history yelling "Stop!"

SAUDI AMERICA
How Energy Is Remaking the U.S. Economy

To understand fully how the shale revolution has remade the American economy over the past decade, consider the unlikely transformation of North Dakota, once one of the slowest growing states, with brutally cold winters and an economy dominated by wheat farms and ranches. Consider in particular the town of Williston.

Sitting atop the Bakken shale, Williston gives you an idea of what the mid-nineteenth-century Gold Rush must have been like. The oil rush of 2007–2014 made North Dakotans rich in a hurry. One retired farmer boasted to us that, thanks to the oil rigs churning on his property, he suddenly has a net worth of more than $30 million. North Dakota now has more millionaires per capita than any other state.

Williston was once a town of about three thousand wheat farmers. It is many times that size today, but no one knows exactly how many people live there. Hundreds of workers slept in their trucks, and hotel rooms went for as high as $500 a night. The town put up temporary encampments, and new homes were popping up as fast as they can be built. At the height of the boom, the local McDonald's was offering workers up to $18 an hour plus a "signing bonus" of as much as $500; the minimum wage was irrelevant here.

The oil wells of Williston seem to be bottomless. In 1995, the U.S. Geological Survey estimated there were one hundred fifty million "technically recoverable barrels of oil" in the Bakken shale. By 2013, geologists were estimating twenty-four billion barrels. Current technology allows for the extraction of only about 6 percent of the oil trapped one to two miles beneath the earth's surface, so as the technology advances, recoverable oil could eventually exceed five hundred billion barrels. That's more than Saudi Arabia has. North Dakota has surpassed California and Alaska in oil production for the first time and now ranks second behind Texas.

The Census Bureau reports that North Dakota led the nation in the rate of job and income growth from 2007 to 2011. At the height of the boom, 2008–2013, the state's unemployment rate fell below 3 percent, though even that astonishingly low official figure was misleadingly high in a state that had ten thousand more jobs than skilled workers to fill them.

The North Dakota miracle is the result of technology and know-how and entrepreneurship, not just abundant natural resources. No one has been more surprised by the shale revolution than the federal government, which under Presidents George W. Bush and Barack Obama lavished more than $75 billion on wind, solar, ethanol, and other "clean energy" initiatives.

With the fall in oil prices from three figures to below $50 in the fall of 2015, the boom in North Dakota has shifted into a lower gear, and new drilling has slowed to a crawl for now. But with the development of more effective technologies, we are only at the beginning stages of the shale revolution.

Texas vs. California: A Tale of Two States

Before we discuss the national implications of the oil and gas boom, it's instructive to look at two states with diverging economic fortunes over the past decade.

For years, Texas and California, America's two most populous states, have been competing against each other as alternative models of growth. One state has embraced the shale revolution, while the other has spurned it in favor of green energy. The Golden State had long been one of America's big three oil producing states, along with Texas and Alaska. Its replacement by North Dakota isn't a matter of geological luck but of good and bad policy choices. California has plenty of oil and natural gas.

Though few outside the energy business have noticed, Texas nearly tripled its oil output from 2005–2014. Even with the surge in output from North Dakota's Bakken region, Texas produces as much oil as the four next-largest-producing states combined. Barry Smitherman, a former chairman of the Texas Railroad Commission (which, despite the name, regulates the energy industry), predicts that "total production could triple by the early 2020s" from the nine and a half million barrels produced per day in 2015.[1]

The two richest oil regions of the United States are in Texas: the Permian Basin (including the Wolfcamp formation) and the Eagle Ford shale formation in South Texas, where production was up 50 percent from 2012 to 2015. The Midland-Odessa urban area in the Permian, surrounded by millions of acres of remote and arid rangeland, is one of America's fastest-growing metropolitan areas.

Nearly four hundred thousand Texans are employed by the oil and gas industry (almost ten times more than in California), and the average salary in the industry has gone as high as $100,000 a year. The industry in Texas generates about $80 billion a year in economic activity, exceeding the annual output of all goods and services in thirteen individual states.

Now look at California, where oil output was down 21 percent between 2001 and 2012, according to the U.S. Energy Department, even as the price of oil remained at or near $100 a barrel. See Figure 3.1. That's not because California is running out of oil. To the contrary, California has huge reserves offshore and even more in the Monterey shale, which stretches two hundred miles south and southeast from San Francisco.

Why the Reddest State Is Covered with Wind Turbines

Even in Texas, the capital of oil and gas, the federal subsidy for wind power has led to the installation of more than twelve thousand MW of wind generation but the state has not directly subsidized this green energy. Local governments, however, have given tax abatements for renewable installations. Indirectly, the state has socialized the cost of constructing over thirty-six hundred miles of new transmission lines to connect the wind farms in the remote far western regions of the state to the urban areas in central Texas.[2] These lines extend as far as seven hundred miles from the source of wind-generated electricity to the urban end-user. The $7-billion cost of building what are called, ironically enough, the Competitive Renewable Energy Zone lines, will be imposed on retail consumers of electricity.

The Texas legislature did establish a mandatory Renewable Portfolio Standard in 1999 that obliges utilities to use a minimum amount of renewable generation. Compliance with the standards can be satisfied by purchase of "renewable energy credits." The initial goals were staggered and quite modest, with a final target of two thousand megawatts of installed renewable capacity by 2009. This proved to be a piece of cake. Texas hit twelve thousand megawatts by 2010 thanks to a generous federal subsidy. The increasingly lavish federal subsidies for construction of new renewable facilities, favorable wind conditions, wide-open spaces, and guaranteed transmission led to rapid installation of wind farms.

The Department of Energy estimates that the Monterey shale contains about fifteen billion barrels of oil—more than the estimated technically recoverable supply in the Bakken.

Unfortunately, much of California's oil lies under federal land. The Sierra Club and the Center for Biological Diversity sued to stop Occidental

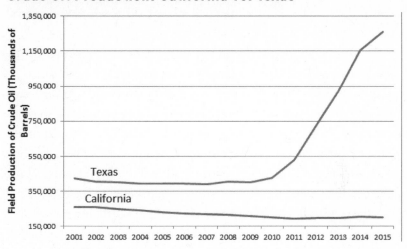

FIGURE 3.1

Crude Oil Production: California vs. Texas

Petroleum from fracking in the Monterey shale, and in 2013 a federal judge blocked fracking in California and ordered an environmental review of the drilling process that Texas, North Dakota, and other states have safely regulated for years. "We're very excited. We're thrilled," exclaimed Rita Dalessio of the Sierra Club in response to the ruling. "I'm sure the champagne is flowing in San Francisco." No doubt. Meanwhile, the oil is flowing in Texas.

Even if the oil is on private land, California can make it politically difficult to get to it. Getting approval for an oil rig can take months in California. In Texas, the average is four days. In short, Texas embraces the oil industry because almost everyone benefits from it, while Californians, brainwashed into believing that oil and gas are "dirty fuels," are embarrassed by it. Which is odd, since who drives more than Californians?

California has also passed cap-and-trade legislation that adds substantially to the costs of conventional energy production and refining. The politicians in Sacramento and their Silicon Valley financiers have made multibillion-dollar, and mostly *wrong*, bets on biofuels and other green energy. In his article "The California Green Debauch," George Gilder laments, "Sadly, the bulk of the new venture proposals harbor a 'green' angle that turns them from potential economic assets into government dependencies that ultimately deplete U.S. employment and tax revenue."[3]

Texas's open attitude toward the energy industry explains why the Lone Star State led the nation in job creation from 2007 to 2013. See Figure 3.2. In fact, Texas created more jobs than the rest of the nation combined on net over those years. The energy boom created thousands of jobs directly related to drilling but also in hundreds of service industries, such as transportation, high technology, and construction. Ancillary industries—processing oil and natural gas and the manufacture of petrochemical products, for example—also contributed to the explosion of jobs. The Census Bureau reports that from 2004–2014, net in-migration

FIGURE 3.2

Carrying the Load in the Lone Star State

Not counting Texas, fewer people are employed across the U.S. since the last recession started in late 2007

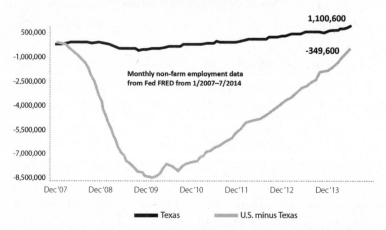

Source: Bureau of Labor Statistics

to Texas was 1.23 million people, while California suffered a net out-migration of 1.39 million people.

The Texas treasury benefits from oil production. In 2012, oil and gas production generated $12 billion in state taxes—a painless source of revenue that helps Texas avoid a state income tax. Californians, on the other hand, face a top marginal income tax and capital gains tax rate of 13.3 percent.

The only reason California lags so embarrassingly far behind Texas is that it chooses to. California's problem is not a lack of resources. The Monterey shale alone is thought to contain about $2-billion-worth of oil and natural gas. But the politicians—at the behest of their green-energy allies—have decided to wall off the state from developing its fossil fuels. Prohibitive environmental regulations, a misguided cap-and-trade law, costly renewable energy mandates, and forty years of prohibitions on almost all offshore drilling amount to a "Keep Out" sign for the energy industry. So the oil remains locked in the ground as one million Californians look for work, as its schools and roads deteriorate, and as it keeps raising taxes to balance the budget. What a tragedy.

Imagine how fast the U.S. economy would grow if California were more like Texas. Imagine how fast the U.S. economy would grow if *all* states were more like Texas. Shale oil and gas aren't the whole story of the state's success. Texas has many policy advantages over its sister states, including no income tax. But if the rest of the United States had grown as Texas did from 2007 to 2013, America would have had an additional ten million people working in 2014.

The National Energy Opportunity

Now let's look at the national economic picture. The economic recovery in the United States from 2009 to 2015 has been the slowest since the Great Depression. Figure 3.3 shows how meager it has been. Our economy has fallen about $1 trillion below the trend of growth from a normal recovery and $2.9 trillion behind the pace of the Reagan-era expansion. Job growth has been about six million behind pace. The

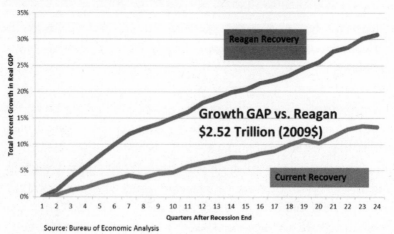

FIGURE 3.3

Recovery's Growth Gap vs. Reagan's Recovery

Source: Bureau of Economic Analysis

income of the average middle-class family fell by $500 from the beginning of the recovery through 2014. No wonder almost half of Americans surveyed in 2014 believed that the nation was still mired in a recession.

The economy's weakness wasn't for want of governmental effort. Under Presidents George W. Bush and Barack Obama, we had trillion-dollar bank and housing bailouts, $830 billion in "stimulus" spending, minimum wage hikes, cash for clunkers, $3.5 trillion of new money created by the Federal Reserve Bank, Obamacare, and tax increases on the rich. But nothing Obama or the Fed or Congress did pulled us out of recession. (Some of those measures probably *hurt* the economy.) What ended the recession was the shale revolution.

This burst in output has changed the economic landscape in important ways that most Americans still don't fully appreciate. In fact, plenty of high-powered economists undervalue the dynamic role energy plays in our economy. You can't calculate the economic value of energy using only the government data for the so-called energy sector, for those data measure only the upstream production activity, excluding the horde of service businesses directly connected to oil, natural gas, and coal and the many petrochemical industries that use petroleum and natural gas to make thousands of products. Traditional assessments of the energy sector exclude its role throughout the entire economy. From the healthcare industry to the digital universe, energy is as important to the U.S. economy as the nervous system is to the human body. The growth in the world global economy over the last century has tracked the increased consumption of fossil fuels.

FIGURE 3.4

$3 Trillion Growth Deficit

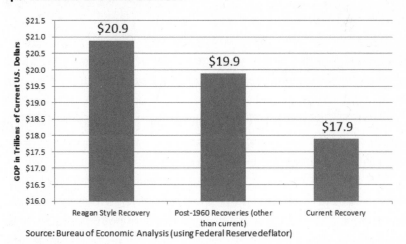

Source: Bureau of Economic Analysis (using Federal Reserve deflator)

Fracking for Jobs

As weak as the recovery from the Great Recession of 2008–2009 has been, there would have been none at all without the oil and gas industry. It created more than a hundred thousand jobs from the beginning of 2008 through the end of 2013, while the overall job market shrank by 970,000.

In 2011 alone, oil and natural gas producers and suppliers added $1.2 trillion to GDP—7.5 percent of the total. They directly contributed over $470 billion to the U.S. economy in spending, wages, and dividends—more than half the amount of the 2009 federal stimulus package. Of this spending, $266 billion was for developing new energy projects, improving existing ones, and enhancing refining and related processing operations.[4]

The Manhattan Institute's Mark Mills finds that "about 10 million Americans are employed directly and indirectly in a broad range of businesses associated with hydrocarbons." Prior to the shale revolution, the number of energy jobs in America had been falling for thirty years, but that industry is once again one of the major employers in the nation.[5]

Made in America

The collateral job growth and community redevelopment from the shale revolution have been phenomenal. In Youngstown, Ohio, steel plants have been rebuilt. Fracking has revitalized Wheeling, West Virginia, a city left for dead when the steel mills, coal mines, and factories closed. Farmers in Pennsylvania and North Dakota have gotten rich leasing their land for drilling. Pittsburgh, the capital of Marcellus shale natural gas production, is back as an oil and steel town.

Outside the Rust Belt, the petrochemical industry is enjoying massive new investment thanks to cheap natural gas. Price Waterhouse Cooper reports that $125 billion in new capital has been poured into 197 new plants.[6] The petrochemical industrial complex in the region around Houston, already the largest in the world, is dramatically expanding. The low price of natural gas has put ten thousand people to work constructing a giant new Exxon Mobil ethylene plant that will add four thousand jobs to the local economy. Terminals on the Texas Gulf coast built not long ago to handle imports of natural gas are now being reconfigured to serve as export terminals, though the Obama administration is holding up the export of liquefied natural gas with meaningless bureaucratic delays.

American manufacturing has made a comeback in recent years, and low energy prices attributable to fracking have been a major springboard

FIGURE 3.5

Electricity Industrial Prices per kWh, 2013

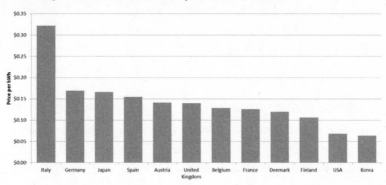

Source: United Kingdom, Department of Energy & Climate Change, International industrial energy prices in the IEA (QEP 5.3.1). Adjusted to USD using exchange rates from the report.

for this recovery. The United States now has lower electricity prices than any of its major industrial competitors except Korea (see Figure 3.5). American industries pay one-half to one-fifth of what industries in the European Union pay for power, and electric rates for American households are a third of those for German households.

In 2014, the organization Energy in Depth documented the effect of cheap oil on American manufacturing, citing more than one hundred major manufacturing facilities with $80 billion in capital investment and five hundred thousand jobs. In a series of reports tracking new capital investments in the chemical industry since 2011, the American Chemical Council points to $125 billion invested in increased production capacity that was made possible by cheap and abundant natural gas extracted from shale.[7] These investments will create over five hundred thousand permanent jobs and generate billions of dollars of new tax revenue for local, state, and federal government.

Abundant natural gas has revived the competitiveness of U.S. manufacturing that was long lost to foreign countries with far lower production costs. And the energy output of U.S. shale fields has not only brought jobs back home, but our low-cost shale energy is attracting investment from foreign companies. "Roughly half of the announced investments [in the American Chemical Council report] are from firms based outside the U.S. Our country is poised to capture market share from the rest of the world, and no other country has as bright an outlook when it comes to natural gas."[8]

Europe's Green Energy Flop

Now for the flip side of the story. One of the most dimwitted energy strategies of modern times is the Euro zone's infatuation with green energy. What Europeans have discovered in their well-meaning crusade to save the planet from climate change is that "go green" means go expensive or go infeasible or go in reverse. Europe's green blunder has sent its electric power costs soaring relative to the United States'.

Nowhere is the damage more visible than in Germany, which in 2005 passed the most aggressive renewable energy law in the world. The short-term goal was 30 to 50 percent reliance on renewables, with an eventual goal of 80 percent over the next several decades. The process of force-feeding industry and households green energy has increased utility costs and in some cases crippled manufacturing production. In 2013, a *Deutsche Welle* headline read "High Energy Costs Drive German Firms to U.S." For example, in 2014 nearly one hundred German chemical companies announced plans to invest in the United States. Everybody in Germany—including the renewables industry—has lost. And to add insult to injury, Germany's energy transformation has *increased* emissions of carbon dioxide. From 2009 to 2013, Germany's emissions of carbon dioxide rose by more than 9 percent, while U.S. emissions rose only 1.3 percent.[9]

In many cases, especially Germany, that difference is the result of the costly rush to renewable sources of electric generation. Germany drained $32 billion from its economy spent on renewable subsidies in 2014, and its former minister of energy and the environment Peter Altmaier predicts that renewable subsidies will reach one trillion euros by 2030.[10] The loss of capital assets in conventional energy infrastructure, moreover, will cost another trillion.

Subsidizing uneconomical renewable-derived electric power inevitably leads to subsidizing lots of other things: the energy-intensive industries dependent on high-priced green electricity, the conventional generators that cannot profitably compete with heavily-subsidized renewables, and the low- and fixed-income consumers who can't afford soaring electric rates. Consider the contrast with the energy transition from renewable fuels (wind and wood) to fossil fuels that distinguishes the Industrial Revolution. In England, the price of coal and of the products whose manufacture depended on coal declined and productivity rose. The cost of consumer products fell, and the average wage increased. In time, a growing and enduring middle class emerged for the first time in history. Yet the green energy policies now in vogue, gambling on uneconomical, diluted, and unreliable renewable energy sources, would force a return to pre-industrial energy scarcity that had trapped most of mankind in poverty before the Industrial Revolution.

The *Wall Street Journal* charitably calls the German renewable energy push a "gamble" that doesn't appear to ever have a chance of paying off. "Many companies, economists, and even Germany's neighbors worry that the enormous cost to replace a currently working system will undermine the country's industrial base and weigh on the entire European economy. Average electricity prices for companies spiked across the European Union, soaring by 54 percent in Germany, for instance, over the five years from 2009 to 2013 because of costs passed along as part of government renewable energy mandates."

Five years ago, many of the European nations expected the rest of the world to follow their lead and spurn fossil fuels, says Daniel Yergin, an international energy expert. That hasn't happened, and it isn't likely to. Companies cannot compete when they pay two or three times more for power than their rivals do. We will look at Europe's green blunder in more detail in a later chapter.

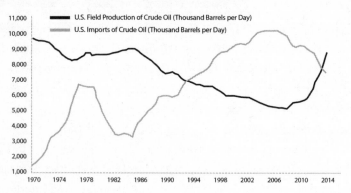

FIGURE 3.6

Imports Fall as U.S. Production Rises

Source: U.S. Energy Information Administration (EIA)

How the Malthusians Got It Wrong

The shale revolution took even the most prescient energy experts by surprise. Many economic forecasters expected oil and natural gas prices to double or triple in the years to come, and those predictions were the rationale for massive subsidies for renewable energy. President Obama betrayed his own inability to see what's coming in a statement from 2010: "Oil is a finite resource. We consume more than 20 percent of the world's oil, but have less than 2 percent of the world's oil reserves. And that's part of the reason oil companies are drilling a mile beneath the surface of the ocean—because we're running out of places to drill on land and in shallow water."[11] The next year, as the shale revolution roared on, Obama declared that oil and gas were "yesterday's energy sources."

A sustainable energy abundance is no longer in question. We now know that energy resources that were thought to be running out will be plentiful for several hundred more years. Figure 3.6 shows how domestic production has soared while imports have declined, putting America on the verge of being energy independent for the first time in nearly half a century. And because the United States is so far ahead of the other oil-producing nations in energy technologies, before the end of the decade, we can move from being energy dependent to energy dominant. It is now realistic to think about wiping out our balance-of-trade deficit.

Now for a Real Stimulus: Low Gas Prices

No one was more surprised by the swift decline in oil prices in 2014 and 2015 than President Obama. As a candidate, he had announced that his policies like cap and trade taxes would "necessarily raise gas prices." In 2009, his secretary of energy said the administration's renewable energy policies would be a success if U.S. gasoline prices reached a European level—that would be around $10 per gallon. And during his 2012 reelection campaign, he derided those who insisted that drilling could alleviate the high cost of energy. "[A]nyone who tells you we can drill our way out of this problem doesn't know what they're talking about—or isn't telling you the truth."[12]

Then between June 2014 and April 2016, the price of oil fell from $105 a barrel to below $40 a barrel. The average price of a gallon of gasoline fell to around $2. Those oil and gas prices translated to a $200-billion savings for American consumers and businesses. That's $200 billion a year we don't have to send to Saudi Arabia, Kuwait, and other foreign nations. Now that's an economic stimulus par excellence.

We don't know if oil will remain in the $30–50-a-barrel range. But it is clear that low energy prices are a gigantic economic windfall for consumers. A fall in energy prices is a massive tax cut for the world's consumers. The rule of thumb is that a one-cent reduction in the price of gas at the pump saves consumers $1 billion a year. The typical household in America spends about $5,000 a year on energy. Cutting these costs by 30 percent produces a windfall of nearly $1,500 for each family. Because low-income families spend more than twice the percentage of their budget on energy than high-income families do, falling prices for energy help the poor the most. That is the payoff from fracking and shale oil.

Are Lower Oil Prices a Saudi Plot?

We hear over and over that low oil and gas prices are actually a curse because they will drive American producers out of business and then the price will shoot up again. That's happened before. And it is true that Saudi Arabia began deluging the world with oil in 2014. This surge in supply drives the world oil price relentlessly lower. They may be strategically driving marginal wells out of business with the low prices. The Saudis are still the lowest-cost producers, so they can withstand lower prices and still make money. And indeed, oil exploration and permitting in the United States have been cut by well over half as the prices have tumbled. Nevertheless, productivity per rig increased by 400 percent from 2008 to 2014—by 40 percent alone in 2014.[13] Many wells have been drilled but await the hydraulic fracturing to extract the oil and gas, the most expensive portion of the process. And the turnaround time for completion of the wells is short.

Is the Saudi strategy working? In the short term, it has shut down many operations in the United States, but it is obvious that the most efficient wells are producing. In June 2015, one year after the plunge in oil prices, half of the drilling rigs had left the shale fields, and more than one hundred thousand jobs had disappeared. But rig counts, although widely cited by the media as the indicator for production volumes, can be misleading. This is especially the case with hydraulically fractured wells. There is a great difference in the cost of drilling, fracking, and output among these wells. "Shale technology," Mark Mills points out, "allows astonishingly fast increases in production and at volumes that can move global markets; furthermore, U.S. capital markets are inherently flexible, fast, and have plenty of capacity to fuel shale expansion almost overnight if prices and profits creep back up."[14]

The U.S. Energy Information Administration reported a production level in the United States of more than 9 million barrels a day in March 2016 and projects that the average production of the entire year will remain around 9.5 million barrels per day. That is a colossal figure and not far behind Saudi Arabia's near-record of 10.3 million barrels in May 2015. Even when prices fell by 50 to 70 percent in the course of a year,

U.S. oil production rose by 1.2 million barrels per day in 2014—the largest increase in one hundred years. Lower prices have not derailed the shale industry. It appears that the most cost-efficient and productive wells are still in operation and even setting records. Rapidly improved drilling techniques that lower costs and increase oil output have been the hallmark of the shale boom, and both trends are likely to accelerate.

The Arabs detected the emerging shale boom early on and understood its potential to make energy cheaper for decades to come. In 2011, the head of Saudi Arabia's nationally owned oil company, Aramco, predicted a shift of the global axis of energy from OPEC to North America. This shift was well underway in 2015 as Aramco ceded to the United States the role of the world's swing producer. Instead of reducing production in a time of over-supply—the economically logical response—the Saudis are maintaining production. If the U.S. shale industry can weather the glut, keep reducing its costs, and increase its output, the advantage is for the United States, which is well suited to be the swing producer, ramping up or ramping down in swift response to demand. With a massive inventory of oil in storage and as many as five thousand wells drilled but not yet fracked, U.S. producers inadvertently developed a rapidly deployable spare capacity—previously the Saudis' exclusive advantage. What an amazing shift in global geopolitics such a development would portend!

The plunge in oil prices in 2014–2015 was good for consumers, but if prices continue to drop, could we bankrupt our domestic industry? Many wells can still make money at prices well below $50 a barrel. The speed with which drillers have reduced costs while they increased output should give the pessimists a pause. Those who worry about low oil prices need to read Henry Hazlitt's classic *Economics in One Lesson*. Would it be a bad thing if OPEC and energy companies started giving their oil away for free?

In a free enterprise system, as productivity rises and technology improves over time, resources become more abundant, not less. Meanwhile, prices of those things fall. Food is the classic example. Fewer farmers today grow more food for more people than ever before, and at

lower prices to consumers. This process makes us all richer. It is true that
lower prices are not good for energy producers. For Texas, Oklahoma,
and North Dakota, the nearly 60 percent fall in prices is bad news. But
for everyone else, it is a glorious financial windfall—an early Christmas
gift from heaven. Since energy is a component of everything we produce
and consume, lower oil prices make everything cheaper—from candy
bars to MRIs to computers to airline tickets.

Lower oil prices cripple our adversaries. Fracking has helped break
the back of OPEC, now a powerless cartel, defund ISIS and other terrorist networks, and restrain Russia's territorial ambitions. What's the
problem with that? Investors may lament the decline of energy stocks,
but almost every industry other than upstream oil and gas production
benefits from lower energy prices.

Our Energy Potential

Life and politics are often rich with irony. One of the richest is that
Barack Obama, a president who wants "to end the era of fossil fuels,"
has in his two terms in office presided over the biggest explosion in oil
and gas production in history. This surge in production happened in spite
of Washington, not because of it. Mr. Obama tries to take credit for the
jobs and GDP growth from fracking even as his EPA, State Department,
and Interior Department try to tear it all down.

The United States is now the world's richest nation in energy in part
because of our vast resources but just as importantly because of our
technological prowess. What is most exciting about the potential for
expanded growth of this industry is that no government subsidies are
needed. And though some at the Department of Energy take credit for
inventing fracking, this was all private-sector driven. Al Gore did not
invent the Internet. And DOE did not invent fracking or horizontal drilling. They are simply trying to stop it.

THE LIGHT OF THE WORLD

Steve Moore was once quoted in the *New York Times* as saying that "our oil supply is infinite. We will never run out," a statement that provoked outrage. One high school science teacher wrote, "Mr. Moore: Even my fourteen-year-olds know that oil is finite." That teacher probably became a top science advisor to President Obama.

Oil is the master resource because everything else depends on it. But it is also the most unappreciated resource. Political and opinion leaders are convinced that we have a moral obligation to "conserve" energy, that every barrel of oil we use is one that our children and grandchildren won't have. Yet the truth is, as the *Financial Times* has reported, the world "is drowning in oil."

The Institute for Energy Research recently published a study showing (1) the government's best estimate of how much oil we had in America fifty years ago, (2) how much of that oil has been drilled out of the ground since then, and (3) what reserves remain (see Figure 4.1 on the following page). Today we have twice the reserves that we had in 1950.

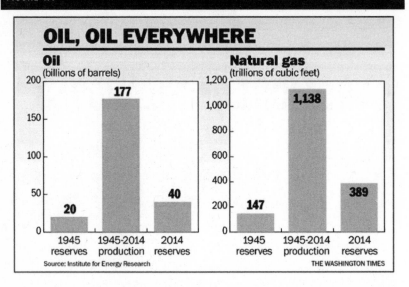

FIGURE 4.1

OIL, OIL EVERYWHERE

Oil
(billions of barrels)

- 1945 reserves: 20
- 1945-2014 production: 177
- 2014 reserves: 40

Natural gas
(trillions of cubic feet)

- 1945 reserves: 147
- 1945-2014 production: 1,138
- 2014 reserves: 389

Source: Institute for Energy Research

THE WASHINGTON TIMES

And we have already produced almost ten times more oil than the government told us we had back then.

Technology and innovation have constantly increased the amount of "finite" oil we can produce. Because we discover new sources of oil much faster than we deplete known reserves, oil and natural gas supplies are for all practical purposes nearly inexhaustible. Fracking is the latest game-changer, and the access it gives us to shale oil and gas resources has virtually doubled overnight. And this technology boom in drilling is just getting started.

To become more prosperous over time, we don't want to conserve energy, we want to use it. Why? Because high energy consumption is an indispensable condition for a modern, prosperous society. Try to imagine your life without the man-made energy flowing through every moment of your day. We are so dependent on energy that its presence, action, and value go unnoticed. And almost all of that energy comes from fossil fuels. Anyone who talks about "decarbonizing" our economy is talking about demodernizing it as well.

Modern Life Uses *a Lot* of Energy

What do we use our energy resources for? That seems like a question with a patently obvious answer, but it's shocking how few people know where energy comes from and how it is used. When we speak to high school and college kids, we ask, "Where does your electricity come from?" And most of the kids point to the outlet in the wall. Ah, the millennials. They know everything, don't they? For those who are wiser and know what they don't know, here are some energy basics.

The United States consumes around one hundred "quads" of heat energy—that is, one hundred quadrillion British thermal units—every year.[1] We use about 40 percent of our energy for electricity, 30 percent for mobility, and 30 percent for "raw heat" to warm ovens and hair dryers and to power countless manufacturing processes. And approximately six of the one hundred quads are converted into "ordered forms of precise power capable of driving radios, microprocessors, lasers and CAT scanners."[2] As Peter Huber and Mark P. Mills remind us in their provocative book *The Bottomless Well*, since the Industrial Revolution, the conversion of raw heat into focused power has been on a trajectory toward faster, lighter, stronger, cleaner, and more precise power generated within less space.[3] The modern wind turbines and solar farms covering millions of acres represent a regression from this improving environmental trend.

Mechanical power was the first pivotal, man-made conversion of thermal energy. Power to move and lift is no longer derived from the backs of men or the muscle of animals. "It is precisely the availability of inanimate sources of power that has enabled man to transcend the limitations of biology and increase his productivity a hundred times over."[4] Electricity was another transformative refinement of thermal energy that vanquished darkness, easing and amplifying human life. Electric power still fuels our work and personal freedoms all day every day. It gives us instant, automatic, compact, silent, clean access to individualized energy services of limitless variety. It provides our food, materials, and mobility and does the work that once required "relentless drudgery," as the historian Gregory Clark characterizes hard manual labor.

In a more recent development, electricity now delivers knowledge. Electric power is "the sole energizer of electronically transmitted information with unmatchable control, precision, and speed."[5] No energy, no Internet, no Google, Facebook, or Netflix. The vast system supporting the information-communication-technology (ICT) universe now consumes 10 percent of all electric generation, a share that is projected to grow enormously as the use of digital technology increases in developing countries. This estimate accounts for data centers, wired and wireless broadband networks, and devices like personal computers, tablets, and smartphones. This tally does *not* include the energy powering the manufacture of this hardware. As Mark Mills puts it, "The cloud begins with coal."[6]

The ICT system uses approximately 50 percent more electricity than global aviation. Imagine consumers' response to an EPA rule rationing our access to that system! The essential data centers must have reliable electric power twenty-four hours every day. Wind and solar power, inherently intermittent sources of electric generation, are incapable of providing the digital universe with the reliable generation for which coal remains the mainstay.

Hydrocarbon energy is also embedded in the majority of all the materials used in every home and workplace. Compounds derived from fossil fuels are the raw materials for thousands of synthetic materials. How would a zero-carbon economy replace these goods and the services they provide?

Utterly Dependent on Fossil Fuels

The increase in energy consumption since the Industrial Revolution is staggering. Western Europeans consume on average six to seven times more energy per day than did their forbears of two centuries ago,[7] and the average American's daily consumption of energy is twice that of the Europeans. Some condemn our consumption as profligate, while others simply stand in wonder at how abundant energy has enhanced the lives of people of every income level.

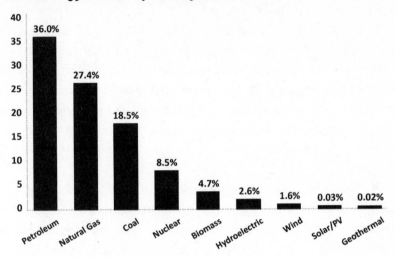

FIGURE 4.2

U.S. Energy Consumption by Source, 2013

Source: U.S. Energy Information Administration (EIA)

Only a trace of those hundred quads that Americans annually consume derives from renewable energy sources. Modern civilization is still utterly dependent on fossil fuels. Non-fossil-fuel energy sources—wood, wind, solar, hydro, geothermal, and nuclear—make up less than 15 percent of the world's total primary energy supply.[8] Nuclear power and hydroelectric power generate far more electricity than all the other renewable sources combined. After several decades of aggressive subsidy, promotion, and even mandates, non-hydroelectric renewable energy sources (wind and solar) in the United States account for only about 3 percent energy consumption.[9] See Figure 4.2 above.

Nevertheless, senior policymakers in the wealthiest and most educated Western countries remain intent on quickly deriving at least 80 percent of our energy from renewables. Their refusal to take into account fundamental laws of arithmetic and physics threatens the supply of affordable energy and therefore the foundations of modern prosperity. Michael Kelly, a professor of engineering at Cambridge University and a fellow of the Royal Society, explains the scope of what they propose: "Since 90 percent of global improvement in mankind's estate since 1800 has been enabled by burning fossil fuels, the scale of the decarbonization project is without historical precedent."[10]

Exponential growth in energy consumption is a defining characteristic of industrialized countries. Developed countries already consume enormous amounts of energy and will continue to do so. And developing countries, if they wish to become developed countries, will consume more energy as well. The global supply of fossil fuels and primary electricity has *increased more than one hundred and sixty times since 1850,*[11] and the supply must continue to grow unless mankind is going to take a giant step backward.

As long as the sun continues to shower us with light and heat, our energy supply will be unlimited. But "energetic order"—*usable power*—can be costly. We spend more "on equipment used...to concentrate and convert energy—generators, furnaces, car engines, motors, and light bulbs, for example"—than we spend on raw energy itself.[12] The supply of energy available for human purposes has not only grown by tremendous volumes, but the extraction, processing, conversions, and end uses of energy have achieved astonishing economic efficiencies as well as environmental sensitivity in prosperous countries. In developed, industrialized economies, we get two to four times more power per unit of energy source than a century ago. Societies are spending less money for far greater energy output. And the physical footprint of our energy infrastructure keeps shrinking. If every computer was as large as the 1960s mainframes, the Internet would not exist. Thanks to tiny microprocessors that operate as the intelligent engines of our computers, we have the Internet, the cloud, and our super smartphones.

And here we encounter the fatal flaw of the renewables so enthusiastically promoted today as a means of averting dangerous climate change. Technologically enhanced from their pre-industrial forms, today's renewable energy systems are less energy efficient than their hydrocarbon counterparts. In some cases, it takes more electricity to

generate electricity from a wind turbine than the turbine produces—
hardly a formula for sustained economic growth.

Energy and the Poor

No one has a bigger stake in sound energy policy than the billion
human beings in poor countries who still live without electricity. The
policies of the U.S. government and of institutions like the World Bank
and the International Monetary Fund condition financing for electrifica-
tion on the use of inferior and expensive renewable energies. As Bjorn
Lomborg notes, "In a world in which malnourishment continues to claim
at least 1.4 million children's lives each year, 1.2 billion people live in
extreme poverty, and 2.6 billion lack clean drinking water and sanitation, this growing emphasis on climate aid is immoral.... Green energy
sources may be good to keep on a single light.... But they are largely
useless for tackling the main power challenges for the world's poor."[13]

The callousness of the doctrinaire warmists is chilling. In an editorial
titled "Sacrificing Africa for Climate Change," Caleb Rossiter, a professor of statistics at American University and a former fellow of the Institute for Policy Studies (IPS), scathingly observed, "Western policies seem
more interested in carbon dioxide levels than in life expectancy."[14] For
departing from the left-wing orthodoxy on climate policy, Dr. Rossiter's
twenty-year fellowship at IPS was summarily terminated.

Just What Is Energy?

Definitions and distinctions are important. Basic physics distinguishes "energy," "power," "force," and "work." Aristotle coined the
word "energy" by combining the Greek preposition *en*, meaning "at" or
"in," with the noun *ergon*, meaning "work." The dictionary definition
of energy—"the capacity to do work"—is useful, but mechanical, or
kinetic energy, expended in physical work like typing, pounding a nail,
or lifting a book, is only the most visible form of energy; there are many

others. "Power," frequently confused with energy, is defined as energy "at work," the "rate of energy use," or more precisely, "the rate at which work is done."[15] "Work" is defined as force multiplied by the distance or resistance through which force acts.

Although it's everywhere, energy remains an elusive phenomenon even to scientists who have devoted their lives to studying it. Most of the public discussion about global warming reflects an understanding of energy that is shallow at best or totally incorrect at worst. Perhaps the most damaging misconception is the prevalent assumption that wind, solar, or biomass (wood and plants) can accomplish the work now performed by oil, natural gas, and coal. Policies intended to reduce man-made carbon dioxide by 80 to 85 percent represent a huge gamble with humanity's future.

A grasp of a few hard facts, a little arithmetic, and some basic physics are necessary to avoid calamitous blunders in energy policy. We will therefore take a detour through eighth-grade biology and tenth-grade physics to clarify some fundamental properties about energy. We will examine basic forms, measures, and functions of energy usually missing from current policy debates about fossil fuels.

Forms of Energy

Basic physics distinguishes multiple forms of energy observable in both natural and human processes. The most fundamental forms are heat (thermal), motion (mechanical or kinetic), chemical (food and fuel), and light (electromagnetic). We also live under the earth's gravitational energy. Damming the flow of rivers in order to generate hydroelectric power is an example of converting gravitational energy.

Thermal

The most fundamental form of energy is heat. The heat energy generated by the sun, converted into chemical energy in food, and then digested by the human body sustains life. Conversion of the high temperatures in fire to useful heat was mankind's early attempt to control energy, and the overwhelming majority of current systems for generating electricity are still based on heat energy, whether they use fossil fuels, uranium, or concentrated solar power.

Kinetic

Also known as mechanical energy, kinetic energy is associated with all motion and moving objects. Mechanical energy operates in wide-ranging natural and human process—weather, weapons, and every motion of the body. The muscles of human beings and animals act as a kind of heat engine to generate mechanical energy for movement and work.

The signal breakthrough of the Industrial Revolution was generation of mechanical energy by means of steam. The steam engine converted into rotary motion the thermal energy released by combustion of the chemical energy stored in coal. A machine could now perform the work that human or animal muscle had performed. With mechanized kinetic energy, the inherent energy limits of pre-industrial societies based on the products of recent photosynthesis were shattered.

The polymath Matt Ridley provides a vivid example of the magnitude of mechanical power gained in the shift from animal muscle to inanimate machine. By 1870, Ridley notes, the mechanical power provided by England's steam engines was equivalent to the work of six million horses.[16]

Chemical

Chemical energy is the most pervasive form of energy. The functions of the human body illustrate the potency and versatility of chemical energy. The human body, of course, depends on the daily consumption of what was originally solar energy stored in food to sustain life. A marvelous chemical reactor, the human body transforms the original solar energy stored in plants, a result of photosynthesis, as well as the meat and dairy products derived from animals nourished by plants, into chemical, thermal, mechanical, and electromagnetic energy.

Through the pathways of the body's metabolism, the human body converts the chemical energy in food and inhaled oxygen to power breathing, maintain temperature, pump blood, digest food, and transmit the brain's nervous signals. Whether at the intracellular level or in brute bodily motion of the most regular or exceptional form, physical human life is driven by a finely-tuned energy system known as metabolism.

Measuring Energy

Despite its diverse manifestations, energy can be measured in consistent quantitative units. Enabling us to compare different sources, forms, conversions, and uses of energy, these measurements throw considerable light on current debates about fossil fuels and green energy from renewable sources. All energy sources are not created equal, and they are not all suitable for every job.

For example, the energy content of coal is approximately two–four times that of wood, which makes coal a far more efficient and less costly fuel. And the power density of natural gas-fired electric generation—at its maximum efficiency—is almost two thousand times greater than that of wind-generated electricity.[17] When all the energy used to produce a gallon of corn-based ethanol is calculated—planting, fertilizing, harvesting, distilling, and transporting—a gallon of ethanol is a net energy loss. In many instances more energy is consumed in producing ethanol than is gained by burning ethanol in the internal combustion system of a vehicle. Not surprisingly, the fuel efficiency of ethanol measured in miles per gallon is about one-third that of gasoline.[18]

Throughout this book we will examine such variables as energy density, energy content, energy efficiency, energy intensity, and the energy cost of energy. To understand these concepts, you need a little

FIGURE 4.3

SI Units for Energy

Joule (energy)	J
Newton (force)	N
Watt (power)	W
Length	L
Temperature Celsius	C
Kilogram (mass/weight)	kg
Volume (liters)	L3
Area	L2

arithmetic and physics. The numbers, units, and symbols for quantifying energy may be a tedious menu for many readers, but with a little patience, these basic units of measurement are readily intelligible, and they are valuable for understanding the many conundrums of energy policy. These measurements are less intimidating than you might think. In fact, they are similar to the nutritional information printed on food labels. The calorie figure on a soup can is a measure of the energy or heat content of the soup. You'll be able to compare the flux of energy stored in an egg from a large hen with the energy in a barrel of crude oil. The egg stores almost as much energy as the barrel of oil![19]

Energy Measurements

The International System (commonly abbreviated "SI," from the French version of the name) is the world's most commonly used units of measurement in science, commerce, and government. English-speaking countries, on the other hand, have been slow to adopt the metric system and the SI units for energy, but they are gradually moving in that direction. Outside of science, the SI units are still not commonly used in the United States. Clinging to miles, foot-pounds, horsepower, calories, and British thermal units (Btu), the customary units remain a dominant system of measurement in this country. There are formulas for converting the measures from one system to another, but this is a cumbersome process for the layperson. For reasons of simplicity and clarity, this book will rely on SI measures with equivalents in customary units wherever necessary.

The most familiar customary measure of energy in the United States is the calorie, which measures the amount of energy—or heat value—in food. For example, one loaf of bread contains roughly 1,400 calories, or 5,714 Btus. As a measure of energy understood as "the capacity to do work," one person would have to eat twenty-two loaves of bread to complete the same work as a car engine burning one gallon of gasoline, which contains 126,000 Btus.[20] One Btu represents the amount of thermal energy (heat) necessary to raise the temperature of one pound of water by one degree Fahrenheit.

Energy Density

Energy density is a straightforward measurement of the amount or content of energy per unit of weight (gravimetric) or per unit of volume (volumetric). Measured in Joules (J) per unit of weight or volume, energy density is a measurement of the heating value of the fuels. Measurement of energy density explains the many energy choices in daily life, historical progress, and economic productivity. Concentrated energy sources confer enormous advantages for extraction, transport, and storage and allow versatile conversions. The relatively higher energy density—and even more so the power densities—of coal, oil, and natural gas is, in large part, why the British Industrial Revolution and its aftermath achieved such unprecedented gains in economic productivity.

By weight, energy density is calculated as Joules per gram (J/g) or megajoules per kilogram (MJ/kg). By volume, energy density is calculated as Joules per cubic centimeter (J/cm3) or megajoules per liter (MJ/L).

FIGURE 4.4

Energy Density by Weight and Volume

From Table A.6, Smil, *Energy in Nature and Society*, at 392

Energy Density by Weight		Energy Density by Volume	
Hydrogen	142–120 MJ/kg	Hydrogen	0.01 MJ/L
Bituminous coal	29–28 MJ/kg	Jet Fuel	33 MJ/L
Natural Gas	39–29 MJ/kg	Natural Gas	35MJ/m3
Propane	50–45 MJ//kg	Crude Oil	35 GJ/m3
Methane	55–50 MJ/kg		
Oil refined product	42 MJ/kg		
Gasolines	47–41 MJ/kg		
Diesel	46–41 MJ/kg		
Dry wood	16–12 MJ/kg at best		
Granola Bar	17 J/g		
Carrots	1.7 J/g		

FIGURE 4.5

Power Density[21]

Power Source	Power Density in Watts per square meter (W/m2)	
	Low	High
Natural Gas	200	2000
Coal	100	1000
Solar PV	4	9
Solar CSP	4	10
Wind	0.5	1.5
Biomass	0.5	0.6

Source: Vaclav Smil

In Figure 4.4, note that the volumetric density of crude oil, measured in gigajoules (GW), is a thousand times higher than that of natural gas. This is why, without compressing or liquefying natural gas, the transatlantic shipment of natural gas does not make economic sense. And natural gas is not a suitable fuel for aviation, where volume or weight is limited. Hydrogen has an energy density by weight far higher than that of any other fuel at 143 MJ/kg, but its volumetric density is minuscule compared with that of crude oil. Kerosene, the traditionally preferred fuel for aviation, has a volumetric density of 33 MJ/L—more than three thousand times that of hydrogen.

Quantifying the power density of different fuels reveals glaring contrasts between renewable energy sources and fossil fuels. If energy density measures the energy content per unit of weight or volume, power density measures the energy flow that can be harnessed from a given unit of volume, area, or mass. Although there are different formulas for quantifying power density, the broadest measure estimates in watts per square meter (W/m^2) and may include all the ancillary area beyond the generating site to include production of materials, transport, and related infrastructure.[22] Different methods of measuring the power density yield different numbers. What remains constant across different numbers is the massive differential between the power densities of renewable gen-eration and of conventional fossil-fueled and nuclear generation.

Watts per square meter is a measure of how much of the surface area of the earth is required to generate electricity. This measure can also include the amount of land used to extract and process raw materials and transmission infrastructure to calculate the power density of the entire system.[23] Coal, natural gas, and nuclear generation have far greater power density than wind, sunlight, or wood (biomass) as a source of generation. That the power densities achievable in fossil-fuel-fired electric generation can be *thousands of times greater* than in renewable systems was the key insight of Google's RE<C engineers.[24]

Generating electricity from renewable sources requires huge amounts of land and material.[25] When used as a generating fuel, the power densi-ties of wind and wood range from 0.5 to 1.5 W/m^2, whereas natural-gas-fired generation systems can achieve a power density of two thousand W/m^2.[26]

In a brief essay, Vaclav Smil points out meeting 20 percent of the world's demand for electricity with wind would be a Herculean task.[27] This is a modest amount of wind generation compared with what is envisioned in most climate policies. Because the wind blows intermit-tently, wind has a capacity factor on average of only 20–30 percent. Thermal power plants using the heat from the combustion of fossil fuels can reach a capacity factor of 75 percent or higher. Thus, to meet demand with wind requires far more generating hardware (turbines and land area) on which to erect that hardware than fossil fueled power plants. Even with the larger, improved wind turbines of 3 MW installed capac-ity, you would need to manufacture, transport, and install four hundred thousand new turbines to meet 20 percent of demand.[28] This is the insight of Google's engineers when they noted, "The scale of the building would be like nothing ever attempted by the human race."[29]

Replacing our current fossil-fuel-based electric system with wind, solar, or biomass would require thousands of times more land than is now used for fuel extraction, electric generation, and transmission, encroaching on millions of acres of the surface of the earth. Most advocates of rapidly replacing fossil fuels with renewable fuels seem unaware of this challenge. The implications of trying to use energy fuels with the inherently inferior power densities of wind, solar, and biomass will be addressed throughout this book.

Energy and Climate

The theories of man-made global warming and predictions of catastrophic climate change are based on assumptions about the earth's climate system that are not confirmed by observational evidence. The empirical sciences have long understood that measurement, observation, and experiment are the essential means of validating a scientific hypothesis. Claims of consensus cannot trump physical evidence. As the renowned paleogeologist Ian Plimer, of the University of Adelaide, argues, "The theory of human induced global warming is not science because research is based on a pre-ordained conclusion, huge bodies of evidence are ignored, and the analytical procedures [climate models] are treated as evidence."[30]

To oversimplify, it is said that the relatively small increment of man-made carbon dioxide added to the natural atmospheric concentration of carbon dioxide since the Industrial Revolution disrupts the natural dynamics of climate. Adding more carbon dioxide, a greenhouse gas, to the atmosphere could lead to some warming, but could the relatively small additional increment of man-made carbon dioxide overpower the natural variables of climate, leading to planetary catastrophe?

Since 1988, the "official" scientific account of global warming has been under the aegis of the United Nations' Intergovernmental Panel on Climate Change (IPCC), composed of scientists appointed by member countries. Every four or five years, the IPCC issues an "assessment report" on the current state of the science. The IPCC is charged with providing the science to support the theory that mankind's consumption of fossil fuels is causing global warming (the physical science), predicting the symptoms (effects, adaptation, and vulnerability), and prescribing remedies (mitigation) to human-induced emissions of carbon dioxide

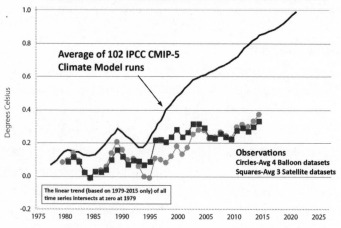

FIGURE 4.6

Global Bulk Atmospheric Temperature (Surface–50k ft)
IPCC Modeled Predictions vs. NASA's Observations

Average of 102 IPCC CMIP-5 Climate Model runs

Observations
Circles-Avg 4 Balloon datasets
Squares-Avg 3 Satellite datasets

The linear trend (based on 1979-2015 only) of all time series intersects at zero at 1979

Degrees Celsius

Source: John R. Christy, University Alabama in Huntsville, Testimony before the U.S. House Committee on Science, Space & Technology (2 Feb 2016); model output, KNMI Climate Explorer.

assumed to cause the alleged disease of global warming. The panel's multiple roles of scientist, soothsayer, and policy maker corrupted the scientific process from its inception. As Richard Lindzen, a revered professor emeritus of atmospheric sciences at MIT, puts it, "The charge to the IPCC is not simply to summarize [the state of climate science], but rather to provide the science with which to support the [UN's] negotiating position whose aim is to control greenhouse gas levels. This is a political rather than a scientific charge."[31]

In a 2009 scandal popularly known as "Climategate," e-mails between key authors of the IPCC's 2008 assessment report revealed an even darker side of the IPCC: active efforts to suppress, destroy, and manipulate data, to exaggerate temperature records and to prevent the publication of works by dissenting scientists in academic journals.[32] Several investigations followed, and some leading scientists called for a dissolution of the IPCC, but the UN-driven process limped on.

To the surprise of many, the 2013 IPCC assessment report acknowledged the gap between the modeled predictions of warming and physically observed temperatures lower than the models. The report also concluded that meteorological records do not indicate a higher incidence of extreme weather events.[33] The political alarmists, including President Obama and many European leaders, however, continue to issue urgent warnings about catastrophic climate change in the here and now that are at odds with the IPCC's latest assessment report. (The IPCC document that makes headlines and is fodder for politicians and activists is not the extensive report written by the scientists but the "Summary for Policy Makers," written by appointed government officials and only a few of the scientists.)

The politicians, the media, and the activists bombard the public with horror stories of imminent and irreversible climate catastrophe. Yet many of the most scientifically prominent alarmists recognize that the evidence does not support such stories. Gavin Schmidt of NASA's Goddard Institute of Space Studies grants that "general statements about extremes are almost nowhere to be found in the [scientific] literature but seems to abound in the popular media."[34] And he is not alone.

Energy: From the Cosmos to Your Body

The climate issue now pervades our culture and is institutionalized in law. The phrase "climate change" has been used in so many vague ways that it has become virtually meaningless. Of course the climate changes. The real issue is energy: the natural forces operating in the galaxy in which the earth resides as well as the energy now harnessed for human purposes. A consideration of some basic physical realities about energy in its many forms and pathways is a useful filter for the exaggerated nonsense typical of official discourse about climate change.

Energy operates incessantly throughout our physical world, within our solar system, atmosphere, plant and animal life, and the human body. Everything and everyone are constantly moving and changing. The sun orbits the gravitational center of the Milky Way galaxy; the earth orbits the sun, and our moon orbits the earth. Energy pulses through the universe on a galactic scale and through your body as it digests this morning's breakfast.

There are fundamental parallels between the pathways and transformations of energy in the natural world, in the human body, and in fossil-fueled societies. For instance, the way the human body burns the chemical energy contained in food is similar to the way the internal combustion engine of an automobile burns the chemical energy in gasoline.

Both natural and man-made energy systems rely on a constant supply of energy, require water, and emit heat. Both systems oxidize carbon. But while the body's natural metabolic system is fixed, the man-made energy system is continuously expanding—amplifying, ordering, and accelerating the transmission of energy and power for human use whenever someone flips a switch or taps on a smartphone. The evolution from Edison's first light bulb to low-emission diode bulbs to state-of-the-art diode lasers is marked by improved efficiency, performance, access, and speed.[35]

Modern man's energy system is still interconnected with nature's energy system. Like the man-made system operating across the world, the earth's biosphere is "an intricate, interactive assembly of energy stores and flows." The term "biosphere," in this regard, refers to the physical home of human beings—the earth and its atmosphere. The earth's biosphere is unique in the known universe. Indeed, as Paul Davies shows in his provocative book *The Cosmic Jackpot*, given all the conditions that had to coalesce with astonishing precision to support life, the earth is an extraordinarily lucky planet.[36] It is the only planet in our solar system—the only one known at this time—with enough atmospheric oxygen to support human life. And oxygen is a kind of waste product of photosynthesis!

The carbon cycle—the earth's system that supports animal and plant life—operates through the constant reception and conversion of external energies.[37] And among those conversions of energy necessary to maintain animal life is inhalation of oxygen and exhalation of carbon dioxide. Plant life operates in the reverse, inhaling carbon dioxide and exhaling oxygen. Atmospheric carbon dioxide is an essential nutrient for life on this planet and hence called the gas of life. Human beings exhale 4 to 5 percent more carbon dioxide by volume than they inhale.[38] This makes the concentration of carbon dioxide in human expiration about forty thousand parts per million (ppm)! The current atmospheric concentration of carbon dioxide is now about four hundred ppm, including man-made contributions from the combustion of fossil fuels.[39] Atmospheric levels of carbon dioxide in 1850 are thought to have been about 280 ppm.

The earth's location in our solar system is also essential to its ability to support life. The position of the earth gives it continuous access to a massive source of energy—the star we call the sun. The earth is a planet orbiting one of two hundred to four hundred million stars within the constellation Sagittarius in the Milky Way. Unlike Venus, which is too hot to support carbon-based life, or Mars, which is too cold, the earth rotates on its axis at an optimal angle and distance from the sun.[40]

The sun is the original source of almost all the energy accessible to mankind.[41] With the exception of the geothermal energy inside the earth and tidal energy driven by gravitational forces, the energy generated by the sun is the source of all energy on the earth, including wind. Geothermal energy is responsible for tectonic shift, volcanoes, and earthquakes. And the heat inside the earth played an important role in transforming dead plant and animal matter into fossil fuels over millions of years of compression. Tidal energy originates from shifting gravitational interaction of the orbits of the sun, earth, and the moon.

"That the sun influences our climate should not be surprising…when we consider that 99.98 percent of the total energy of the world's climate comes from the sun."[42] Oddly, the UN's IPCC, whose "science" is the authoritative support for climate policy to supplant fossil fuels, largely dismisses the sun's effect on climate.[43] The IPCC assumes that the increased man-made emissions of carbon dioxide over the previous two centuries overpower the influence of the sun—and of all other natural climactic variables, such as water vapor, clouds, and aerosols—on climate.

The question of the climate's sensitivity to anthropogenic carbon dioxide added to the atmosphere is crucial to the IPCC's predictions of warming in the future. IPCC models assume anthropogenic carbon dioxide amplifies the greenhouse effect of natural water vapor and thus may double warming caused by carbon dioxide. Since the mid-1990s, the rate of warming predicted by the IPCC's models has not occurred. The temperatures actually measured by NASA's remote sensing satellites and balloons are substantially lower than the IPCC's modeled forecast. As shown in Figure 4.6 on page 86, the average warming of the IPCC's 102 climate models is one degree Celsius for the period 1979–2013. Observational measurement of global temperature over the same period is only 0.2 degree Celsius. This means that the climate sensitivity (or warming) expected from the doubling of atmospheric carbon dioxide is more likely to be three times lower than the IPCC models assume.[44]

In its Fifth Assessment Report, issued in 2013, the IPCC concedes that its models may assume too much sensitivity to man-made emissions of carbon dioxide and too little natural variability. Yet the first pages of the report's "Summary for Policy Makers" conclude with high degree of certainty that human influences prevail. Although climate sensitivity to man-made carbon dioxide is a core assumption of the models, the IPCC's acknowledgment of its uncertainty is buried under a host of qualifications.[45]

Human Activity Trumps the Power of the Sun?

To get a sense of the power of the sun, consider that it burns over six hundred million metric tons of hydrogen every second. If the resulting heat were converted to electricity, it could meet the energy needs of the earth's current human population for eons.[46] The sun's energy is produced through nuclear fusion, in which the atomic nuclei of hydrogen

Just Where Does Energy Come From?

Energy and how it operates are questions that have preoccupied philosophers, scientists, engineers, and artists for thousands of years. Energy is so intimately connected to life itself that it almost seems equivalent to physical life. Major advances in the scientific understanding of energy and its engineering applications have occurred only within the past two centuries. Although we know more about how energy operates in the natural world and how it can be harnessed for human purposes, we still lack a clear understanding of what energy *is*. Is it a particle or a wave? Is it a capacity or something physical? Albert Einstein's famous formula—energy equals mass times the speed of light squared ($E = mc^2$)—and that formula's practical applications in nuclear physics make this much clear: matter itself is a repository of massive energy.

Understanding the operation of energy in our lives, society, and the natural world is important, because if now misunderstood, current government actions to supplant fossil fuels and to decrease energy consumption could reverse the trajectory of progress enjoyed over the last century by an increasing percentage of the world population. The late Nobel laureate physicist and author of many popular books Richard Feynman concluded that energy remains an elusive, subtle concept. "It is very, very difficult to get right."[47] Current energy policies to replace coal plants with subsidized solar panels and wind turbines do not get energy right unless a return to energy scarcity is the goal.

and helium are fused. Man has applied nuclear fission, in which atomic nuclei are split, but the practical applications of nuclear fusion remain elusive. If nuclear fusion were commercially viable, we would have at our disposal an almost infinite and pollution-free source of energy. Clearly, the physical dynamic of our planet generates a surfeit of energy. The challenge is how to access and convert the energy into forms affordable, adaptable, and acceptable to human societies.

Made of Sunlight

The human body—like all complex plant and animal life on earth—depends on transformations of the sun's light energy. Solar radiation—also known as visible sunlight—is a form of the electromagnetic energy generated by the sun in between infrared and ultra-violet radiation on the electromagnetic spectrum.

To a large extent, our bodies are constructed by sunlight. And the agent is the most fundamental natural energy conversion on the earth, commonly known as photosynthesis catalyzed by atmospheric carbon dioxide. The transformation of solar radiation into chemical energy sustains the growth of the tissue in living plants. Carbohydrates, the food base on which human life depends, originate through photosynthesis.

Typically taught without inspiration in eighth-grade science classes, photosynthesis is the most important energy conversion on the planet. James Watt's steam engine, which converted the heat energy in coal to mechanical energy in a machine, is the most important anthropogenic conversion of energy. Before mankind harnessed fossil fuels on a large scale in the Industrial Revolution, the energies available for human use were limited to what recent photosynthesis could provide in the form of fuel for heat, food, and raw material for clothing and shelter.

All human beings depend on the chemical energy available in plants for food, and the world's poorest societies still depend on it for heating fuel as well. Developed societies, on the other hand, no longer rely on woody plants as a source of thermal and chemical energy. For that purpose, they depend on the products of ancient photosynthesis—the remains of life from long-dead plants and organisms transformed and concentrated through millions of years of compression and heat inside the earth—that is, fossil fuels.

Don't Forget the Diamonds!

Carbon, indeed, is the stuff of life. It occurs in countless forms. Diamonds represent a relatively pure form of carbon, noted for their incomparable hardness and conductivity. Graphite—good old pencil lead—is another relatively pure form of carbon. The opposite of a diamond, graphite is dark and soft.

In the second decade of the twenty-first century, humanity sits atop two centuries of major advances in physics, biology, and chemistry that have applied hydrocarbon compounds for mankind's benefit. Yet the doomsayers of our age employ the term "carbon" as if it were a poison threatening the survival of civilization.

The *American Heritage Dictionary* provides a concise explanation of photosynthesis: "Almost all life on earth depends on food made by organisms that can perform photosynthesis such as green plants, algae, and certain bacteria. These organisms make carbohydrates from carbon dioxide and water using the light energy from the sun.... Almost all of the oxygen in the earth's atmosphere was produced as waste by photosynthetic organisms."[48]

The primal energy conversion for life on the earth, photosynthesis is relatively inefficient. The amount of solar radiation that reaches the earth is the energy equivalent of twenty million calories per day per surface acre, and the average percentage of that radiant energy that plants capture and convert into plant tissue is relatively minute—averaging less than 0.3 percent.[49]

Human beings, however, digest carbohydrates produced by photosynthesis with an energy efficiency (the ratio between the amount of energy input and the actual energy output) of 99 percent.[50] Many machines, or "prime movers" as engineers call them, that convert energy from one form to another, like the turbines used by modern thermal

Questions about Climate Science

Climatological research over the past three decades, supported by hundreds of billions of dollars from taxpayers world-wide, nominally excluded research on natural climate variables such as the sun and water vapor. In the U.S., the federal government selects the research projects and provides the majority of research funds. The overwhelming majority of those research grants were devoted to studies that reinforced—but did not prove by empirical evidence—the original theory that mankind's use of fossil fuels will lead to "dangerous interference with the climate."[51]

As shown in Figure 4.6 on page 86 (modeled temperature predictions), the IPCC's all-important computer models have substantially exaggerated predicted warming for decades. Many senior scientists in the field conclude that it is time to declare the IPCC's methodology and computer models a failure. A portion of the federal research funds should be allocated to those highly credentialed scientists—now marginalized as skeptics—to assess the IPCC's work over the last several decades and to offer alternative theories and evidence.

President Obama often speaks of the "dictates" of climate science. Yet the predictions of computer models that are contradicted by measured observation—actual temperatures—hardly offer scientific justification for eliminating the energy sources on which modern society is utterly dependent.

power plants, can convert 99 percent of the turbine's mechanical energy into electricity.[52] Given that the sun's radiant energy is showered on the earth every day, the energy that goes into the photosynthetic conversion is largely irrelevant. In this sense, the earth is not a closed system of energy. The sun will come up again tomorrow, and human innovations will continue to surprise us.

As we shall see later, the chief factor limiting plant productivity—photosynthetic efficiency—is the level of atmospheric carbon dioxide, which is currently at a relatively low level compared with previous eras in the earth's long history. Yes, you read that correctly. Agricultural productivity would be substantially increased if the atmospheric concentration of carbon dioxide were much higher. This is why nurseries often pump carbon dioxide into greenhouses.

The earth's atmosphere is now 78 percent nitrogen and 20 percent oxygen; the remaining 2 percent consists of trace gases such as carbon dioxide and argon. Natural carbon dioxide accounts for a minuscule 0.039 percent of the atmospheric gasses we actually breathe at the tropospheric level. Human activity—breathing as well as burning oil, natural gas, and coal—accounts for 3 to 5 percent of the atmospheric level of carbon dioxide, that is, about 0.002 percent of all the gasses in the atmosphere.[53] We wonder how this trace of carbon dioxide from human activity could override the power of the sun in matters of climate or weather. Observed temperatures do not reflect the assumed climate sensitivity to carbon dioxide that drives the models.

Carbon: The Chemical Basis of Life or a "Weapon of Mass Destruction"?

The political use of the word "carbon" to denote a pollutant that, if not eliminated, will lead to a planetary meltdown is utterly detached from reality. In an address to a large international gathering, Secretary of State John Kerry stated that carbon is "among the worst weapons of mass destruction." President Obama and Christina Figueres, head of the UN's climate program, regularly declare the urgent need to decarbonize human societies. This is a shorthand slogan for eliminating the use of fossil fuels now providing 80 to 90 percent of energy across the world.

Communism, says Figueres, is more likely to save the planet than democracy.[54] The long-sought goal of a global agreement on reducing carbon emissions assumes mandates imposed by strong central governments. Surprisingly, the long-awaited climate agreement reached in Paris in 2015 does not appear to bind any country in a legally enforceable manner, but international politics may be a different story. The Paris climate pact incorporates "pledges" to reduce greenhouse gases submitted by each country. The pledges—known as "Intended Nationally Determined Contributions" (INDCs) to reducing greenhouse gases—are voluntary, but the text repeatedly speaks of the agreement's legal effect and "entry into force." At the least, a huge international bureaucracy is now empowered to badger national governments about their pledges.

Governments and the private sector have already directed hundreds of billions of dollars to ridding the world of carbon. Betting on the success of this effort would be a highly risky investment. Carbon, after all, is defined as "the chemical basis of all known life."[55] Have people forgotten this fact?

How can carbon be a weapon of mass destruction *and* the basis of all known life? As Humpty Dumpty said to Alice when she asked if a word can mean anything you like, "The question is, which is to be master—that's all."[56] Climate policy is ultimately about power—will energy be controlled and allocated by big, centralized governments or by free persons acting in competitive market economies?

Hydrocarbon compounds represent a host of useful natural chemicals and synthesized compounds, providing the chemical building blocks for such ubiquitous materials as plastics, polyester, lubricants, and solvents. With the addition of phosphorous and other elements, carbon also naturally forms DNA and RNA as well as adenosine triphosphate (ATP). ATP is the most important energy-transferring molecule in all living cells. Decarbonizing anyone?

Policy vs. Reality

One of our favorite *New Yorker* cartoons shows a giant electric fan blowing into a windmill to get the turbines to rotate. It's a humorous reminder that the aggressive political pursuit of green energy as the dominant source of electric power runs afoul of some basic physical realities. Given the magnitude of the human damage and geopolitical weakness that would follow a collapse of the complex energy systems on which modern societies depend, a more critical assessment of renewable energy is urgently needed. Engineers and physicists typically have an intuitive understanding of why wind and solar power are not promising candidates to provide base load electric power for large cities. Climate scientists and most policy makers do not.

Energy remains an elusive concept, easily misunderstood by policy makers who would impose grand plans on society. The late economist Julian Simon reminded us that energy is the master resource because it allows the extraction, transport, and transformation of all other natural resources. If world leaders continue to impose energy policies that contradict fundamental energy realities, the damage will extend far beyond higher electricity rates and could lead to a world much poorer and less free.

Without abundant, affordable, reliable, and versatile energy, economic growth will be undermined. The productivity achieved through man's relatively recent energy enrichment, commonly known as the Industrial Revolution, will be unraveled. Poverty will increase and the middle class will shrink, a trend already occurring across the world, even in the United States. The ruling elites will go unscathed, protected as they were before the Industrial Revolution, while the rest of mankind reaps the bitter harvest of false green hopes.

The global warming alarmists and many educated elites have lost their faith in man's ability to adapt and to tame his natural surroundings. Making carbon the enemy of the planet means that mankind is the enemy of the planet. Our bones, blood, and flesh are made of carbon. As in so many earlier fits of pessimism, the source of these damaging policies is the misanthropic view that the "common enemy of man" is man.[57] The prophets of doom have the story backward: the abundant energy that is a product of human ingenuity makes our planet habitable, not inhabitable.

DARKNESS REIGNED
The Pre-Industrial Era

"Civilization," writes Matt Ridley, "like life itself, has always been about capturing energy."[1] The quests for food, relief from back-breaking labor, and the expansion of human horizons beyond sheer survival dominated man's efforts to capture energy throughout most of history. As late as 1800, 80 to 90 percent of the population of the United States worked in agriculture. With the bulk of the population laboring to harvest natural materials—food, fuel, and fiber—for mere subsistence, the number and variety of goods were necessarily scant. Then came the Industrial Revolution, and the percentage of the U.S. population working in agriculture declined to 41 percent by 1900. Today that figure is 1.5 percent.[2] Man-made energy now does most of the work that human or animal muscle had to perform in pre-industrial societies. No longer are the "fortunes of the harvest" equivalent to the "fortunes of the economy," as was the case in pre-industrial eras.[3]

Our energy-enriched lives—characterized by convenience, comfort, recreation, information, and mobility—would have been unimaginable for an average family even in the early twentieth century. Indeed, economic historians have documented the extreme poverty in which the overwhelming majority of humanity across the world was trapped until around 1800. (See Figure 1.1 on page 5.) The great breakthroughs in productivity and the political reforms of the nineteenth century delivered the populations of the Western world from the poverty and oppression that most of mankind has taken for granted. How essential, therefore, that we not take for granted our liberty and affluence, for which abundant energy remains a necessary condition.

Before the British harnessed and converted the inanimate, concentrated energy stored in coal, the energy supply available for human use was diffuse, sparse and expensive, and it offered only limited power to amplify the muscles of men or animals. The historian Carlo Cipolla summarizes the magnitude of the transition from pre-industrial energy scarcity to industrial energy abundance: "The Industrial Revolution opened the door to a completely new world, a world of new and untapped sources of energy such as coal, oil, electricity, and the atom; a world in which man found himself able to handle masses of energy to an extent inconceivable in the preceding rural world. From a narrowly technological and economic point of view, the Industrial Revolution can be defined as the process by which a society gained control over vast sources of inanimate energy."[4] Vaclav Smil calculates that global consumption of fossil fuels amounted to no more than 1.5 EJ as late as 1800 but had risen to 443 EJ by 2005.[5] (1 exajoule (EJ) = 10^{18} joules.)

The Malthusian Trap

The pre-industrial era has been called mankind's long sojourn in the "Malthusian trap." The British cleric and scholar Thomas Malthus (1766–1834) is known for his theory that the growth of human population is limited by the fixed amount of land on which food can be grown. Although Malthus's theory accurately described the energy limits in pre-industrial economies, it has been repeatedly refuted by modern economic growth and energy-enriched agricultural output.

Two hundred years later, you can still attract attention by predicting that we shall run out of natural resources or exceed the planet's carrying capacity. Paul Ehrlich, Lester Brown, White House science adviser John Holdren, and the other pessimistic purveyors of these gloomy forecasts—none of which ever has come true—are aptly called Neo-Malthusians.[6] Human nature is drawn to predictions of colossal disasters, and scary news sells more than good news. We easily forget what the late economist Julian Simon and others have shown—human creativity is the "ultimate resource," continually expanding our access to the master resource called energy.[7]

When Malthus wrote his *Essay on the Principle of Population*[8] in 1798, Britain was in the early stages of the Industrial Revolution—a revolution in economic growth that his theory precluded. He assumed that the world's supply of tillable land and timber was an insuperable barrier to economic growth. "Elevated as man is above all other animals by his intellectual faculties," he wrote, "it is not to be supposed that the physical laws to which he is subjected should be essentially different from those which are observed to prevail in other parts of animated nature."[9] Yet even as he penned those words, men were exercising their intellectual faculties on technologies that would transcend the physical laws by which Malthus believed they were permanently limited.

Malthus argues that when good harvests increased the food supply, income per capita would temporarily rise, only to be brought back down by increases in population. When drought or pestilence ravaged the supply of food and heat energy, nature would "cruelly" check growth. Incomes would decline, malnutrition would inevitably decrease fertility or shorten life span, and the population would decrease. In a Malthusian world, mankind is trapped by the same natural laws that apply to animal populations.

According to Malthus, birth rate must match death rate. If it does not, nature will inevitably check growth by reducing the standard of living. As he argued, population expands geometrically (i.e., 1, 2, 4, 16, 32, 64, 128, etc.), while food supply can increase only arithmetically, acre by acre, on an assumed fixed area of land (1, 2, 3, 4, 5, 6, etc.). "The power of population is indefinitely greater than the power of the earth to produce subsistence for man."[10] In other words, increasing human numbers must outstrip the productive capacity of a fixed extent of land. Great Britain had made important improvements in agricultural techniques, but they were marginal compared with the great hydrocarbon enrichment. The huge gains in agricultural productivity later made possible by fossil fuel–based fertilizer, transportation, and refrigeration were simply unfathomable to Thomas Malthus.

The energy breakthrough that undermined Malthusian pessimism, of course, was not confined to a single decade or even century. England and a few other countries, particularly in Europe, had been using coal for heat energy from the late sixteenth century. The Dutch economy, relying on windmills and the younger fossil fuel peat, advanced beyond England's for a time. Then peat became scarce, and the Dutch economy waned. British coal was another story. From 1800 on, the energy contributed by coal dwarfed energy delivered by human muscle, draft animals, and firewood combined.[11]

Back to Photosynthesis: Nature's Most Important Energy Conversion

Prior to the harnessing of fossil fuels little more than two hundred years ago, human societies relied on the limited and variable supply of energy annually captured in recent plant growth. Mankind was at the mercy of the weather and the productivity of the land for an adequate food supply and almost everything else necessary for survival. Heating fuel, essential for households and almost all production, was derived from trees and woody plants. Food, clothing, and shelter came from plants or animals dependent on plants that human beings cannot digest. The mechanical energy necessary for agriculture and production of all goods came from human and animal muscle. Although water wheels, wind mills, and other creative devices stretched the available mechanical power in some places, their contribution was marginal, as it is today.

The average person enjoyed a small range of goods. The production of textiles, metals, glass, and ceramics required wood for heat energy and so was extremely limited. Clothing was expensive and thus remarkably limited even for the more affluent members of society. The small clothes closets in even the grandest of homes built before 1950 indicate the relatively higher cost and lower availability of energy. Turning cotton, wool, and animal hides into material suitable for clothing was an energy-intensive, and therefore expensive, process. Today, 60 percent of all fibers derive from synthetic materials for which oil and natural gas are the raw materials as well as the fuel source for manufacturing power. The result is enormous growth in the supply and diversity of textiles. The price of clothing as a percentage of income has dramatically declined.

Metals like steel, so associated with the industries arising in the Industrial Revolution, provide another good example of energy constraints based on plant growth within a fixed area of land. Naturally occurring metals such as iron ore, although perhaps plentiful in some areas, required massive volumes of wood for smelting. Wood was also in high demand for buildings, home heating, and almost all fledgling industries.

Hard Lives and Grim Deaths

Human innovation could substantially stretch the land's bounty to increase the harvest, income, and population, but increased demand and bad weather could reverse those gains. Unavoidably subject to nature's destructive whims—drought, flood, famine, pestilence—or to human foibles such as war, man's subsistence was precarious, particularly for children and the infirm. For most of recorded history, global average life expectancy hovered around only twenty-five years.[12] Many people reached an advanced age, but 30 percent of children died before fifteen.[13] In the early phases of industrialization, England achieved a longer average life span than any other country—thirty-five years.

Carlo Cipolla provides a vivid description of the unrelenting proximity of death in pre-industrial societies. "Mortality was very high in

A Short History of Fossil Fuels

Coal is the most abundant fossil fuel and has the longest history. China may have used coal to smelt metals as early as 1000 BC, long before it was used in Europe. Archaeological evidence indicates that coal was used for limited purposes in ancient Greece and Rome.[14] American Indians used coal long before European explorers discovered it in 1673. Commercial coal mining began as early as 1740 in Virginia. Thomas Edison opened the first central power plant fired by coal in 1882 to provide lighting for four hundred lamps and eighty-two customers.

With a far higher energy density and heating value than wood, coal has been long valued as the heating fuel in a wide variety of applications. In the industrial age, coal provided the heating fuel to make steel and to power steam turbines in ships, railroads, and power plants. Coal use has slightly declined in the United States but accounts for 30 percent of global energy consumption and global use of coal is increasing faster than any fossil fuel.[15]

Natural gas (mostly derived from coal) was put to commercial use in the early stages of British industrialization. The widespread commercial use of natural gas is relatively recent, although natural gas seeping from the ground had been recognized in ancient Greece and Rome. In 1816, Baltimore, Maryland, became the first city to light houses and streets with processed natural gas. Robert Bunsen's invention of his eponymous burner in 1885 opened many opportunities for this versatile fossil fuel.

Although Herodotus described oil pits near Babylon, and Marco Polo reported the collection of oil near the Persian city of Baku in the thirteenth century, the first sustained commercial application of petroleum did not occur until the middle of the nineteenth century in the United States—also the era when the internal combustion engine was invented. Petroleum is an extraordinarily versatile energy source. Refined oil can be separated into different parts called fractions, from which we get propane, butane, multiple petrochemicals, gasoline, kerosene, jet fuel, home heating oils, ship fuel, lubricating oils, and asphalt, to name just a few. Perhaps six thousand products in daily use are derived from petrochemicals.[16]

medieval and modern Europe. A woman who managed to reach the end of her fertile life, let us say at age 45, had normally witnessed the deaths of both of her parents, the majority of her brothers and sisters, more than half of her children, and often she was a widow. Death was a familiar theme. And it was a 'grim business.' With no alleviation of pain, the bitterness of death was very real."[17] It's still true, as John Wayne said, that "nobody gets out of this alive," but the grim reaper no longer hovers so close to our children.

The elites were not spared the sorrow of early mortality. Only two of Thomas Jefferson's six children survived childhood, and one of them, his daughter Mary, died at twenty-five. Only his daughter Martha survived to adulthood. His wife, also called Martha, died at forty-four, probably from complications in childbirth.[18]

Stretching the Pre-Industrial Energy Limits

However a pre-industrial society might have stretched its energy supply, there was an inherent limit to the productivity of land. Innovations may have abounded, but the majority of the population dependent on a fixed area faced limits to the improvement of its living conditions and real income per person.

Where coal seams, oil deposits, or gas vents were near the surface of the earth, ancient civilizations made limited use of fossil fuels.[19] Still, as long as man depended primarily on the sun and vegetation for mechanical and heat energy, a dramatic improvement in his living conditions was out of reach.[20] When the timber, cropland, pasture, water, peat, or human labor ran out, notes Matt Ridley, the economic good times ended.[21] The vast majority of the population lived lives of "laborious poverty," in the memorable words of the nineteenth-century economist W. S. Jevons, just a poor harvest away from starvation.[22]

Human living standards, especially in Western Europe, had made gains in many areas centuries before the Industrial Revolution. Improvements to agricultural methods increased the food supply, supporting a larger population. Roads, canals, and ships brought more commerce and trade. Universities emerged in Bologna, Paris, Oxford, and elsewhere in the eleventh and twelfth centuries. The development of the printing press in the fifteenth century enhanced the accumulation and transmission of knowledge and spurred inventive technologies. The arts flourished, though they were mostly inaccessible to the bulk of the illiterate population. And of critical importance, long before 1800 much of Europe—especially Great Britain—had legal institutions that secured the rule of law, property rights, and contracts.

Although we tend to see the great achievements of history as a cumulative and unitary historical process, such a view overlooks the critical role of energy in determining life expectancy, real income, and other elements of man's material well-being. There were few sustained gains in life span, per capita income for the majority, and population until after 1750.

In the historian Edward Wrigley's view, the poverty to which the bulk of humanity was long consigned in pre-industrial eras cannot be attributed exclusively to pre-democratic political systems. All economies dependent on the limited and variable energy harvested from the land are subject to severe physical constraints.[23] "The main bottleneck for pre-industrial economies was the strictly limited supply of energy," according to Cipolla.[24] The energy factor is often overlooked in economic histories or subsumed under the categories of land, raw materials, technology, or machines. Abundant, cheap, dense, and versatile energy, as

Cipolla, Wrigley, and other historians argue, was necessary to sustain the economic growth begun in the English Industrial Revolution.[25]

From Organic to Mineral

Another way to understand the fundamental difference between pre-industrial and industrial societies is in the contrast between an *organic* economy and a *mineral* economy. The energy supply in an organic economy depends on plant growth—often called an "animate" source. In a mineral economy, energy supply depends on a vast store of inanimate minerals—a class of natural resources which typically includes coal, oil, and natural gas. Yet fossil fuels contribute so much more than minerals. Another telling difference between pre-industrial and industrial energy sources is the difference between the former's origin in "living nature" and the latter's origin in "ancient nature." As Matt Ridley put it, "The secret of the industrial revolution was shifting from current solar power to stored solar power."[26]

The energy capacity of coal, oil, and natural gas is on a completely different scale from that of plants or minerals such as iron or copper. The stored heat and chemical content in fossil fuels can generate thermal, mechanical, or chemical energy or can be transformed into synthetic materials. These minerals are the "master resource," as Julian Simon pointed out, because the energy capacity of fossil fuels can transform all the other natural resources into a host of different materials, and fossils can be used as a raw material to make synthetic materials.[27]

Fossil fuels are hydrocarbon chemical compounds, originating from the physical remains of once living plants and animals, which have been compressed and heated in the earth and below the ocean floor for millions of years. You too could become fossil fuel in a few million years. What an astonishing circle of life! The fossilized remains of once living plants and organisms rejoin the biosphere to amplify life. And the carbon dioxide emitted in the combustion of these once living but now geologically cooked plants and animals enriches the growth of living plants.

Mankind's Energy History

Man's first energy advance came around 8000 BC when human groups began to cultivate crops and raise livestock instead of hunting and gathering what unassisted nature might provide.[28] Nomadic populations shifted to permanent settlements to tend crops and animals, laying a foundation for cities, trade, and the division of labor so closely associated with economic growth. Curiously, this seismic shift in the patterns of human society arose in at least seven different locations on three continents around the same time.[29]

This Neolithic agricultural revolution augmented the supply of food and materials needed for human survival. For thousands of years, however, the gains could not sustain a continuously increasing population while improving living standards for the bulk of that population.

A brief review of the energy sources on which all human societies relied until Britain inaugurated the great energy enrichment should make us appreciate the gifts of energy we enjoy.

Food Energy

Provision of an annual food supply plentiful and cheap enough to meet the basic needs of every member of a given population has been a chronic challenge for human societies until quite recently. Living generations are the heirs to a monumental expansion of the global food supply. Against all odds, the twentieth-century agricultural revolution achieved colossal gains in productivity that generated more food for a much larger population. Between 1961 and 2007, the world population doubled from 3.1 billion to 6.7 billion, but food supply per person increased by 27 percent.[30] This growth would have been inconceivable in pre-industrial eras. Fossil fuels, indeed, have allowed mankind to transcend what was an intractable limit on food supply—the fixed acreage of earth's arable land.

Although innovative cropping methods and animal-derived fertilizers stretched agricultural productivity in various societies, the gains were usually on the margin and could be rapidly reversed by natural, political, or economic conditions. England had achieved the greatest gains in

The Simple Story of Energy according to Matt Ridley

"The story of energy is simple. Once upon a time all work was done by people for themselves using their own muscles. Then there came a time when some people got other people [a.k.a. slaves] to do the work for them, and the result was pyramids and leisure for a few, drudgery and exhaustion for the many. Then there was a gradual progression from one source of energy to another: human to animal to water to wind to fossil fuel. In each case, the amount of work one man could do for another was amplified by the animal or machine. The Roman empire was built largely on human muscle power, in the shape of slaves.... The European early Middle Ages were the age of the ox.... With the invention of the horse collar, oxen then gave way to horses, which can plough nearly twice the speed of an ox, thus doubling the productivity of a man.

"In turn oxen and horses were soon being replaced by inanimate power. The watermill...became so common...that by the time of the Domesday Book (1086), there was one for every fifty people in southern England.... The windmill appeared first in the 12th century and spread rapidly.... But it was peat, rather than wind, that gave the Dutch the power to become the world's workshop in the 1600s....

"Hay, water, and wind are ways of drawing upon the sun's energy: the sun powers plants, rain and wind. Timber is a way of drawing on a store of the sun's energy laid down in previous decades—on solar capital, as it were. Peat is an older store of the sunlight—solar capital laid down over millennia. And coal, whose high energy content enabled the British to overtake the Dutch, is still older sunlight, mostly captured around 300 million years before. *The secret of the industrial revolution was shifting from current solar power to stored solar power* [emphasis added]."[31]

agricultural productivity and population on the eve of industrialization. Many historians note that a larger population combined with a food supply to nourish that population were factors key to England's ascension in the Industrial Revolution. And the fruit of the "ghost acres" England imported from America bolstered that food supply.

Throughout most of history, increased agricultural yield was the result of putting additional acres under cultivation rather than increasing the productivity of each acre. Over time, this approach did not appreciably increase the food supply and often encountered the law of diminishing returns from marginal, less fertile soils. Over the millennia, human societies played a game of tug-of-war in which a bountiful food supply led to an increased population, which eventually overpowered the available foodstuffs, followed by a reduction of population—an economy subject to the same rules, really, as wild animals. The relation of the size of a human population to the supply of land and food was radically altered by fossil fuels.

Fuel

Wood and woody plants overwhelmingly dominated the fuel supply throughout the pre-industrial era, as they still do in the poorest of nations. Alarmingly, some major European countries, committed to rapidly replacing fossil fuels with renewable fuels, are reverting to wood for home heating and generation of electricity. The European Union estimates that wood accounts for 50 percent of the renewable energy consumed in its member countries—a development that the *Economist* rightly describes as "environmental lunacy."[32]

The return of wood as a major source of energy is the result of the spike in European electrical rates cause by the rush to wind and solar. The United Kingdom is subsidizing wood-burning stoves, demand for which has skyrocketed. Even as the most prosperous and educated Western countries revert to wood as fuel, wood-burning cook stoves are responsible for the deaths of four million people a year in developing countries. European wood-burning cook stoves may be more efficient than their Indian and African counterparts, but the reappearance of wood smoke inside the home is a pitiful step backward.[33] According to Environment and Human Health, Inc., "Although wood smoke conjures up fond memories of sitting by a cozy fire, it is important to know that the components of wood smoke and cigarette smoke are quite similar, and that many components of both are carcinogenic."

In addition to the adverse environmental effects of burning wood, use of wood on a large scale has an obvious drawback: replenishment requires many decades if not more than a century of tree growth. Fast-growing varieties of trees and woody plants are now cultivated in some parts of the world, but it still takes decades to replenish this source of fuel.

Charcoal derived from wood was the most energy-dense heating fuel in the pre-industrial era, but it was highly inefficient. With an energy density of 29.7 MJ/kg, charcoal has a heating value far higher than that of wood, which ranges from ten to fourteen MJ/kg.[34] Charcoal was the only fuel adequate for smelting iron ore and other naturally occurring metals, but the production of charcoal was extremely wasteful. More wood—and thus more heat energy—was required to make charcoal than could be generated from the final product. And the power density of wood relative to the amount of land required to grow it is only 0.5 to 0.6 W/m²—a power density thousands of times weaker than the most efficient power plants fueled by natural gas.[35] Such energy constraints on pre-industrial metallurgy were reflected in widespread deforestation in Europe prior to the Industrial Revolution.

For a sense of the energy cost of charcoal, consider that the production of 10,000 tons of iron could involve burning the trees felled on 100,000 acres of forest.[36] Fossil fuels have shrunk the human footprint on the surface of the earth as will be discussed in a later chapter. With coal, the output of metals could eventually be measured in the millions, not thousands, of tons. And thus steel—the iconic metal of the steel cathedrals (factories) and machines of the industrial age—was accessible on a vast scale without deforestation.

Muscle Power

Until fossil fuels provided the motive power for the plethora of machines invented from the seventeenth through the nineteenth centuries, mechanical power was severely constrained by what human and animal muscle could provide. For the majority of mankind, the muscles of human and animal bodies remained the dominant source of mechanical energy until the mid-twentieth century. The grueling degree of some forms of human labor in the early stages of the Industrial Revolution is chillingly depicted in the accompanying photo of a young "drawer" pulling a tub of coal up a narrow mine shaft in England.

This job was typically performed by a child or woman working twelve hours per day. Common in the early 1800s, the drawers pulled wagons filled with coal up an underground shaft as small as sixteen inches in height. In 1842 Parliament forbade employment of women and girls in the coal mine.[37] In contrast to this horrific job, the typical manufacturing labor in prosperous modern societies (even in coal mines) might be described as managing—rather than bodily generating—energy flows through mechanical devices.

A young "drawer" pulling a coal tub up a mine shaft.

Before machines did the heavy lifting, the hard limits of animate mechanical energy could be achieved only with a huge concentration of labor or by creative devices like levers and pulleys. Early civilizations amassed labor not for manufacturing but to construct architectural monuments such as the pyramids of ancient Egypt and the cathedrals of Europe. Men were true beasts of burden.

"Without mechanical devices to overcome the effects of gravity and friction, individual human capacities to lift and carry loads are limited to modest burdens," observes Vaclav Smil.[38] Ingenious devices were developed that amplified the work of human muscles. Wheels, axles, levers, pulleys, wedges, inclined planes, tread wheels, and other devices were used, but the mechanical power gained was inherently limited. The maximum sustained human exertion of muscle, Smil calculates, was fifty to one hundred Watts. Animals are much stronger. Draft animals with the appropriate rigging and collars can sustain power of four hundred to eight hundred Watts, with an average of six hundred Watts—six to eight times greater than the capacity of human muscle.[39] Oxen, mules, and horses meaningfully amplified mechanical power and were indispensable over the centuries, but they also competed with human demand for limited arable land and calories. But it is the huge power differential between horses—overall the most powerful animate source of mechanical energy—and the early machines that shows why the Industrial Revolution was indeed an epochal shift for mankind.[40] (See Figure 5.1 below.)

FIGURE 5.1

Power Capacity in Horsepower of Mechanical Prime Movers

Ox pulling a load	0.5
Donkey mill	0.5
Vertical water mill	3
Post windmill	8
Newcomen's steam engine	5
Watt's improved steam engine	40

Source: Power to the People, p. 77

Watt's steam engine could produce forty times the power of one horse. Matt Ridley correctly notes, therefore, that by 1870, "the capacity of the country's steam engines alone was equivalent to six million horses or 40 million men, who would otherwise have eaten three times the entire wheat harvest."[41]

Water and Wind Power

Waterwheels and windmills—which ultimately depend on solar radiation—were important in augmenting mechanical energy, especially in the most advanced societies, on the eve of the Industrial Revolution. These energy converters were used as early as the first century AD[42] and were popular in Europe from the Middle Ages onward. William the Conqueror's Domesday survey counted at least six thousand water wheels in the kingdom of England in 1086. By 1300, the number had grown to twelve thousand.[43] Waterwheels were the "most advanced energy converters of the early modern world," writes Smil, because they could operate continuously, an impossibility for manual or animal-driven mills.[44]

The contribution of waterwheels and windmills to the energy supply, however, was remarkably small given their proliferation and refinement. In time, the far more efficient and powerful fossil-fuel-driven engines quickly supplanted waterwheels and windmills. Paul Warde estimates that windmills and waterwheels contributed no more than 1 to 3 percent of energy consumed in England and Wales in the early nineteenth century.[45]

Light

Darkness reigned in the pre-industrial world after the sun set. What light there was was extremely costly and quite messy. Pre-industrial towns and cities had almost no outdoor lighting. If they had some form of lighting it was likely weaker than what a full moon would generate. Indoor lighting, if used at all, consisted of candles made from animal fat or dried plant stocks dipped in animal fat, both of which were smoky, dangerous, and smelly.

Summarizing the history of energy before the industrial age, the economic historian Edward Wrigley writes, "Thus, the production horizon for all organic economies was set by the annual cycle of plant growth.... This set physical and biological limits to the possible scale of production.... Above all, access to a mineral rather than a vegetable energy source expanded the production horizon decisively."[46]

An Extreme View of Pre-Industrial Humanity

In *A Farewell to Alms*, the historian Gregory Clark paints a startling, if somewhat exaggerated, picture of life in pre-industrial societies: "The average person in the world of 1800 was no better off than the average person in 100,000 B.C.... Before 1800 there was no fundamental distinction between the economies of humans and those of other animal and plant species."[47] Referring only to man's *material* goods, Clark continues, "The basic outline of world economic history is surprisingly simple.... Before 1800 income per person—the food, clothing, heat, light, and housing available per head—varied across societies and epochs. But there was no upward trend. A simple but powerful mechanism...[known as] the Malthusian Trap, ensured that short term gains in income through technological advances were inevitably lost through population growth."[48]

A closer look at other basic indicators of human well-being tells a dramatic story not unlike Clark's. The bulk of mankind enjoyed no meaningful, sustained gains in income and lifespan throughout history until the Industrial Revolution. (See Figure 1.1 on page 5.) To be sure, there were temporary booms and busts, but there was no sustained upward trend in living conditions for the average human person for thousands of years. In England, real income per person was relatively static from 1200 until around 1850 when income rose sharply and steadily. Around 1750, the rate of improvement began a turn toward what rapidly became a steep trajectory toward continuous economic growth, longer and wealthier lives with more choice and individual freedom.

In the United States, we have become so accustomed to oceans of energy in our homes, workplaces, and everywhere we go that we are oblivious to our dependence on constant and immense flows of man-made energy. Insulated from the vagaries of wind and sunshine, destructive weather, chronic scarcities, and darkness, mankind not only has access to a prodigious supply of energy, industrial civilization has achieved remarkable control of the flow of energy.

The residents of modern, prosperous nations assume that effortless access to this energy bounty is inviolable. Yet the health, wealth, and comforts we enjoy are the fruits of human innovations transforming the distinctive energy available in coal, oil, and natural gas. According to Vaclav Smil, "Energy conversions are required for every process in the biosphere and every human action, and our high energy, predominantly fossil-fueled civilization is utterly dependent on unceasing flows of fuels and electricity."[49]

The Myth of the Happy Peasant

For many, the word "industrialization" evokes images of factories bellowing pollution, workers trapped in mindless, repetitive jobs on assembly lines, and children laboring in coal mines. Yet the hardships that working men suffered in the early stages of the Industrial Revolution were substantially eliminated in later decades, and we should not romanticize the supposedly simple rural life of an earlier epoch.

In a spirited assessment of the industrial breakthrough titled "The Great Enrichment," Deirdre McCloskey dispels the myths of the happy peasant: "Well it was a 'happiness' of constant terror, of disease at all ages, of dead children, of violent hierarchy, or women enslaved and silenced, of *sati*, of five-percent literacy.... An income of $3 a day affords no scope for the exercise of vital powers along lines of excellence, a flourishing human life."[50]

How short is mankind's societal memory! Could the wealthiest countries in the world actually risk these phenomenal improvements in human well-being wrought by abundant, affordable, and versatile energy because of an increasingly uncertain risk of global warming? Current policies to supplant fossil fuels overlook the magnitude of human improvement made possible by fossil-fuel-derived energy, for which there is now no comparable alternative.

Until the great political changes and sustained economic growth in the nineteenth and twentieth centuries, the physical living conditions of the mass of humanity hovered around subsistence levels. The favored few may have enjoyed wealth, comforts, and high culture, but grinding poverty was the common lot of mankind. The economic growth following the Industrial Revolution—of which we are the greatest beneficiaries— provided an escape from what seemed like intractable poverty for most of humanity. Until superior energy sources are available, this is the most profound gift of fossil fuels—a gift for which over a billion human beings are still waiting.

THE INDUSTRIAL REVOLUTION
Humanity's Great Energy Enrichment

I f an inherently scarce energy supply explains the limited economies and grim living standards of the pre-industrial era, energy abundance and improved human well-being remain the distinguishing characteristics of modern, industrialized society.

In the second half of the eighteenth century, England found an escape route from the energy scarcity that had constricted economic growth in agrarian societies over most of history. As the historian E. A. Wrigley of Cambridge University points out, "The [pre-industrial] energy flow was insufficient to underwrite increased output on the scale associated with an 'industrial revolution.' Only by gaining access to a vast store rather than a limited flow could this problem be solved."[1] England found that "vast store" of energy in coal, though in the nineteenth and twentieth centuries industrial societies found even more in oil and natural gas.

The creative applications of the dense and versatile energy stored in abundant fossil fuels that began around 1800 and are still spreading across the world have transformed human life and the productive capacities of economies. "The ability to transcend both the land constraint through the use of fossil fuel and the muscle constraint by mechanization which increased power (largely fueled by coal) were founding acts of the modern world."[2] Among the profound benefits of such energy enrichment, life expectancy has tripled and global real income per person has increased at least ten to thirtyfold.

In his world history *A Farewell to Alms*, Gregory Clark explains what this change meant: "Around 1800, in northwestern Europe and North America, man's long sojourn in the Malthusian world ended.... Between 1770 and 1860...the English population tripled. Yet, real incomes, instead of plummeting, rose.... A new era dawned."[3]

The hockey-stick graph at the beginning of this book, charting human progress from AD 1 to 2000, tells many stories but none more dramatic than the story of mankind's great energy enrichment, otherwise known as the Industrial Revolution. The vertical trajectory, beginning around 1800, shows the extent to which man-made emissions of carbon dioxide (indicating the consumption of fossil fuels) track sustained economic growth and the continual rise of income for the majority of the human race. Increasing use of fossil fuels still tracks rising economic growth with a statistical correlation of over 95 percent—about as close as such a correlation ever gets.[4]

When the chemical energy in coal was converted to heat and then to mechanical energy by a machine in the latter part of the eighteenth century, man was liberated from the physical limits of muscle—his own and animals'—that had consigned the majority of men to lives of arduous physical labor and poverty with extremely limited mobility. When electricity became available for lighting, heat, and power in now countless household appliances, industrial motors, and electronics, a second energy revolution took place, amplifying human well-being beyond measure. And the internal combustion engine that still powers our vehicles vastly expanded the horizons of individual liberty, mobility, and choice. By converting electric energy into photons (light) our minute digital devices transmit to each person an endless stream of information, communication, and entertainment.

Energy Enrichment as a Necessary Condition

Historians and economists have long debated the origin, causes, conditions, timing, and even the appropriate name for the great change that emerged in England in the nineteenth century. The most common name, the "Industrial Revolution," is typically attributed to the historian Arnold Toynbee (1889–1975), although French historians used the name earlier than Toynbee. Instead of identifying the breakthrough as an industrial revolution, some scholars argue that the great change is more properly understood as either a technological, economic, capitalist, market, cultural, promethean, or energy revolution. Although many historians give little weight to the energy factor, we are persuaded by Wrigley, David Landes of Harvard, and others that an exponential increase in the energy available in fossil fuels was not a cause but a necessary condition of the sustained productivity, economic growth, and human enrichment that distinguish this historical transformation.[5]

But for the abundance and the versatility of the energy stored in fossil fuels, the *sustained* economic growth per capita and improvements in human welfare that the Industrial Revolution produced would have been impossible. "The quantity of energy needed," Wrigley concludes, "to underwrite the scale of material production reached in England by the middle of the 19th century would have been far beyond attainment in an organic economy and, in the absence of coal, this would have prevented growth on a comparable scale."[6] In other words, the many technological advances occurring during the eighteenth century in England are conceivable without coal, but the sustained growth of the economy in the nineteenth and twentieth centuries would have been impossible without the vast store of fossil fuels and their countless, innovative applications. Fossil fuels do not explain why the Industrial Revolution began but why it continued and gained steam along the way.

In fact, what we call the Industrial Revolution might be more aptly called the Great Energy Enrichment, a term we borrow from the inimitable polymath Deirdre McCloskey.[7] The sea change in man's material horizons, widely characterized as industrial or economic, arose from physical, biological, and chemical factors: a shift from reliance on a variable flow of energy derived from annual plant growth to reliance on a huge store of the remains of once-living plants and organisms geologically concentrated over millions of years, that is, coal, natural gas, and oil.

The key development that propelled the Industrial Revolution was therefore physical. Now there's no doubt that the economic system known as capitalism, articulated in 1776 by the classical economist Adam Smith in *An Inquiry into the Nature and Causes of the Wealth of Nations*, was also a necessary condition of the unprecedented growth that marked the Industrial Revolution, as were English legal institutions. Indeed, the coincidence of tapping into a vast store of energy, the development of transformative technologies like the steam engine, and capitalism, was an extraordinarily powerful—although fortuitous—dynamic.

We would also submit that fundamental Judeo-Christian principles regarding the value of the human person also played a powerful role. The Declaration of Independence imbeds this principle as a foundation of our country when it declares the inalienable rights of the individual to "life, liberty and the pursuit of happiness." It is, perhaps, not merely a coincidence that in 1807, when the British Parliament finally passed William Wilberforce's bill to end the English slave trade, the largest industrial complex in the world using steam power and lighting generated by coal opened in Manchester, England.

With the energy enrichment made possible by fossil fuels, an enduring middle class with upward mobility emerged for the first time in history.[8] "[N]othing has ever furnished so many opportunities to rise in the social scale as the Industrial Revolution," writes Landes.[9]

Public discourse about global warming and climate policies ignores fundamental physical realities about energy and overlooks the profound benefits of carbon-rich energy. Our healthy, comfortable, affluent lives depend on our high consumption of fossil fuels. The complex and intricate global systems that constantly deliver the energy services we assume in developed countries are the result of miraculously fine-tuned engineering that evolved over the past century. We are a fossil-fueled civilization.

Without fully comparable energy alternatives, climate policies to rapidly subvert the energy-rich hydrocarbons risk a necessary foundation for human well-being and economic productivity.

From an Organic Economy to an Energy-Enriched Mineral Economy

Until coal was harnessed on a massive scale in the English Industrial Revolution, mankind's energy and material horizons were physically bounded by the energy harvested from natural materials such as wood, plants, animals, human muscle, and diffuse flows of wind and water. "As long as the supplies both of mechanical and heat energy were conditioned by the annual quantum of insolation [solar radiation received by the earth] and the [relatively low] efficiency of plant photosynthesis in capturing incoming solar radiation," Wrigley explains, "it was idle to expect a radical improvement in the material conditions of the bulk of mankind."[10] Fossil fuels vastly expanded the scope of mankind's material horizon and energy budget.

The contrast between an agrarian economy reliant on organic sources of energy and raw materials and a mineral economy reliant on mineral fuels and inorganic raw materials throws light on the wellsprings of the unprecedented growth generated by the Industrial Revolution. The word "organic" is now used vaguely to describe anything considered "natural." But to speak precisely, organic material is derived from living matter.

Organic—also known as agrarian—economies derive almost all energy and raw materials from the annual cycle of plant growth. All fuel, food, fodder, and fiber needed for human subsistence depend on organic materials produced from the land. Human creativity may stretch the yield of land and products made from wood, wool, flax, leather, hops, barley, reeds, straw, fur, bone, and horn. The material base and energy budget for all manufacture in an organic economy, however, is inherently limited and subject to nature's whims such as floods and droughts. With coal, the productive capacity of the economy was no longer limited to the "fortune" of the harvest from the soil.

Minerals are not derived from living matter. There are perhaps four thousand identified minerals, of which iron ore, aluminum, clay, copper, and silica may be familiar to our readers. Coal, oil, and natural gas are considered mineral energy fuels, but that classification gets complicated. The carbon content of fossilized plants and animals that lived millions of years ago is higher than that of most minerals. The point, however, is that fossil fuels are not subject to the vicissitudes of plant growth nor do they compete with other needed resources for land use. And most importantly, they offer a massive, concentrated source of fuel with much higher energy content than wood. More than any other so-called organic resource, chronically scarce wood—the sole organic source of heat energy—was the bottleneck of pre-industrial economies.

To appreciate Wrigley's emphasis on the inescapable physical realities of energy, consider that the harvest from a hayfield may capture a year's worth of energy flow from the sun,[11] while the harvest of mature timber might capture a century of solar insolation. As a source of heat energy, peat contains a store of energy concentrated over thousands of years. But coal, natural gas, and oil provide a more accessible, larger, and more concentrated store of solar energy highly compressed over millions of years. "The secret of the Industrial Revolution," according to Matt Ridley, "was shifting from current solar power to stored solar power."[12]

As a mineral fuel, coal not only provides a massive stock of heat energy that breaks the energy bottleneck of wood. Coal also allows the energy-intensive extraction and processing of a wide variety of minerals that were previously precluded for reason of costs. The major industries that developed during and after the Industrial Revolution were based on mineral raw materials. Metals, chemicals, pottery, glass, bricks, plastics, building materials, and many textiles all depend on raw materials.

The shift from the organic economy to a mineral economy was slow, but step by step it opened a path for growth that did not strain a resource in fixed supply—as occurred with wood for centuries before. As Wrigley explains, "[It] meant that expansion no longer entailed a call upon a flow [of energy] whose scale could be enlarged only with much difficulty, but was accommodated instead by increasing calls on a capital stock [of energy] that was often large enough to pose no problems even when demand grew to unprecedented levels."[13]

In contrast to other minerals, fossils generate enough heat energy in volumes large enough to extract and convert "unpromising" mineral substances into useful materials. These versatile hydrocarbons also can serve as raw materials which the "ultimate resource"—human intellect and imagination—can turn into "synthetic" materials, as we call them. With the master resource and the ultimate resource, we will never run out of energy. Given the now irreplaceable marvel of fossil fuels, however, the highest caution should greet political demands that we end the era of fossil fuels right now.

Every production process (and each human breath) involves the expenditure of energy. The shift from an economy circumscribed by the annual flow of energy from the sun, inefficiently captured by photosynthesis in plants, to an economy based on a store of solar energy concentrated over millions of years revolutionized the material basis of all production.

In England, it was not until around 1850 that a full-fledged, energy-intensive, mineral economy propelled substantial economic growth both in the aggregate and per person. Conventional explanation in pure economic terms overlooks something more fundamental about the energy escape route from pre-industrial energy scarcity. The analytical framework, largely based upon Adam Smith's view of the division of labor, capital, and market economies, may explain the economic growth in the golden age of the Netherlands, but it cannot explain the exponential growth in the aggregate and per capita that later appeared in England and now extends across the world.

Smith, Ricardo, Malthus, and many of today's neo-classical economists conclude that sustained growth that could indefinitely improve real income per person was impossible. According to economist George Gilder,

"The leading economic growth model, devised by the Nobel laureate Robert Solow of MIT, assigned as much as 80 percent of this advance to a 'residual'—a factor left over after accounting for the factors of production in the ken of economists: labor, capital and natural resources. In other words, economists can pretend to explain only 20 percent of the apparent 119-fold expansion."[14] We submit that the kind of energy stored in affordable fossil fuels helps to explain a meaningful portion of the exponential growth that indeed did occur.

Earlier we shared Ridley's vivid portrait of the scale and intensity of the energy enrichment. His jaw-dropping numbers bear repeating. The magnitude of the energy gain that coal contributed to England's economy in the late nineteenth century is staggering. By 1870, coal provided an amount of heat energy equivalent to the caloric needs of 850 million additional laborers. For perspective, England's population was about twenty million in 1870. And the mechanical energy available in England's steam engines was equivalent to the mechanical power available in six million horses. Without that steam engine, the horses would have consumed three times the wheat harvest. Need we point out the magnitude of the energy gain involved? Indeed, England's nineteenth-century

FIGURE 6.1

Energy Consumption in England and Wales (1561–1570) Compared with Italy (1561–1570)

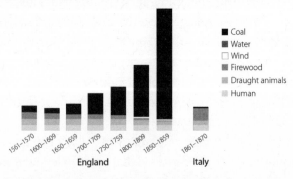

Source: E.A. Wrigley, *Energy and the English Industrial Revolution*, p. 95

The Improving State of the World

Between 1900 and 2015, life expectancy increased from forty-seven to seventy-nine years in the United States. "Americans now have more creature comforts, they work fewer hours in their lifetimes, their work is less physically demanding, they devote more time to acquiring a better education, they have more options to select a livelihood and live a more fulfilling life, they have greater economic and social freedom and they have more leisure time and greater ability to enjoy it. And these trends are evident not just in the United States but, for the most part, elsewhere as well."[15]

economic miracle was energy enrichment unlike anything seen before. "That is how impossible the task of Britain's nineteenth century miracle would have been without fossil fuels."[16]

By around 1800, the human population reached one billion people. Within two centuries, human numbers increased more than sevenfold. Yet the gross world product increased more than seventyfold, and real income per capita rose at least tenfold as a conservatively estimated global average. The productivity of the world economy meant that there was more than enough life-sustaining energy "stuff" and "material" to meet the basic needs of all human beings. Poverty was no longer an ineluctable fate for the majority of people.[17]

Instead of population pressure forming a Malthusian ceiling on growth—or worse, a collapse, as predicted by the classical economists and the modern doomsayers—living standards for the much larger human population have continuously improved in developed and developing countries with the exception of those regions wracked with violence and corrupt rulers. As Indur Goklany shows, "Never before had the indicators of the success of the human species advanced as rapidly as in the past quarter millennium."[18] Improvements advanced earlier and at a more rapid rate in

Western countries, but since 1950, global indicators of human well-being have advanced more rapidly than population.

"And in truth," Deirdre McCloskey spiritedly argues, "the amount by which average material welfare multiplied under actually existing innovations exceeds by far the official and cautious statistics. Stuff unimaginable in 1700 or 1820 crowds our lives from anesthesia to air conditioning. The new stuff makes the factors 16 or 18 or even 30 [i.e., by what multiple real income per capita has increased] into gross understatements."[19] And the speed of economic development in some countries has been amazing. England's Industrial Revolution took three centuries, but South Korea's took only four decades.

How the Great Energy Enrichment Began

England was not the first country to harness fossil fuels. Some societies with coal seams, oil deposits, and gas vents near the surface of the earth used fossil fuels for a certain period to great advantage. The Netherlands made highly productive use of peat, a relatively young, less concentrated hydrocarbon, and was primed to outpace England in industrialization. And then peat became scarce, and Holland's economy stalled.

So why was it England—a small, island country—that changed the world? Historians still debate the multiple, reinforcing, and interrelated factors that led to England's breakthrough. The physical presence of large deposits of coal alone doesn't explain why or how England initiated the great change of industrialization.

Britain was more advanced than other countries in a number of categories. In food supply, population, life span, literacy, and the energy availability in coal, England had progressed further than any other country. In 1750, life expectancy in England was thirty-five years, while the global average was twenty-five, having risen by only a year since AD 1000. Global per capita income likewise had barely budged since 1000, whereas per capita income in England was rising at an annual rate of 0.36 percent, according to Angus Maddison's numbers.[20]

Another advantage Britain enjoyed was the flurry of scientific activity from the mid-seventeenth century, exemplified by the work of Isaac Newton. Practical application of science led to many creative devices and instruments. Political and economic theory, such as Adam Smith's *Wealth of Nations*, as well as legal and financial institutions that protected property rights and economic freedom also primed the pump for the English Industrial Revolution.

The use of the word "revolution" to describe the origins of industrialization is misleading because it connotes an abrupt change. What is commonly called the Industrial Revolution was indeed a monumental change, but it occurred over several centuries. The energy enrichment that literally fueled the economic productivity for which this revolution is known did not occur at a certain date, decade, or even century. England and other countries, particularly in Europe, had been using coal for heat energy from the late sixteenth century, but wood remained the dominant source of heat energy for centuries.

England's use of coal steadily increased in the latter decades of the sixteenth century. Coal's initial use was to provide heat energy to mine more coal, but wood, draft animals, and human muscle still provided the majority of energy consumed. By the middle of the nineteenth century, coal had become the predominant source of energy consumed in England.[21]

Industrialization of the more pervasively agrarian United States took off a little later than in England. Raw materials and foodstuffs exported from the United States to England were an important supplement to the needs of England's industries and growing population. Without these "ghost acres," many historians question whether England's comprehensive industrialization would have been as successful. The story of American industrialization, however, is quite the same as England's: dramatic rise in life expectancy, GDP per capita, population, and carbon dioxide emissions.

The proponents of a fast transition from fossil fuels to renewable fuels assume that energy sources are readily interchangeable. But the value of coal, natural gas, and crude oil is not only in their abundance and affordability but also in their chemical potency and versatility. An affordable, abundant, dense, versatile, reliable, controllable, and portable source of heat energy, coal was a source of thermal energy with a far higher heat content than wood. It made economical the energy-intense extraction and processing of metals and other mineral raw materials previously precluded or limited by energy cost. The flurry of scientific advances and energy innovations that emerged in the seventeenth century and continued through the next three centuries took beneficial advantage of these distinctive chemical properties of fossil fuels.[22]

This shift from the diffuse and variable flows of energy to the massive store of hydrocarbon minerals was a turning point for human progress. Energy was no longer inherently scarce.

Productivity Unleashed

The hallmark of the Industrial Revolution was the rapid and radical expansion of the productive powers of an economy. Efficiency is the amount of work completed per input of energy. Power is the amount of work performed per unit of time.[23] Efficient and profitable enterprises produce more output per unit of input and thus can generate profit. The magic of fossil fuels is that their creative applications can exponentially increase output and thus overall efficiency. Let's look at a few examples of the promethean gains in productivity.

Cotton

Cotton textiles were the flagship English industry at the time of the Industrial Revolution. According to Clark and Wrigley, the textile industry accounted for more than 50 percent of the increased productivity, and thus growth, in England during the entire nineteenth century. "Efficiency in converting raw cotton to cloth increased 14-fold from the 1760s to the 1860s, a growth rate of 2.4 percent per year, faster than productivity growth in most modern economies."[24] In 1760, transforming a pound of cotton into woven cloth took approximately eighteen man-hours. By 1860, the same work was completed in 1.5 man-hours.[25] Similar gains were achieved across many industries.

Metals

Steel and cast iron are the raw materials for the physical infrastructure of modern societies. A huge supply of cheap coal revolutionized metallurgy and access to mineral resources previously limited because of the energy-intensity of extraction and processing. The concentrated energy in coal dramatically expanded the production of iron, steel, and other metal resources that had long remained scant and expensive. Transforming iron ore into steel requires tremendous heat energy, making the energy cost of metallurgy extremely high without an inexpensive, dense, and controllable source of thermal energy.

Before the Industrial Revolution, smelting required large volumes of wood or charcoal. Coal, where available in a huge store, eventually replaced wood to provide heat energy to smelt hundreds of millions of tons of iron ore at far less cost. Wales, without much timber but abundant coal, became one of the world's major steel-producing regions. "Coal use permitted a rapid expansion of metals at low prices and in previously unimaginable quantities."[26]

Light

Another example of the productivity achieved by the hydrocarbon energy enrichment is the staggering decline in the cost of basic services such as light itself. Could there be a greater gift of fossil fuels than the affordability of indoor and outdoor illumination? George Gilder calls the fall in the cost of lighting "one of the most astonishing increases in wealth in the history of mankind, a million-fold increase in the abundance and affordability of light itself...."[27]

In 1800, six hours of work in England at the average wage bought one hour of light from a tallow candle. In 2009, one half-second of work paid for an hour of illumination from a light bulb. The difference in labor costs in 1800 and 2009 means that the price of lighting decreased to one-tenth of 1 percent of its price in 1800.[28] Modern versions of Thomas Edison's incandescent light bulb deliver light three orders of magnitude greater than a candle.[29]

And fossil fuels saved the whales! In early industrial societies, whale blubber was the preferred source for lighting among the elites. Tallow candles made out of the rendered fat from sheep and cattle—a much smokier and smellier source of light, although still expensive, were used by the masses. The demand for whale blubber eventually decreased the population of whales. Kerosene derived from petroleum then replaced blubber and was a more efficient source of illumination.[30]

At the Heart of the Industrial Revolution: Mechanical Energy

The invention of a steam engine that translated the heat energy stored in coal into mechanical energy, replacing dependence on human or animal muscle to perform work on which all human societies had relied, unleashed the productivity, efficiency, and inventiveness for which the Industrial Revolution is known. These machines were far more powerful, tireless, and controllable than the amassed muscle of even hundreds of horses. This was a turning point for mankind. The transformation of the energy in coal and petroleum into mechanical power is the most important energy conversion in industrial civilization. If photosynthesis is the most fundamental natural energy conversion, the steam engine is the most fundamental anthropogenic conversion.

As the historian David Landes notes, "It was precisely the availability of inanimate sources of power that has enabled man to transcend the limitations of biology and increase his productivity a hundred times over....It is no accident...that the growth of capital has been proportional to the consumption of fossil fuels."[31]

Watt's Steam Engine:
The Emblem of the Industrial Revolution

The first true steam engine that could convert heat energy into mechanical energy was the invention of Thomas Newcomen around 1712. His engine, developed to pump water out of the coal mines, an instance of consuming energy to generate more energy, was extremely inefficient, converting only 1 percent or less of the heat energy released from burning coal, and the high cost limited its application. It was James Watt's later steam engine, patented in 1769, which deservedly became the symbol of the British Industrial Revolution.

Watt's machine converted 10 percent of the heat energy, consuming a fourth of the coal that Newcomen's engine did, and was much faster.[32] "This was the decisive breakthrough to an age of steam, not only because of the immediate economy of the fuel,... but even more because this improvement opened the way to continuing advances in efficiency that eventually brought the steam-engine within reach of all branches of the economy and made of it a universal prime mover."[33] Further refinements of the steam engine throughout the nineteenth century revolutionized transport.

Conversion of the heat energy in fossil fuels to mechanical power launched yet another chapter of the great energy enrichment when the internal combustion engine was developed. The passenger car made personal liberty possible on a scale unimaginable to our ancestors a century ago.

Landes stresses that "the key to the steam engine's revolutionary effects on the pace of economic growth" was that "it consumed a mineral fuel [fossil fuel] and thereby made available to industry, for provision of motive power [movement] as against pure heat, a new and apparently boundless source of energy."[34] The value of an "apparently boundless," concentrated store of energy in versatile fossil fuels remains a foundational driver of economic growth. And the young shale revolution that has unlocked the mother lode of oil and natural gas resources means that our store of hydrocarbon is virtually boundless—sustainable for centuries or millennia to come.

Choosing Energy Austerity?

Most climate policies assume the developed world will embrace "planned austerity" to decrease consumption of energy and a shift to the renewable energy sources of the past: wood (now given the more distinguished name "biomass"), wind, and solar. The policy makers behind these plans evidently discount the burgeoning growth of the world's information-communications-technology (ICT) system—often considered the clean and green industry of the future. At the moment, the digital universe consumes 50 percent more energy than global aviation. "Shortly," as Mark P. Mills calculates, "*hourly* Internet traffic will exceed the Internet's *annual* traffic of the year 2000."[35] This ICT universe is totally dependent on highly reliable, affordable electric generation.

Our small smartphones may need a negligible electric charge to run for hours, and they may appear absolutely clean at the point of use, but they depend on thousands of data centers across the world, broadband wired and wireless networks, and the factories that manufacture our devices and related ICT hardware. The data centers consume huge volumes of electricity twenty-four hours per day. For a sense of the scale of energy use: "The average square foot of data center uses 100–200 times more electricity than does a square foot of a modern office building. Put another way, a tiny few thousand square foot data room uses more electricity than lighting up a one hundred thousand square foot shopping mall."[36] And there are tens of thousands of these data centers housed in huge warehouses.

Wind turbines and solar panels cannot power data centers. Google tried it, and it was a complete flop. Coal, natural gas, and nuclear are the only generating sources right now that can reliably power the data centers. The administrator of the Environmental Protection Agency may nonchalantly announce that coal is no longer "marketable." The more sober Energy Information Agency, however, projects that fossil fuels will continue to meet 80 percent of global demand through 2040.[37] Coal remains in high demand in developing countries, especially China, India, and Africa, because their leaders understand that the availability of electricity transforms the lives of the world's most impoverished people.

Sustainable Fossil Fuels?

At least one of the classical economists' contemporaries understood the role of energy in England's Industrial Revolution. William Stanley Jevons (1835–1882) correctly assessed the magnitude of the energy revolution taking place around him—mankind's liberation from the Malthusian trap. In *The Coal Question* he wrote, "With coal almost any feat is possible or easy; without it we are thrown back into the laborious poverty of earlier times."[38]

But he too overlooked the factor of human ingenuity and was captured by Malthusian logic. Jevons expected that as England used more and more coal, the price would rise and thus arrest the phenomenal growth that he had witnessed. Coal, however, did not become scarce or more expensive. Indeed, coal-fired energy produced more energy, productivity, and income. More than 150 years later, the world's coal supply remains massive.

Until the English Industrial Revolution, every other economic boom in human history eventually burned out because resources dwindled—whether timber, cropland, pasture, labor, water, or peat. These resources, in principle unlike coal, natural gas, and oil, are renewable and so replenish themselves but at a pace far too slow to meet ongoing demand. Coal in the English Industrial Revolution was a different story. As England used more coal, it actually became more accessible and cheaper.

Although not in principle renewable, fossil fuels remain abundant enough to sustain economic growth for many centuries until fully comparable or superior energy sources are genuinely available at scale. After

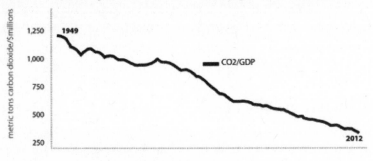

FIGURE 6.2

Carbon Intensity of the U.S. Economy, 1949–2012

Source: U.S. Energy Information Administration (Oct. 2013).

four decades of predictions of the near-term depletion of oil and gas, the United States has now gained access to the protean store of oil and gas shale. Never underestimate human ingenuity.

More output from less input remains the inherent dynamic of economic growth from fossil fuels. Modern societies are getting more work out of each ton of fossil fuel. According to recent EIA data, the carbon intensity of the U.S. economy has been declining since 1949.[39] (See Figure 6.2.) The United States now uses 50 percent less energy per unit of GDP than it did in 1950.

"A Farewell to Alms"

The greatest gift of the great energy enrichment, available in market economies today unless politics denies it, is the release of entire populations from abject poverty. In the Industrial Revolution, the poorest—not the already wealthy—were the greatest beneficiaries. "The plain fact is that the mechanization of production in the Industrial Revolution raised incomes across all classes," remarks Matt Ridley.[40]

Obviously, the Industrial Revolution did not guarantee a swift release from poverty but the productivity of the economy made such a release physically and economically possible. "The increase in the productive

FIGURE 6.3

Average Annual Rate of Increase for Various Time Periods

	1 AD–1000 AD %	1000 AD–1750 AD %	1750 AD–2009 AD %
Life Expectancy	0.01	0.00	0.41
Income	0.00	0.05	0.98
Population	0.02	0.14	0.88
Carbon Dioxide Emissions			3.23

Source: Indur Goklany, Humanity Unbound, p. 6.

powers of an industrialized society were such," Wrigley concludes, "that for the first time in human history the miseries of poverty, from which previously only a minority of the population were exempt, could be put aside for whole populations. There were no guarantees but the potential for such a change existed."[41] By the second half of the twentieth century, major improvement in health, education, and general welfare was widespread, and a middle class was growing.

The historian Gregory Clark of Princeton University, who titled his global economic history *A Farewell to Alms*, states his theme in bold terms:

The Industrial Revolution, a mere two hundred years ago, changed forever the possibilities for material consumption. Incomes per person began to undergo sustained growth in a favored group of countries.... Moreover the biggest beneficiary of the Industrial Revolution has so far been the unskilled.[42]

Figure 6.3 shows the barely measurable increase in global income per capita from 1 AD until 1750. The dramatic increase from 1750 to 2009 is strongly correlated with the first measurable increase in man-made emissions of carbon dioxide in human history, that is, the first intensive use of fossil fuels.

Clark's figures on England in Figure 6.4 show what he characterizes as "the unprecedented, inexorable, all-pervading rise in incomes per person since 1800. The lifestyle of the average person in modern economies was

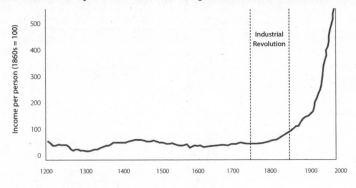

FIGURE 6.4

Real Income per Person in England (1200–2000)

Source: Gregory Clark, *A Farewell to Alms*, p. 195

not unknown in earlier economies: it is that of the rich in ancient Egypt or ancient Rome. What is different is that now paupers live like princes and princes live like emperors."[43] As Goklany more soberly characterizes these numbers, "Never in human history had indicators of human wellbeing advanced so rapidly."[44]

Greatest Gains to the Poor

Real income per capita calculated as an average may be highly misleading. But the most distinctive feature of the economic boom fueled by the Industrial Revolution is that the income gains accrued more to the poorest and the average worker than to the wealthy. The average English income headed upward around 1800. By 1850, it was 50 percent above the level of 1750 even though the population had tripled. As Ridley notes, "The rise was steepest for unskilled workers.... The share of national income captured by labour rose.... Real wages rose faster than real output throughout the nineteenth century, meaning that the benefit of cheaper goods was being garnered by the workers as consumers, not by bosses and landlords."[45]

As the abundant heat, mechanical, and chemical energy supplied by coal increased productivity, the supply of goods increased while the price declined. A winter coat, which may have cost a month's wages in 1800, may have cost only a week's wages by 1850. As productivity increased, factory workers were more able to afford to buy the products they helped produce.

Ridley writes: "In Gregory King's survey of the British population in 1688, 1.2 million laborers lived on four pounds/year and 1.3 million 'cottagers'—peasants—lived on two pounds/year. That is to say, half of the entire nation lived in abject poverty; without charity they would starve. During the Industrial Revolution, there was plenty of poverty but neither as widespread nor as severe."[46] The violent protests of the nineteenth-century textile workers known as the Luddites against the labor-saving machines were short-lived. Although factory workers in the early stages of the Industrial Revolution may have worked, by modern standards, in dangerous and dirty work conditions, their living conditions were better than their tenant farming ancestors', which is why they flocked to the factories from the farms.[47]

The Puzzle of Industrialized Economic Growth

Many traditional economists remain puzzled that the increased productivity and associated economic growth begun in the Industrial Revolution have never stopped. In *Knowledge and Power*, George Gilder reflects on the perplexing magnitude of modern economic growth. "The central scandal of traditional economics," George Gilder writes, "has long been its inability to explain the scale of per capita economic growth over the last several centuries. It is no small thing. The sevenfold rise in world population since 1800 should have attenuated growth per capita. Yet the conventional gauges of per capita income soared some seventeenfold, meaning a 119-fold absolute increase in output in 212 years."[48]

The pivotal role of energy as a driver of sustained growth was also not foreseen by the classical economists who lived during the early days

Added Mechanical Power at the Elbow

As Fred Cottrell explains: "A coal miner who consumes in his own body about 3,500 calories a day, will, if he mines 500 pounds of coal, produce coal with a heat value of 500 times the heat value of his food which he consumed while mining it. At 20 percent efficiency, he expends about 1 horsepower of mechanical energy to get the coal. Now if the coal he mines is burned in a steam engine of even 1 percent efficiency, it will yield about 27 horsepower-hours of mechanical energy. The surplus of mechanical energy gained would thus be 26 horsepower-hours, or the equivalent of 26 man-days per man-day. A coal miner who consumed about one-fifth as much food as a horse, could thus deliver through the steam engine about four times the mechanical energy which the average horse in Watt's day was found to deliver."[49]

And these were the gains in productivity at an early stage of the Industrial Revolution!

of the English Industrial Revolution. Adam Smith (1723–1790), David Ricardo (1772–1823), and Thomas Malthus (1776–1834) assumed that the "fortune of the economy" was intractably circumscribed by the annual harvest of food and natural raw materials from the "land," as they named the material factor. These early economists also concluded that sustained growth in wages that could offer an escape from poverty for the majority of a growing population was impossible. The harvest of their organic economy could be extended by innovation and trade, but all three of these economists concluded that the law of diminishing returns would eventually slow and then arrest economic growth.

Their pessimistic outlook for enduring growth that could lift all boats was soon undermined by application of fossil fuels. Tapping into a massive store of mineral fuels and mineral raw materials provided an escape from the bottleneck in an agrarian economy reliant on fruits of the land for all energy sources and raw materials. The availability of fossil fuels, indeed, made the extent of land a less important production factor than the classical economists understandably then assumed.

Many modern economists still downplay the energy factor or subsume it under other economic factors such as technology, stock of machinery, or equipment. Without the vast store of controllable energy in fossil fuels, however, the substantial and sustained gains in real income per capita that distinguishes modern economic growth would have been physically impossible. The innovative use of fossil fuels on a massive scale helps explain, not necessarily why modern economic growth began, but why it never stopped.

Many historians also overlook the role of energy—this physically necessary variable—in their account of the radical changes associated with industrialization. And many economists don't include energy in their models for economic growth. They recognize the technologies of power (machines that convert fossil fuel into mechanical power) but not the energy source itself. Yet the prodigious increase in the availability of concentrated hydrocarbon energy sources and advances in their conversion account for the difference between pre-industrial and industrialized societies.

Until the historical data were collected and analyzed in the second half of the twentieth century, many economists and historians viewed human progress—from the cave to the farm to the factory to the jumbo jet to the semi-conductor—as an incremental, cumulative, and unitary march of knowledge through time. While advances in ideas, technology, legal institutions, and economic systems may have followed that pattern of steady progress, advances in the basic living conditions of most human families did not until the great energy enrichment.

The historical data show that most of mankind was trapped in subsistence poverty for thousands of years until the Industrial Revolution. Periods of material progress followed by regression—not continuous improvement—appear to have been the common lot of mankind until a phenomenal departure from this trend around two hundred years ago on the island of Great Britain.

Smithian and Promethean: Two Kinds of Capital

The Industrial Revolution and the sustained economic growth it spawned—a decisive departure from previous history—cannot be adequately explained as yet another incremental, cumulative advance. The unprecedented economic growth associated with industrialization had a dual nature that was the product of happenstance: Adam Smith and fossil fuels. The advent of capitalistic economic systems explains a lot about the emergence of the Industrial Revolution, but it is the energy revolution—which we call Promethean—that explains why the economic growth—aggregate and per capita—did not slow and then halt as all previous booms in history had done. The coincidence of Smithian capitalism, with its understanding of the division of labor, trade, and accumulation of capital, and Promethean capitalism explains the uniqueness of the Industrial Revolution.

Smith especially stressed the connection between specialization of labor and productivity, yet output per worker was increased not only by specialization but also by the availability of fuel and mechanical power "at the elbow" of labor, as Wrigley puts it.[50]

Satanic Mills?

For many, the word "industrialization" evokes bleak images of Blake's "dark satanic mills"—smoke-belching factories where workers trapped on assembly lines performed their mindless, repetitive motions. Karl Marx, Charles Dickens, and other writers decried the pollution, filth, and squalor in the new factories and urban apartments. Later writers, however, have pointed out that worse poverty, disease, pollution, and child labor certainly existed in England before the Industrial Revolution. Rural poverty may have been worse than urban poverty.

The poverty of early industrial England may be memorable because it was the first time politicians and writers expressed concern. The prosperity that industrial growth made possible indeed increased and helped institutionalize compassion. In the nineteenth century, when industrialization was spreading and the related commerce was exploding, slavery and child labor were abolished in most Western nations.

The Great Energy Divergence

Although the Western world now enjoys the greatest energy bounty, a larger portion of the developing world's population also has access to electricity, the form of modern energy with transformative advantages for economic growth, health, and general well-being. Yet billions of people, mired in miserable poverty, still lack access to electricity. The energy poverty in Sub-Saharan Africa is likely far worse than that of our ancestors in pre-industrial societies.

The farewell to alms that modern economic growth made possible clearly has not eliminated chronic hunger in all countries. "Material consumption in some countries is now well below the pre-industrial norm.... Just as the Industrial Revolution reduced income inequalities within societies, it has increased them between societies," Clark notes.[51] The causes of this "Great Divergence" are analyzed in a book by that name by Kenneth Pomeranz. The gap in incomes between the poorest and richest countries is now of the order of fifty-to-one.[52]

In much of the developing world, better nutrition and increased access to modern medicine have extended life expectancy, and the rate of population growth has slowed. Yet many of these countries have not engendered stable, enduring legal institutions, and they don't have the energy availability on which economic growth rests. Perhaps half of the world's population still lacks access to low-cost, reliable, and safe electricity.[53] Electric heat, lighting, and refrigeration still remain unavailable for a substantial portion of the population in many developing countries. As in all pre-industrial societies, energy scarcity perpetuates life spans still much briefer than in developed countries as well as poor health and harsh poverty in many African and Asian countries.

Contaminated drinking water, inadequate disposal of waste, and inadequately ventilated cook stoves burning dung and biomass remain major killers.[54] Modern treatment plants for water and waste, although not expensive, cannot operate without electricity. And without electricity, an estimated one billion people receive poor healthcare in clinics and hospitals, where vaccines and medicines cannot be refrigerated and equipment cannot be sterilized. Without electric power, X-ray machines and incubators are useless.[55]

Half of all children in developing countries attend primary school without electricity. Power shortages and unplanned outages stall business activity. In Pakistan, outages of twelve to eighteen hours a day have amounted to a loss of 6 percent of gross domestic product and five hundred thousand jobs in recent years.[56]

These populations don't need a diffuse flow of intermittent, far more expensive green energy. Subsidized, costly, and unreliable renewable systems of electric generation will not alleviate the energy poverty in these countries. They need base-load, reliable, cheap, on-demand electricity with basic emission control technology.

Fifty percent of Africans lack access to reliable electricity.[57] In India, almost three hundred million people have no electric power at all, and another seven hundred million live without electricity in their homes.[58] Blackouts in South Africa similarly stymie growth.[59]

The world's poor don't want "climate aid" to force them to buy wind turbines and solar panels. A survey conducted by the United Nations of over nine million people in developing countries found that taking action on climate change ranked last on a list of sixteen major needs, among which education, healthcare, jobs, and government reform led the list. So the United Nations, the wealthiest countries, and the scores of non-governmental organizations swarming around the climate crusade would impose their green dreams on countries still fighting tuberculosis, malaria, and malnutrition? Caleb Rossiter clarifies the issue: "Real years added to real lives should trump the minimal impact that Africa's carbon emissions could have on a theoretical catastrophe."[60]

Denial of the severe limitations of renewable energy has been institutionalized in national governments and global organizations such as the United Nations. In an editorial in the *Wall Street Journal* titled "This

Child Does Not Need a Solar Panel," the Danish environmentalist Bjorn Lomborg denounces the moral callousness of the green delusion: "Providing the world's most deprived countries with solar panels instead of better healthcare or education is inexcusable self-indulgence. Green energy sources may be good to keep on a single light or to charge a cellphone. But they are largely useless for tackling the main power challenges for the world's poor."[61]

Increasingly over the last six years, the United States, the European Union, and major international institutions such as the International Monetary Fund and the World Bank have been limiting aid for energy development to those projects based on renewable energy. A study in 2014 by the Center for Global Development found that thirty-eight of forty projects receiving funding over the past five years from the U.S. Overseas Private Investment Corporation (OPIC) were renewable projects. The same study found that sixty million additional persons would have gained access to electricity if OPIC had been allowed to invest in natural gas projects and not just renewables.[62]

The United Nations and rich countries are not only conditioning aid for energy development on green energy sources, they are diverting existing funds dedicated to economic development and education to "climate aid"—that is, more wind, solar, and biofuel projects. This is a tragic waste of billions of dollars that could enrich the lives of the billions of human beings still living in a dark, smoky world.

Since the Industrial Revolution, we have learned how the availability of affordable and reliable electricity is essential to fundamental human welfare and economic development. Rather than throwing away billions of dollars to inefficient renewable energies that make the green elites feel good, wealthy nations could assist poorer nations in developing electric systems based on hydrocarbons with effective emission controls for genuine pollutants, not carbon dioxide.

China's urban skies are not darkened by the invisible, harmless natural compound that is carbon dioxide but by the uncontrolled emission of real pollutants that can impair health. The environmental record of the United States shows that this conventional pollution can be reduced by more than 80 percent. The energy-poor nations of the world need that technology rather than the ideologically-driven climate aid.

"But it is a strange moral calculus," Indur Goklany write, "that endorses policies that would reduce existing gains in human wellbeing, increase the cost of humanity's basic necessities, increase poverty and reduce the terrestrial biosphere's future productivity and ability to support biomass, all in order to solve future problems that may not even exist or, if they do, are probably more easily solved by future generations who would be richer economically and technologically."[63]

Historically Clueless:
Climate Policies to Supplant Fossil Fuels Deny History

Climate policies to eliminate fossil fuels without fully comparable alternatives threaten to rupture the energy foundation of the modern world. Without authority in law, the Obama administration is dismembering the coal industry in the United States. Coal still provides the cheapest and most reliable source of electricity, and billions of dollars already have been invested successfully to reduce coal's emissions of genuine pollutants.

The regressive effect of high-cost but low-performing green energy systems already harms middle-, low-, and fixed-income households in Germany and England. And energy intensive industries are leaving these countries for places with stable and lower energy costs but with fewer emission controls. In testimony before the U.S. Senate in December 2014, Dr. Benny Peiser, of the Global Warming Policy Foundation, concluded that current renewable mandates represent "undoubtedly one of the biggest wealth transfers from poor to rich in modern European history."[64]

Such a wealth transfer is an about-face from the phenomenal improvements in human welfare to a regression, indeed a devolution, from the Industrial Revolution—a cruel policy choice by the wealthiest countries in the world. The ruling elites will not be affected, as was the case in all pre-industrial eras, but the majority of the population will bear the brunt of the economic decline. We doubt the average citizen is aware of the already damaging repercussions of the grand decarbonizing programs. Poll after poll demonstrates that a strong majority of Americans put climate change at the bottom of their long list of worries. Would the leaders of the wealthiest countries of the world actually force a return to the energy-scarce world of the pre-industrial era in which the rulers lived comfortable lives but the majority of a population lived in misery?

Take note of history. As Isaiah Berlin put it, "Disregard for the preferences and interests of individuals alive today in order to pursue some distant social goal that their rulers proclaim is their duty to promote has been a common cause of misery for people throughout the ages."[65]

The great energy enrichment that began in England less than two hundred years ago remains a necessary condition of the substantial and sustained economic growth. The novelty of this Industrial Revolution is that the economic growth once ignited, endured and expanded. And the greatest rate of economic growth occurred in the second half of the twentieth century. If not shackled by climate policies, the shale gale of energy secured by innovative private actors in the United States could revive our national economy and open up opportunities for growth across the world.

THE REAL GREEN REVOLUTION
Fossil Fuels Feed the World

*Both the jayhawk and the man eat chickens, but the more
jayhawks, the fewer chickens, while the more men,
the more chickens.*
—American Economist Henry George

Fossil fuels are extraordinarily versatile. Natural gas has been essential for the dramatic increase in the global food supply of recent decades, as has the carbon dioxide added to the atmosphere by burning fossil fuels. Natural gas and petroleum are also the raw material for thousands of synthetic fibers and a dizzying array of new materials from waterproof clothing to plastic heart valves.

Paul Ehrlich's Dire Predictions
In 1970, Paul Ehrlich wrote:

The death of the world is imminent.... Because the human population of the planet is about five times too large, and we're managing to support all these people—at today's level of misery—only by spending our capital, burning our fossil fuels and turning out fresh water into salt water. We have not

only overpopulated but overstretched our environment. We
are poisoning the ecological systems of the earth....

He stands in a grand apocalyptic tradition, beginning with Malthus
in the eighteenth century and continuing with Al Gore in our own day.
Mass starvation is always a few decades away. Since 1800, however,
agricultural productivity has increased by as much as the rest of the
economy. The number of people fed by one hectare of land (2.5 acres)
increased from 1.9 in 1908 to 4.3 in 2008.[1] "While the 20th century
population total has grown 3.7-fold, the global harvest of staple cereal
crops, as well as the total production of crop-derived food energy, has
expanded seven-fold," observes Vaclav Smil.[2] See Figure 7.1. How did
that happen? The late economist Julian Simon explained it best: "Minds
matter economically as much as or more than hands or mouths. Human
beings create more than they use, on average. It had to be so, or we would
be an extinct species."

When Malthus warned of impending famine in 1798, the world
population was around one billion. That figure doubled by the early
1920s and then doubled again by the early 1970s, when Ehrlich, author
of the bestseller *The Population Bomb*, was predicting that "hundreds
of millions of people will starve to death in spite of any crash programs."[3]
In 2012, the year Brown published *Full Planet, Empty Plates*, the world
population reached seven billion, with no famine in sight, except for
those intentionally caused by repressive governments.

Not one of Ehrlich's many predictions ever came true. Food supply per
person has dramatically increased, while the rate of population growth
has substantially declined in those developing countries most contributing
to the rapid increase since 1950. While the human population rose 3.7-fold
in the twentieth century, the food supply, measured by global harvest of
food grains, rose seven-fold. To anyone who's not a misanthrope, the
achievement of twentieth-century agriculture is breathtaking.

In the 1960s, India produced only about two tons of rice per hectare,
a quantity that tripled by the mid-1990s. And the price of rice fell from
about $550 per ton in the 1970s to about $200 per ton in 2001.[4] India

FIGURE 7.1

Agricultural Gains

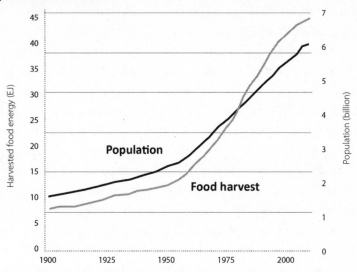

Source: Vaclav Smil, *Enriching the Earth*, p. 201

is now a major rice producer, exporting almost 106 million tons in 2013.[5] The astonishing leap in agricultural production in the twentieth century, known as the Green Revolution, could not have occurred without abundant, affordable fossil fuels. Indeed, the Green Revolution is simply a later chapter of the energy revolution on which the Industrial Revolution relied.

Natural Gas–Derived Fertilizer

The topic of agricultural fertilizers may not intrigue the 81 percent of the U.S. population that now resides in urban areas. Even as we take it for granted that grocery store shelves will be filled with diverse, fresh, and convenient food from across the world, most of us give little thought to agriculture. The development of natural gas–based fertilizers, however, is one of the most important stories in human history.

Natural gas is the main raw material in synthesized nitrogen fertilizers. Without such fertilizers, the phenomenal expansion of the food supply would not have occurred.[6] A study published in *Nature Geosciences* in 2008 found that this type of fertilizer fed 48 percent of the world's population.[7] The *Agronomy Journal* reports, "The average percentage of yield attributable to [natural gas–derived] fertilizer generally ranged from 40–60 percent in the USA and England and tended to be much higher in the tropics."[8] Synthesized nitrogen has enabled the developing world to avoid the famines that so many predicted. From 1950 to 1984, global production of cereal grains increased by 250 percent. "As a result," notes Vaclav Smil, "never before have so many people—be it in absolute or relative terms—enjoyed such an adequate to abundant supply of food. Continuing malnutrition is now caused by unequal access to food rather than by absolute supply shortages."[9]

The upsurge in agricultural yield in the industrial West that began in the early twentieth century reveals the potency of synthetic nitrogen fertilizer, although application of the Haber-Bosch process was limited until after the Second World War, when refinements to the manufacturing process reduced its cost.

Norman Borlaug:
The Father of the Twentieth-Century Green Revolution

The first name to mention in any discussion of the agricultural achievements of the twentieth century is that of Norman Borlaug (1914–2009), the father of the Green Revolution, whose work led to stunning increases in crop yields. Often called "the man who saved a billion lives," he was awarded the Nobel Peace Prize and the Presidential Medal of Freedom for his contribution to an unprecedented expansion of the world's food supply, which prevented the widespread starvation in developing countries that the Neo-Malthusians had predicted.[10]

The term "Green Revolution" could be applied to the entire twentieth century, but it typically refers to the second half of the century, when agricultural productivity rose by leaps and bounds. Most importantly, those gains were achieved in the poorest countries of the world, where malnutrition, hunger, and starvation were still commonplace. Borlaug developed cultivars (plant varieties produced by selective breeding) of wheat, rice, and other cereal grains that maximized the energy stimulus of fertilizers, increasing their yield.

Borlaug's high-yield grains played the same role in the agricultural revolution that James Watt's steam engine had played in the Industrial Revolution. The steam engine converted heat energy into mechanical energy, while the high-yield food grains converted the chemical energy in fertilizer into food energy. In his Nobel Prize acceptance speech in 1970, Borlaug explained what he had done:

> If the high-yielding dwarf wheat and rice varieties are the catalysts that have ignited the Green Revolution, then chemical fertilizer is the fuel that has powered its forward thrust.... The new varieties not only respond to much heavier doses of fertilizer than the old ones but are also much more efficient in its use. The old tall-strawed varieties would produce only ten kilos of additional grain for each kilogram of nitrogen applied, while the new varieties can produce 20 to 25 kilograms or more of additional grain per kilogram of nitrogen applied.[11]

Borlaug's genius was to figure out that smaller, stubbier plants could increase output of the edible portion of the plant. Fertilizer produced more grain in the head of each stalk, but tall-stalked plants could not support the heavier heads. When the stalks collapsed, farmers suffered a complete loss. So Borlaug developed strains of disease-resistant wheat with short, stubby stocks that could withstand the weight of much heavier heads, tripling or quadrupling the output of an acre of land.

One of the first countries in which Norman Borlaug developed his "semi-dwarf" wheat varieties was Mexico. Against the longest of odds, Mexico increased its wheat output by a factor of six in the early 1960s and became a net wheat exporter by 1963. Borlaug had similar success with rice and other cereal grains in India, Pakistan, and the Philippines. Between 1965 and 1970, wheat output nearly doubled in India and Pakistan.[12]

Comparing doomsaying Neo-Malthusians like Paul Ehrlich with doomslaying humanitarians like Norman Borlaug, we might ask ourselves whose team we'd want to join. Ehrlich's remedy for food shortages, pollution, and now supposed man-made global warming is for all-powerful government to reduce the number of human beings, who are despoiling the natural world, going so far as to oppose emergency shipments of food to alleviate crises until the rulers of those starving people get "the population under control." His followers supported some of the most inhumane acts of genocide in history, their population-control ideology leading to forced abortions, sterilizations, one-child policies, and other statist dictates on human reproduction. Thanks to China's demographically distorting one-child-per-couple policy, tens of millions of girls are missing. Women were abused and sterilized in Egypt, China, and Africa, all in the name of population stabilization and saving the planet. From what? Many rich Americans who profess to believe in reproductive rights of women and the "right to choose" hypocritically fund these controls that are now euphemistically called "family planning."

Borlaug was a liberator and one of the great life-savers in history. The Malthusians were and are oppressors, some of them even mass murderers. The history of what happened in China under Maoist thuggery is no longer a secret. Yet the United Nations gave an award to China for the effectiveness of its evil one-child policy.

Another instructive contrast is that between Norman Borlaug's Green Revolution in agriculture and the green revolution in energy for which the environmental Left longs. Borlaug's work vastly expanded available food energy and may have saved the lives of a billion harshly impoverished human beings. A low-carbon energy transformation, on the other hand, would make the energy scarcity that now afflicts the low- and fixed-income population of some European countries a universal misfortune.

Increased Atmospheric Concentrations of Carbon Dioxide Increase Agricultural Yield

Global warming alarmists refuse to acknowledge a fundamental truth about carbon dioxide. This natural molecule, which Secretary of State John Kerry calls a "weapon of mass destruction," amplifies life.

Carbon dioxide is essential to the growth of plant life on which all human and animal life depends for food. The physical life of the human body is part of the carbon cycle in which plants inhale carbon dioxide and exhale oxygen. Human activity over the past two centuries has inadvertently enriched the atmosphere with carbon dioxide. At the same time, fossil fuels have shrunk the human footprint on the natural world by amplifying the food supply per acre of arable land through natural gas–based fertilizers and other fossil fuel inputs. Spread the news! Man's carbon footprint shrinks his physical footprint on the earth.

The environmental Left, including America's senior policy makers, resolutely ignores the benefits of a fossil-fueled civilization. Without fossil fuels, the amount of land devoted to agriculture would have to increase by 150 percent.[13] As the world's population was tripling from 1961 to 2007 and the food supply per person was increasing by 27 percent, the amount of cultivated cropland increased by only 11 percent.[14] Vaclav Smil states it dramatically: "In effect, in 2007, the global food and agricultural system delivered, on average, two and a half times as much food per acre of cropland as in 1961."[15]

The Environmental Protection Agency now calls carbon dioxide a pollutant. Yet atmospheric carbon dioxide—the chemical compound from which plants construct their tissues—is the "gas of life." Human use of fossil fuels has increased the atmospheric concentration of carbon dioxide from approximately 280 parts per million (ppm) at the beginning of the Industrial Revolution to approximately 400 ppm in 2015. To put those figures in perspective, consider that in an ordinary greenhouse, which uses heightened levels of carbon dioxide to stimulate the rate and quality of plant growth, a carbon dioxide concentration of 1,000 to 1,200 ppm is considered ideal.[16]

According to hundreds of scientific studies, the relatively slight increase in the atmospheric concentration of carbon dioxide has enhanced native and cultivated plant productivity, growth, moisture retention, and resistance to pests. An increase of 300 ppm in the air's carbon dioxide content enhances herbaceous plant biomass by 25 to 55 percent.[17]

The fertilizing effect of increased atmospheric carbon dioxide has been recognized for a long time. A conference at Duke University in 1977 noted such benefits as increases in plant photosynthesis, less water loss, greater leaf area, and increases in plant branch and fruit.[18] Another conference in 1992 concluded that a doubling of atmospheric carbon dioxide would increase photosynthesis in plants by 50 percent.[19]

Craig Idso's analysis of the social benefits of atmospheric carbon dioxide offers a welcome scientific retort to the federal agencies' wildly speculative scenarios about carbon dioxide's harmful cost to humanity. "Numerous studies conducted on hundreds of different plant species testify to the very real and measurable growth-enhancing, water-saving, and stress-alleviating advantages that elevated atmospheric carbon dioxide concentrations bestow upon the Earth's plants."[20] Unless feeding the world's seven billion human residents is not a priority, the increased atmospheric concentration of carbon dioxide attributable to human activity is unquestionably a huge social benefit.

Although fertilizer, pesticides, irrigation, and new plant varieties spurred the twentieth century's agricultural revolution, substantial credit also goes to the addition of man-made carbon dioxide to the atmosphere. The bureaucrats who created out of thin air a yardstick to calculate the so-called "social cost of carbon"—an official estimate of the economic damages associated with man-made emissions of carbon dioxide—ignore this benefit.[21] This hazy and speculative calculation purports to monetize the cost of rising emissions of carbon dioxide up to three hundred years into the future. Predictions of economic conditions centuries ahead are notoriously flimsy, but surely the value of increasing food supply on the same amount of land is of high social value.

In a carefully researched paper, Idso challenges the EPA's estimates of the social cost of carbon with evidence, offering an estimate of the direct monetary benefits of atmospheric carbon dioxide's contribution to past and future global crop production. Using historical data from the United Nations Food and Agricultural Organization,[22] Idso arrives at an annual monetary value of ambient carbon dioxide enrichment from 1961 to 2010 of $3.5 trillion.[23] And he projects that the future gains in the value of global food production resulting from higher levels of atmospheric carbon dioxide through 2050 will be $11.6 trillion.

Yet the truth about carbon dioxide and food production has been turned on its head. The Left now says that a warmer planet will *reduce* food production. Here is some of the representative propaganda of the Union of Concerned Scientists from its global warming website:

> Climate-related threats to global food production include risks to grain, vegetable, and fruit crops, livestock, and fisheries. [The threats include r]educed yields. The productivity of crops and livestock, including milk yields, may decline because of high temperatures and drought-related stress.

Really? A colder, not a slightly warmer, planet would be the real and obvious threat to agriculture. Alaska doesn't produce much food. Think about it this way: How can a "greenhouse effect" reduce food production?

Other Fossil Fuel Contributions to Agriculture

In addition to fertilizer and carbon dioxide enrichment, the dazzling productivity of modern agriculture depends on energy intensive pesticides, machinery, refrigeration, packaging, and efficient transport—all of which require large amounts of fossil fuels.

The agronomist E. C. Oerke estimates that 50 to 77 percent of wheat, rice, corn, potatoes, and soybeans grown from 2001 to 2003 would have been lost without the use of pesticides, which kept losses to between 26 and 40 percent.[24] Cotton, which accounts for 48 percent of natural fibers, is particularly vulnerable to pests. Oerke calculates that the application of pesticides in 2001–2003 kept global cotton crop losses to 29 percent instead of the 80 percent that would have been lost without pesticides.

Irrigated farm land achieves crop yields more than three times those of dry-land farms. Aside from locations where it can be accomplished with natural gravity, irrigation requires energy to pump water. The wonderful array of equipment that powers modern agriculture—tractors, planters, seeders, spreaders, sprayers, sorters, rollers, rotators, cotton pickers, harvesters, threshers, mowers, rakers, swathers, wagons, bale lifters, wrappers, winnowers, backhoes, front-end loaders, skid steers, and milkers—runs on fossil fuels.

The rapid transport of agricultural products is essential to make food available, both in the developing world and in highly developed countries. This transportation system by road, rail, and air allows food surplus to be shipped to regions with temporary food shortages. On the other end of the spectrum, grocery stores in affluent countries now feature fresh products from all over the world twelve months of the year. The coldest of winter weather is no longer an obstacle to enjoying asparagus. Jets, trucks, and tankers crisscross the world to fill our stores with an epicurean bounty that a king couldn't have dreamt about two centuries ago. Affordable fossil fuels make this transportation system possible. Refrigeration, packaging, and containers reduce food waste that can otherwise eliminate around one-third of food supply.[25] Whether providing fuel for cooling and freezing or synthetic material for packaging, fossil fuels reduce loss of the food supply.

From Omnivore to Locavore

Standing athwart the energy-enriched global agricultural revolution yelling "Stop!" are the "locavores," champions of eating locally grown foodstuffs.[26] Representing an uninformed choice for energy regression, the locavore movement could arise only among affluent urban and suburban populations. Yearning for the imagined agrarian simplicity of an earlier epoch when lots of people went hungry, locavores prefer a "ten-mile" diet, limited to food grown in their own locale. But billions of human beings in developing countries prefer the ten-thousand-mile diet of affordable, fresh, and safe food made possible by global agricultural, transportation, and storage systems. That is their own choice, and next they may choose to grow their own food.

The locavores' agenda covers everything from smoother skin to world peace. Eating locally, they believe, is a way to "heal the planet," create jobs, enjoy healthier food, and enhance spiritual and societal health. As one conservative devotee of locavorism, Rod Dreher, writes, "Learning the names of the small farmers and coming to appreciate what they do is to reverse the sweeping process of alienation from the earth and from each other that the industrialized agriculture and mass production of foodstuffs has wrought."[27] What about eradicating hunger for billions of people? Doesn't that reduce alienation as well?

Locavorism may not be spreading like wildfire, but the U.S. Department of Agriculture likes it. Through an initiative called "Know Your Farmer, Know Your Food," the USDA has established hundreds of "food policy councils" to promote locally grown food and closer relationships between producers and consumers.[28] Support for small farms and local farmers' markets is, of course, a harmless diversion for American urbanites, but billions of people around the world rely on the productivity of U.S. agriculture—productivity that depends on energy-enriched farming and ranching on a large scale.

Ethanol: The Folly of Food as Fuel

The world's elite may not have a keen interest in the global supply of basic cereal grains, but rice, corn, and wheat are the basic foodstuff for the majority of the human beings with whom we share the planet. The UN Food and Agricultural Organization estimates that 842 million people still live in chronic hunger worldwide.[29] Diverting a vitally needed food grain, such as corn, to transportation fuel is taking food from the mouths of hungry millions.

The ethanol policies of the United States, which transform a basic food into an optional fuel, have been widely condemned by international institutions devoted to eliminating hunger. Before the federal ethanol mandate took effect in 2007, the price of corn had averaged less than $2.50 per bushel for many years. In 2008, the price of a bushel of corn rose to almost $8, provoking food riots in Mexico, the Middle East, and Asia. Some commentators attributed the beginning of the Arab Spring to popular unrest stirred by soaring food prices.

Although the recession and some bumper crops lowered corn prices for a few years, the price rose again to $8 in 2012 and remained over $4 for several years. The high price of corn motivates many farmers to dedicate more acreage to corn instead of other food grains. The devotion of more cropland to corn and less to other basic cereal grains—wheat, soybeans, and rice, for instance—drives up the prices of those other grains.

The world has long depended on exports of corn from the United States, the world's largest producer. For decades, U.S. exports of corn have accounted for about 40 percent of all corn exports. But consider how much of the American corn crop is now going to fuel instead of food. In 2015, the federal ethanol mandate diverted—quite unnecessarily—40 percent of the U.S. corn crop to ethanol, an extremely inefficient and environmentally questionable transportation fuel.[30] Gasoline now sold in the United States is roughly 10 percent ethanol—the maximum blend at which auto makers are willing to warrant engine function. A category of engines called "Flex Fuel" is warranted for using "E85"—a blend of 85 percent ethanol and 25 percent petroleum fuel. Good luck finding a station that offers E85 unless you live in Iowa.

If ethanol were to replace conventional gasoline, corn would have to be planted on five hundred million acres of land—substantially more than the 442 million total acres of American cropland.[31] And ethanol is a far less efficient fuel than gasoline refined from crude oil. Ethanol's energy density is 34 percent less than gasoline's, and it delivers one-third fewer miles per gallon than gasoline. The bi-partisan majority of Congress that enacted the Renewable Fuel Standard in 2007 was reacting to rising oil prices and increasing dependence on imported oil. Within a year, however, the shale revolution took off, and by 2014 the United

States was producing more oil than we could store. Yet the ethanol mandate persists.

Ethanol policy occupies a strangely prominent role in our country's politics because the first contest of each presidential campaign is in Iowa, where corn is king. The Hawkeye State has forty-two of the nation's 189 ethanol plants and produces 25 percent of all ethanol distilled in the United States.[32] It is nearly impossible for a candidate from either party to win the Iowa caucuses without supporting ethanol mandates. This political factor alone has perpetuated the counterproductive and ethically dubious Renewable Fuel Standard.

Promoters of ethanol pitch it as a way to reduce greenhouse gas emissions, yet research has shown that ethanol probably increases such emissions. According to a study published in *Science*, biofuels may generate "17–420 times more carbon dioxide than the fossil fuels they replace."[33] At each step of the process before combustion in a vehicle—planting, fertilizing, watering, harvesting, distilling, and transporting exclusively by rail or truck—ethanol production indirectly generates carbon dioxide as well as genuine pollutants.

Using hundreds of millions of acres of fertile agricultural land to produce transportation fuel is a throwback to a time when our needs for food, mechanical energy, and fuel competed for the produce of a fixed amount of land.

A couple of generations ago, human hunger was a major concern. During the depression of the 1930s, poverty and hunger were visible on many American streets. How fast the human condition has changed! Now we worry about an epidemic of obesity, which is more prevalent among the poor than among the wealthy.[34] In many countries of the world the latest nutritional worry is "pet obesity." You know people are well fed when they are worried that they are feeding too much to their pets. Perhaps Europe and America are literally lands of "rich fat cats." Still, hundreds of millions of people across the world rely on corn, wheat, or rice for their daily caloric intake. Only the elite in the most affluent countries, insulated from the human face of subsistence poverty, could devise and mandate policies to shrink the supply of basic food commodities like corn.

The Versatility of Fossil Fuels: Synthetic Materials

We thought we would spare you a full chapter about the wonders of asphalt, plastic, and polyester. Synthetic materials like these, however, are yet another incalculable benefit of fossil fuels. How these materials would be replaced in a decarbonized world is a question left unanswered by environmental extremists, who are uninterested in something as mundane as plastic. The importance of these ubiquitous materials in everyday life, however, is undeniable. Our homes, offices, hospitals, and drug stores are packed with these materials and fibers derived from hydrocarbon.

Versatility is one of the distinctive advantages of oil, coal, and natural gas. The combustion of these materials in transportation, industrial processes, and the generation of electricity accounts for a huge volume of energy, but it is only the tip of the hydrocarbon iceberg. Supplanting fossil fuels with nuclear power or with renewable fuels like wind and solar is imaginable, if currently impracticable. But how would we replace the plastic, synthetic fibers, chemicals, pharmaceuticals, cosmetics, asphalt, and other materials derived from fossil fuels?

Plastic, Asphalt, and So Much More

From petroleum or crude oil, when refined and separated, we can make gasoline, kerosene, asphalt, chemical feed stocks, and pharmaceuticals. The last two categories cover almost all consumer products. Everything "plastic" derives from petroleum or natural gas, including cellophane tape, shotgun shells, soccer balls, guitar strings, pacifiers, aspirin, rubbing alcohol, artificial limbs, fabric softener, hair color, lipstick, shaving cream, electric tape, and Plexiglas.[35]

Fossil fuels enabled huge increases in the volume of materials available for the production of basic consumer goods. In 1900, 144 million metric tons of materials were used to make basic consumer goods in the

FIGURE 7.2

Renewable, Nonrenewable, and Total Material Usage in the U.S., 1900–2006

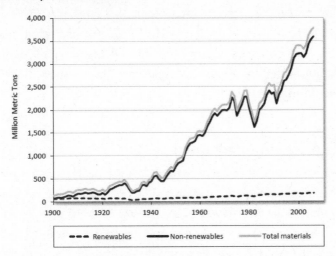

Source: Grecia R. Matos, *Use of Minerals and Materials in the United States from 1900 through 2006*, U.S. Geological Survey Fact Sheet 2009-3008, http://pubs.usgs.gov/fs/2009/3008.

United States. That figure rose twenty-six-fold to almost four billion metric tons in 2006.[36] Most of this increase was in materials derived from fossil fuels and nonrenewable chemicals. The volume of renewable materials declined from 46 percent in 1900 to 5 percent in 2006. Once again, fossil fuels shrank man's footprint on the natural world. See Figure 7.2. And that 5 percent of materials must be processed, shipped, and moved with energy from fossil fuels.

Textiles

The majority of textiles and clothing are now made of synthetic fibers derived from fossil fuels. Synthetic alternatives to natural materials are the primary reason for the mind-boggling abundance of consumer goods. Clothing and household furnishings—the most personal consumer goods—are a compelling example. Until the late 1800s, all clothing and textiles were made from natural materials such as plant fiber (cotton);

wool from sheep, goats, or wild animals; animal skins; and silk from worms. Synthetic fibers derived from fossil fuels currently account for 60 percent of global fibers.[37]

Polyester is the raw material for 80 percent of synthetic fibers, while vinyl, nylon, and acrylic account for 18 percent of synthetics.[38] All these fibers, derived from petroleum, have reduced the cost of clothing across the world and improved the warmth and affordability of winter clothing. For insulation, water repellency, and lighter weight, synthetic fibers are better than natural.

Green Energy = Income Inequality

For many years now, much of the political debate in Washington has centered on income inequality. Thomas Piketty's bestselling economics book, *Capitalism in the Twenty-First Century*, is nothing more than a discussion of the gulf between the rich and the poor. Capitalism leads to inequality, we are told. America's most famous socialist, Senator Bernie Sanders, ran for president in 2016 on the theme that "almost all of the gains of the economy in recent decades have gone to the top 1 percent."

Our point isn't to question the wisdom of Piketty's and Sanders's policy prescriptions. Readers who want to be educated about income inequality can read Steve Moore's book *Who's the Fairest of Them All?* Rather, we are struck by the irony that so many on the political Left who want to redistribute wealth are the same people who want to abandon cheap, safe, and efficient forms of power production in favor of much more expensive, unreliable, and even ecologically damaging forms of energy.

Take a close look at Figure 7.3. It shows the correlation between per capita income and energy consumption by country. Poor countries consume very little energy. Rich countries consume a lot. Cheap energy is one of the greatest economic equalizers in history. It has enabled even those near the bottom to enjoy a better lifestyle than kings had two hundred years ago. It is essential for making food, housing, clothing, technology, healthcare, education, travel, and entertainment affordable for nearly everyone.

FIGURE 7.3

The Correlation between Energy Use and GDP

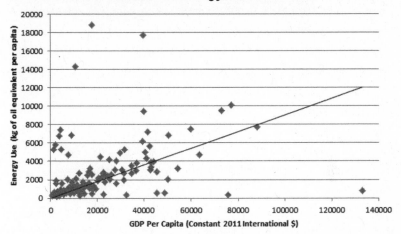

It's astonishing how many young people (and many older people too) to whom we give speeches don't have even the most basic understanding that the chair they are sitting in, the heating system that keeps the room warm, the laptop computer they are tapping on, the iPod they are listening to, the car they drove to get there, the light in the room, the Nikes they are wearing, the apple they are chomping on, the shampoo they used to wash their hair, the textbook they are staring at, and the eyeglasses on their head are all ubiquitous in our society because of affordable energy. Young people—God love them—are idealistic, and they want to save the planet, so it's cool on college campuses to be in favor of green energy. But it isn't cool or smart or "fair" to make energy more expensive—it is impoverishing. The young take what they have as a given, not as the gift of hundreds and thousands of years of the evolution of human knowledge and century upon century of learning by doing.

Every generation stands on the shoulders of its ancestors. Our ancestors have harnessed energy to steadily improve the state of the world. The green agricultural revolution of the last century was, as we've said before, an energy revolution. There is a very good evolutionary reason advanced peoples don't use sun panels and windmills to power their societies. It's called the evolution of knowledge. We use coal and gas instead of windmills for the same reason that wheels aren't made of stone anymore. Windmills are to power generation what carrier pigeons are to communications.

One of the surest ways of increasing inequality and hindering the fight against hunger, disease, pollution, malnutrition, poverty, and deprivation is to make energy more expensive, because doing so makes *everything* more expensive. The rich can afford to fill up their tanks for $75. The poor can't. The rich can afford to pay an extra $150 a month in higher utility bills. The poor, and even the middle class, can't. The rich can afford to pay an extra $200 for a life-saving drug or vaccine. The poor can't.

Fossil fuels have been one of the greatest anti-poverty programs in history, improving the human condition more than all of the trillions of dollars of government welfare programs and foreign aid programs combined. By contrast, most forms of green energy aren't green at all. They're a prescription to make the poor poorer.

THE FALSE HOPE OF GREEN ENERGY

The $5 Billion Man

One of the greatest scams in modern government is the millions and even billions of dollars that Silicon Valley businesses and investors are making off green energy subsidies. And the poster child for green corporate welfare is Elon Musk, CEO of Tesla, SolarCity, and SpaceX. The multibillionaire is a master investor—he "goes where the money is"—and increasingly, the hunt for cash doesn't take place on Wall Street or even in Silicon Valley. It's in Washington, D.C.

Until the price of oil went bust—he lost billions in early 2016—Musk was one of the hottest CEOs in the country, and Tesla stock had been a strong performer. But one key to Musk's success has been that his companies have, according to a 2015 analysis by the *Los Angeles Times*, gathered in $4.9 billion of taxpayer subsidies over the past several years—everything from grants and loan guarantees to property-tax abatements and federal tax credits for buying his products.[1] The new king of corporate welfare, Musk is starting to make Florida's Fanjul family, which lives off sugar subsidies, or former Archer Daniels Midland CEO Dwayne Andreas, who cashed in on ethanol mandates and subsidies, look like pikers.

Many Wall Street investors have gambled that Musk can cut his costs before the taxpayer money runs dry. But it might be that he and his backers are betting that Washington is so tied into the powerful green industrial complex that the tax dollars will never stop flowing, like a fiscal perpetual motion machine. This is what liberals mean by "public-private partnership." It says a lot about the U.S. economy and the role that big government plays that those who reach the top of the federal subsidy mountain are Wall Street's darlings.

Nearly all of Musk's corporate activities—building electric cars, producing solar panels, and launching rockets into space—depend on government's largesse. The secret to his success is finding out what the Obama administration and other politicians want then starting to produce it, regardless of whether it's commercially viable. The solar panel scam is so costly that the government in many cases is paying homeowners to put Musk's product on their roofs. The investment firm Sanford Bernstein found that late in 2015, when Congress extended green energy tax credits, the more than billion-dollar value of the credits was instantly translated into higher stock valuations. So the tax bill effectively took money from American taxpayers and handed it over to the shareholders of green energy firms. That's quite a scam—taxing the poor and giving to the rich.

Challenged on CNBC in 2015 about the size of the subsidies he rakes in every year, Musk replied that they're "helpful" and create jobs. He defended the government support as necessary because "what the incentives do is they are catalysts. They improve the rate at which a certain thing happens." Well, it's true that if the government subsidizes something, you usually get more of it. Even SolarCity's own filings with the Securities and Exchange Commission concede that eliminating all the rebates and other handouts would "adversely impact our business."

The fact is, there might not be a solar industry if the government weren't underwriting it—which it has been doing for thirty years, even though the aid is always sold as "temporary." The real issue is: Why do our governments do it? Why are politicians steering tax dollars to their favorite causes—and contributors?

Who knows if Musk's electric cars will ever become profitable or whether solar energy can compete on its own anytime in the next decade? Oil is going to have to get many times more expensive for that to happen. It's fairly certain that the wise men of Washington who pass out our money don't have a clue whether this will happen. And it's not their money they're handing out as if this were a Monopoly board game. It's the taxpayers'. How many Solyndras do taxpayers have to finance and then watch crash and burn before the government cuts off this cronyism?

The Forty-Year Green Energy Bust

Even against the backdrop of Washington's extensive fiscal malpractice, Uncle Sam's nonstop "investment" in green energy qualifies as one of Uncle Sam's most expensive boondoggles. Bad bets on renewable energy since the 1970s include direct subsidies, government loans and loan guarantees, tax preferences, lavish grants, and regulatory mandates biased in favor of wind and solar power. The payoff has been elusive to say the least.

Let's start with the simple facts. Green energy remains an inconsequential source of energy in America despite more than $80 billion in direct federal taxpayer subsidies under Presidents George W. Bush and Barack Obama. This is shown in Figure 8.1 on the following page. Wind and solar combined produce less than 3 percent of our energy, and only about 5 percent of our electricity.[2]

There are plenty of niche markets for wind and solar power. But the assumption that current renewable technologies can provide the same energy services that oil, coal, and natural gas now handily provide at a vast scale defies reality. Without the lavish subsidies, renewable energy would find its niche markets.

America's $18-trillion industrial economy cannot be powered with windmills and solar paneling unless we can transcend the four laws of

FIGURE 8.1

Renewable Energy Is Insignificant

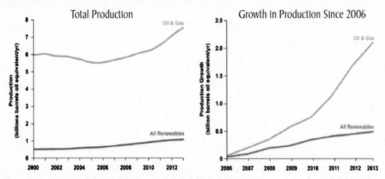

The growth in oil & gas production from America's shale fields in the last seven years exceeds by twofold the total production of energy from all renewable sources (excluding hydro dams).

Data source: U.S. Energy Information Administration

thermodynamics, the application of which put man on the moon, led to micro-processors, semiconductors, and innumerable technological breakthroughs that have extended our life spans and improved human life across the world.

The future of green energy is not much brighter than its dismal past—even according to some of its most vocal proponents. In 2012, the Department of Energy issued an amazing forecast: renewable energy's share of electricity production in America is expected to shoot up—hold on to your hats—all the way to 9.5 percent in 2030.[3] See Figure 8.2. Nevertheless, the Environmental Protection Agency has decreed that renewables must provide around 30 percent of our electricity by 2030.[4] The total share of electricity from wind and solar combined is expected to only reach 6 percent of electricity production by 2040—if all goes according to plan.[5] And even this minuscule increase presumes that the multi-billion-dollar federal subsidy machine keeps running and growing. Europe's pursuit of renewable energy—begun a decade earlier than our own—shows that as more power is generated from wind and sun, the amount of subsidies needed will balloon.

FIGURE 8.2

Sources of U.S. Primary Energy Use in 2030

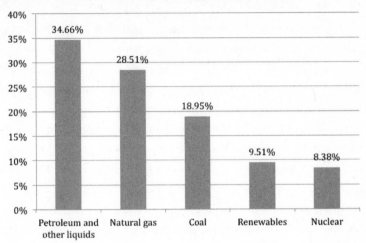

In 2014, Michael Kelly, of the University of Cambridge, published some revealing calculations about potential contribution of renewables to reducing carbon dioxide emissions by 80 percent in 2050—the goal of the United Kingdom's Climate Change Act of 2008. Zero-carbon energy, he found, had been static for twenty-five years, accounting for 12 to 13 percent of the energy consumed. And remember the European Union considers wood, the use of which is increasing, to be a carbon-neutral renewable fuel. If overall energy trends continue as projected, carbon energy will grow—as a portion of energy consumption—seven times faster than the zero-carbon renewable energies.[6] At these rates, the 80 percent reduction in carbon will be reached not in 2050 but sometime around the year 2400.

A more politically correct projection comes from the U.S. Energy Information Administration, which reports that renewable energy projects will be the fastest-growing source of new energy production over the next three decades in terms of percentage change.[7] But this is growth from a tiny base in any case. For example, despite the billions of dollars "invested" in solar projects, solar power accounts for only 0.7 percent of U.S. electricity production—even after growth of 10.3 percent from 2010 to 2012.[8] Then again, an increase to just 1.0 percent would represent a 100 percent growth rate.

The story of the world's largest concentrated solar thermal plant, Ivanpah, illustrates the limitations of this form of renewable energy. Sprawling across four thousand acres of the Mojave Desert that once were home to a federally-protected tortoise, this plant focuses almost 350,000 mirrors (instead of solar panels) on steam turbines to generate electricity. Built at a cost of more than $2.2 billion and subsidized by a $1.6-billion federal loan guarantee, Ivanpah got off to a slow start, as the New York Times noted in an article titled "Huge Solar Plant Opens Facing Doubt about Its Future."[9]

Ivanpah is generating only 40 percent of the time, evidently because cloud cover is more frequent than was expected. To jump-start the turbines in the morning after the sun comes up, the plant uses four times more natural gas than was planned, raising the question whether it is a solar or a natural gas plant. Producing air temperatures of up to a thousand degrees Fahrenheit, it killed 3,500 birds during the first year of operation. The math and physics underlying wind, solar, and biomass renewables—which our ruling class has decreed to be the replacements for steady-state, energy-dense coal, gas, and nuclear sources—do not in fact work. Yet the United States, and much of Europe have bought the renewable lobby's bill of goods.

. By far the biggest source of renewable electricity today (close to 50 percent of all renewable electricity produced) is hydroelectric power, yet it receives almost no subsidies. Wind and solar combined produce less than a quarter of all renewable energy but receive nearly two-thirds of all renewable energy subsidies.[10] Even with these enormous subsidies, in total, the EIA projects that wind will produce only 4.9 percent of our electricity by 2040, up from 4.3 percent today.[11] The high costs and the insuperable problem of intermittency—the wind doesn't always blow and wind speeds fluctuate—preclude wind power from fueling a large industrial base or a major metropolitan area.

Consequently, America will derive upwards of 90 percent of its energy from sources other than wind and solar for at least the next thirty years—mostly traditional fuels like coal, natural gas, nuclear energy, and hydropower. Of course, it's these vital resources which the environmentalists despise.

The International Energy Agency concedes that green energy is in fast retreat and is getting crushed by "the recent drop in fossil fuel prices."[12] It finds that because of the huge price advantage of oil, natural gas, and coal, "fossil plants still dominate recent [electric power] capacity additions."[13] Barack Obama told voters that green energy was necessary because oil is a "finite resource" and we would eventually run out.[14] But as the late economist Julian Simon taught us in his classic book *The Ultimate Resource*, human ingenuity in finding new resources almost always outpaces resource depletion.[15] The recent shale revolution is a stunning example of Simon's insight. (See Figure 2.1 on page 28.)

What does this mean for the future of green energy? Well, for now, it can't possibly compete with fossil fuels in a free and functioning market. But the market works only in countries that allow it to do so. German and British renewable mandates have resulted in a cascade of subsidies, soaring prices, energy scarcity, and industrial flight. Our own EPA Clean Power Plan rule threatens to inflict the same disaster on the United States by eliminating competitive energy markets and mandating that the carbon intensity of electricity trump cost and reliability.

The national leaders who got their countries into this renewable mess bravely insist that necessary energy revolutions may have painful chapters. Held hostage to Vladimir Putin's natural gas prices—two to four times higher than in the United States—the dogmatic European greens have few alternatives. So they are returning to their great-great-grandparents' heating fuel—wood.

Germany and England are learning that the more renewable fuels they dispatch to their electric grids, the more coal they must burn to back up the intermittent generation from wind or solar sources. And since most of their coal plants have been shuttered, not because of government mandates but because they could not compete with lavishly subsidized renewables, these countries are now subsidizing coal plants to come back on line.

On another green energy front, the collapse in the price of oil and natural gas is flattening the market for battery-powered cars. The trade publication *Fusion* noted in 2015 that "electric vehicle purchases in the U.S. have stagnated. According to auto analysts at Edmunds.com, only 45 percent of this year's hybrid and EV trade-ins have gone toward the purchase of another alternative fuel vehicle. That's down from just over 60 percent in 2012."[16] And a major car market website observes, "Never before have loyalty rates for alt-fuel vehicles fallen below 50 percent." It seems that "many hybrid and EV owners are driven more by financial motives [than by] a responsibility to the environment."[17] That's what happens when the world is awash in abundant fossil fuel and technology advances.

Don't bet on the long-promised super batteries storing wind and solar power any time soon. The much acclaimed Tesla "gigafactory" in Nevada is supposed to produce more storage than all the current lithium batteries in the world. In storage capacity, according to our colleague Mark P. Mills, the batteries to be annually produced at the Tesla facility would amount to thirty billion watt-hours of electricity. Yet the United States consumes around 4,000,000 billion watt-hours per year.[18] This means that annual production of batteries at the "gigafactory" would store about five minutes' worth of U.S. electric demand. For context, thirty minutes of the energy output of the Eagle Ford shale field in Texas represents a greater quantity of energy than the batteries produced in a year at the Tesla factory.[19]

Giving Green Energy the Old Google Try

Scientists at Google—the epitome of a modern "green" business—encountered the sobering realities of renewable energy when they searched for a fast path to a zero-carbon future. The RE<C initiative ("Renewable Energy Cheaper than Coal"), launched in 2007, invested in "potentially breakthrough technologies." After four years, Google's

high-powered engineers concluded that renewables "simply won't work" on the scale envisioned. In fact, the grand green plan was damaging to the environment. They wrote:

> Even if one were to electrify all of transport, industry, heating, and so on, so much renewable generation and balancing/storage equipment would be needed to power it that astronomical new requirements for steel, concrete, copper, glass, carbon fiber, neodymium, shipping and hauling, etc., would appear. All these things are made using mammoth amounts of energy: far from achieving massive energy savings, which most plans for a renewables future rely on implicitly, we would wind up needing far more energy, which would mean even more vast renewables farms—and even more materials and energy to make and maintain them and so on. The scale of the building would be like nothing ever attempted by the human race.[20]

The green movement has responded that RE<C simply wasn't "ambitious enough." But unlike governments, private company's don't have unlimited budgets. They have to turn a profit at some point.

Google's setbacks in green energy were even more embarrassing when the firm also had to admit that it couldn't even power its own data centers with the solar panels it had installed. According to the company statement: "The plain truth is that the electric grid, with its mix of renewable and fossil generation, is an extremely useful and important tool for a data center operator, and with current technologies, renewable energy alone is not sufficiently reliable to power a data center."[21] Try lighting up a whole city.

The Google scientists were not "climate change deniers." But they came to a stark realization that other greens should ponder. Transitioning to a green power system would require two to three times more generating capacity to provide the same amount of electricity as a coal or natural gas plant, back-up generation from reliable sources for grid balancing, and energy storage equipment. These structures would in turn require astronomical quantities of steel, concrete, copper, glass, carbon fiber, neodymium, along with shipping and haulage of these raw materials. All this output requires copious amounts of energy inputs. Far from achieving the massive energy savings assumed by most renewable energy master plans, humanity would end up needing far *more* energy.

Nevertheless, Washington clings to the fantasy that green energy is going to replace fossil fuel production. If Google can't make renewable energy work, does anyone really think Washington can?

Government's Fatal Conceit

The practice of fleecing American taxpayers to fund pipe dreams of alternative energy sources goes back to the late 1970s, when the Carter administration spent billions of dollars on the Synthetic Fuels Corporation, one of the great corporate welfare boondoggles in American history. Under Presidents George W. Bush and Obama, Washington demonstrated that it continues to suffer from what F. A. Hayek called the "fatal conceit." Like the central planners of the 1950s Politburo, Congress and the White House thought they knew where the future was headed, and from 2010 to 2015 the U.S. Government poured $150 billion into solar and other renewables.[22] Even as fracking changed the energy world around them, these blindfolded sages stuck with their green fantasy that wind turbines were the future.

It's bad enough when private sector investors are sucked in to placing foolish bets on a medieval energy source like wind turbines. But when politicians play public venture capitalist, they lose our money. To make matters worse, government-backed technologies divert private investment toward those deemed worthy by policymakers and away from more promising innovations. This turns a genuinely competitive market on its head.

We don't know if renewables will ever be a bigger part of America's energy mix. But if they do, it will be because of market forces and technological advances, not central planning.

Who Gets All Those Subsidies?

Which form of energy is most heavily subsidized by taxpayers? This has been a source of raging debate for at least the last decade. If you listened to the Obama administration, you would think all of the tax breaks and subsidies go to oil and gas. But in 2010, the natural gas and oil industry received $2.8 billion, coal got $1.4 billion, hydropower $216 million, and solar $1.1 billion. The grand-prize winner in the government-subsidies sweepstakes was the wind industry, which received $5 billion.[23]

The most meaningful gauge of subsidies takes into account how much electricity each recipient actually produces. The Department of Energy will not provide such a calculation, but the Institute for Energy Research, using DOE data for 2010, has tallied government energy subsidies per unit of electricity produced.[24] Coal received sixty-four cents per megawatt hour, natural gas and petroleum received sixty-four cents, nuclear $3.14, wind $56.29, and solar a whopping $775.64. So for every tax dollar that goes to oil and natural gas, wind gets about $60 and solar about $800, and solar *still* can't compete in the market.

FIGURE 8.3

Electric Shock: Federal Electricity Subsidies, 2010

	% of All Subsidies	$ Per Megawatt Hour
Coal	10.0	0.64
Natural Gas and Petroleum	5.5	0.64
Nuclear	21.0	3.14
Hydropower	1.8	0.82
Geothermal	1.7	12.85
Solar	8.2	775.64
Wind	42.0	56.29

Source: U.S. Department of Energy, 2011; Institute for Energy Research, 2011

The DOE has calculated subsidies for transportation fuels and the story is much the same as for electricity production. Oil and natural gas, which get 20.7 percent of fuel subsidies, account for 80.3 percent of our transportation fuel. The big winner here is "biomass and biofuels"— mostly ethanol, which account for 10.9 percent of fuel production but receive 73.2 percent of the taxpayer assistance. On an equivalent Btu basis, for every dollar of aid to oil and gas, ethanol receives roughly $28.[25]

An important difference between fossil-fuel producers and green energy producers is that the former pay a great deal in taxes, the latter almost none. According to a recent study by the American Petroleum Institute, the oil and gas industry contributes more than $30 billion a year in the form of income taxes, rents, royalties and other fees.[26] Renewables, especially wind and solar, with profits close to zero, pay almost no income tax. The Congressional Research Service reports that the renewables industry will receive nearly $40 billion in tax-related provisions between 2014 and 2018.[27] 18 percent, or $7.2 billion, of this tax-related support comes from a program called "Section 1603 Grants in Lieu of Tax Credit program." These are like earned income tax credit payments to corporations that pay no income tax, and the CRS notes that the "one-time grant" instead of future credits is popular because of the "uncertainty renewable energy investors may have regarding their future tax position."[28] This means there is a good chance they won't have any profits to tax.

In 2012, then-Senator Jim DeMint of South Carolina proposed, as a free-market alternative to this spider web of subsidies, extinguishing all targeted federal tax credits and other subsidies to all forms of energy— coal, gas, oil, wind, solar, bio-fuels, batteries, and nuclear power.[29] This measure would have eliminated about $90 billion of corporate welfare— enough savings to lower the federal corporate income tax rate by almost 1 percentage point. DeMint could muster only twenty-five votes for his proposal. Almost all Senate Democrats and even many Republicans refused to end "green" taxpayer giveaways.

Solar Scam

About half the states have imposed "renewable portfolio standards," which require utilities either to generate or to buy a certain percentage of their electric power from wind and solar energy producers. These standards raise consumers' costs by forcing utilities to buy power from more expensive sources.

Thanks to a slew of solar industry subsidies, homeowners can effectively contract with solar leasing firms that will install those panels for free. But they often get gouged later, as do taxpayers in one of the great corporate welfare scams of modern times. Homeowners buy the solar power system at an ultra-low long-term interest rate while immediately receiving the prized 30 percent tax credit. Or they install the equipment with a long-term, no-money-down lease option. SolarCity offers customers loans with financing from major banks, including Bank of America and Citigroup.

Rooftop solar would probably not survive without these giveaways. According to SolarCity's 2014 annual report, 93 percent of new customers enter into the second option. "Our business," says the report, "currently depends on the availability of rebates, tax credits and other financial incentives. The expiration, elimination or reduction of these rebates, credits, and incentives would adversely impact our business."[30]

In a typical lease, SolarCity owns the equipment and pockets the tax credits. The homeowner pays SolarCity monthly for the energy individually consumed from the panels, while the electric utility credits net metering proceeds to the homeowner.

These solar panels are installed regardless of whether the savings from the electric power generated covers the cost of materials, installation, and upkeep. Often they don't come close. Congressman Paul Gosar (R-Ariz.), a member of the Committee on Oversight and Government Reform, and eleven House colleagues have written to the Federal Trade Commission asking if the booming solar leasing market—a "new industry with a limited track record and little regulatory oversight"—poses a "considerable risk" to homeowners.[31]

Congressman Gosar is not worried only about the taxpayers but also about the families that have been lured by "deceptive marketing strategies" into sucker deals. His investigation has found that "homeowners who signed these zero-money-down leases are struggling to sell their homes" and may not have been "fully aware of the terms of their 20–30-year leases."[32] In some cases these pay-me-later, long-term leases exceed the life of the roof or the homeowner's intention to live in the home.

SolarCity's website claims you can "secure lower, predictable solar energy rates that are guaranteed for years to come." Its advertisements romance customers with slogans like: " Start with no upfront cost" and "Our coverage is the best in the industry, with repairs and a production guarantee at no additional cost."[33] Yet the fine print indicates solar power costs on home systems will increase by up to 2.9 percent annually for twenty to thirty years—hardly a bargain if long-term electricity trends have reversed because of the natural gas boom.

California and Louisiana homeowners have filed class-action lawsuits against solar leasing companies alleging fraudulent marketing campaigns that don't warn customers of true costs and risks.[34] The California lawsuit against SunRun cites a website claim that "nationwide, electricity rates have been increasing 6 percent per year over the last 30 years…and there's no evidence that this trend will reverse anytime soon."[35]

"Net metering" is residential solar's most important subsidy, because it forces the local power company to purchase any excess energy—even at money-losing rates—generated by these home systems, regardless of demand. Under this scheme, a sunny day with below-normal energy demand may lead to a surplus of electric power. The homeowners can sell this unneeded solar power at a tidy profit to an unwilling buyer at full retail cost—a level often four times the wholesale rate. Ultimately these costs must be passed on to other ratepayers.

According to E&E News, a leading energy policy newsletter, "43 states, the District of Columbia, and four U.S. territories have net metering policies in place, with differing capacity limits. Under the Energy

Policy Act of 2005, all public utilities are required to offer net metering to customers upon request."[36]

Solar panel users are guaranteed access to the electric grid when they need it—on stormy or cloudy days, for example. But they fail to pay their fair share for construction and upkeep of the grid, making them free riders.

With power generation plants, fixed costs can make up 20 to 50 percent of electricity's retail price. Thus solar users don't have to pay for the fixed cost of the grid system, but plant owners get to charge for its cost, embedded in the retail price of electricity, when they sell to the grid. In effect, each solar panel home enjoys a $1,000 subsidy paid for by neighbors and other grid users, according to Greg Bernosky of the Arizona Public Service Co.[37]

The Solar Energy Industries Association likes to tout the industry's "amazing success"—but the continued success of this fad depends on a cascade of government subsidies, including a 30 percent federal investment credit that was supposed to expire at the end of 2016. None of these "renewable energy" subsidies to harvest the sun's rays will have more than a tiny effect on greenhouse gas emissions. But when green homeowners can pass the costs on to their neighbors, such schemes can look attractive.

SolarCity boasts that it plans to have one million long-term leases in place by 2018 in spite of the 50 percent drop in oil and gas prices that began in 2014.[38] Don't be surprised if we see taxpayer losses that dwarf the Solyndra debacle.

Anatomy of a Green Energy Flop

One of the premier government-as-venture-capitalist fiascoes was Fisker Automotive, a California-based maker of battery-powered cars, which received a loan of $529 million from the Department of Energy in 2010.[39]

Fisker's success was critical to fulfilling Barack Obama's promise that America would be "the first country to have a million electric vehicles on the road by 2015."[40] Fisker was supposed to build about one hundred thousand of those vehicles,[41] but by the end of 2013 the company had produced and sold only about two thousand of its $100,000 Karmas.[42]

When, during the 2012 presidential campaign, Mitt Romney confronted Obama with this spectacular failure, the administration and the press rushed to Fisker's defense, and the firm's spokesman indignantly declared that "we don't consider ourselves a loser."[43]

Well, judge for yourself. Financial documents from congressional sources reveal that Fisker was crippled by severe financial and production problems that began even before the half-billion taxpayer loan was approved. DOE knew all this but gave the green light anyway. On August 23, 2009, Bernhard Koehler, Fisker's chief operating officer, sent a panicked email to DOE's loan office. The firm was so cash-strapped that it needed funding "in a very short time frame," Koehler warned. "A delay until the end of September is not possible for us or our suppliers." Then he added: "I'm sorry if I'm being very direct right now, but we don't have much time. I have to lay off all of my Fisker Coachbuild employees on Monday and some of the Fisker automotive people." Fisker could raise more equity with the loan, Koehler assured DOE, but was "nowhere without it."[44] No one could mistake Fisker for another Google.

In an internal e-mail, the DOE loan office admitted that it knew Fisker was troubled early on. The "Location of Collateral" report reveals that under even the most generous assumptions the value of the assets would never be close to making taxpayers whole in case of a default. Much more indefensible was issuing a low-interest, under-collateralized loan to a company whose credit rating—CCC+—is a warning of possible bankruptcy. This loan was looking like a Hail Mary pass.

Within months of receiving the loan, Fisker's troubles cascaded. According to the DOE loan office's corporate quarterly credit report of December 12, 2011, "the original business plan, delivered at closing in April 2010, called for a February 2011 launch of the Karma. The February 2011 launch date was included as a required milestone in the Loan Arrangement and Reimbursement Agreement."[45] In March 2011, "Fisker claimed that the milestone had been met." Not until June of that year did Fisker come clean, presenting "new information calling into question whether the milestone had actually been met."

The same report also revealed that in 2011 Fisker's credit rating had been downgraded to an even more dreadful CCC rating. The reason for the downgrade: "Deteriorating financial profile and/or persistent operation inefficiencies." The expected "recovery rate" on the Fisker loan was now put at 50 percent—scarcely better than the return rate of a 2007 subprime mortgage—and even that was optimistic.

Fisker signaled SOS again in November 2011. According to the DOE credit report, "Fisker investors told DOE that Fisker could not raise additional equity cash unless DOE agreed to move financial covenants and milestones that Fisker would begin to breach on December 31, 2011."[46] Like a rich uncle, DOE granted the extension.

Conditions kept getting worse. For example, because of continuing delays in launching the Karma, the estimates of the number of cars steadily declined through 2011.[47] Fisker then admitted that it would not meet its Karma sales milestone for February 29, 2012. The DOE, for good reason, feared the firm would experience a "liquidity shortage"—Fisker's burn rate on capital soared to $244 million in 2011, up from $190 million in 2010 and $90 million in 2009. It was losing money at an accelerating pace.

At the end of 2011, DOE halted further funding of the loan, saving $336 million of taxpayer money after $192 million had been lent out.[48] In late August 2012, more than two hundred of the Karmas on the road were recalled for a faulty cooling-fan after one caught fire while parked at a shopping mall. In 2012, *Consumer Reports* slammed the model as "plagued with flaws."[49] *Bloomberg* reported that the Karma "quit running during a road test" by the consumer magazine.[50]

Fisker, having sold virtually no cars, eventually went belly up. The environment wasn't improved; but taxpayers got soaked with at least $200 million in losses on a loan that should never have been made. The Fisker debacle represents the triumph of Obama's green dreams over common sense. Unfortunately, its lessons were lost on the administration, which has spent $8 billion on the Advanced Technology Vehicles

Manufacturing Program.[51] You can't just look at the losers, the White
House says. Fair enough. But where are the winners?

Biofuels

The spectacular excesses of the Obama administration should not
lead anyone to assume that environmentalist boondoggles are the exclusive preserve of Democrats. In his 2006 State of the Union message,
President George W. Bush proclaimed, "We'll fund additional research
in cutting-edge methods of producing ethanol, not just from corn but
from wood chips and stalks or switch grass. Our goal is to make this
new kind of ethanol practical and competitive within six years."[52] The
seeds of some of the biggest green energy flops were thus planted to "end
our addiction to fossil fuels" an odd goal for a President from Texas to
articulate in one of his State of the Union speeches.

President Bush and Congress went on to establish numerous subsidies
in the hope of launching a viable biofuels industry. They began by fun-
neling nearly $400 million in grants and loans to fledgling producers,
the Solyndras of bio-fuels. Then, to give the industry an extra financial
push, Bush signed an energy bill in 2007 that provided production tax
credits of more than $1 per gallon for the manufacturers of corn-based
and cellulosic fuels. On top of that, he enticed producers with the guaranteed market created by the Renewable Fuel Standard (RFS), which
required oil companies to blend 250 million barrels of cellulosic fuel into
conventional gasoline. The mandate would rise to five hundred million
gallons in 2011, and by the end of the decade the requirements would
jump to 10.5 billion gallons annually. As if the subsidies and mandates
were not enough, American ethanol producers would be protected
through 2011 by a tariff on ethanol imported from Brazil.

When these mandates were established, there were no companies
producing commercially viable cellulosic fuel. The dream was that if you
mandate and subsidize it, someone will build it. But nobody did. Despite
the federal subsidies, by 2011 cellulosic fuel production wasn't as much
as 250 million barrels or even twenty-five million but very close to zero.[53]

In 2010, the EPA revised the cellulosic mandate downward to 6.6 million. Even so, there was *no* cellulosic fuel available, so oil companies had to purchase "waiver credits" for failing to comply with a mandate to buy a product that the feds promised would exist but didn't. In 2010 and 2011, waiver credits cost oil companies about $10 million—a tax on gasoline production eventually passed on to motorists in higher gas prices at the pump.[54]

In 2012, the EPA had to concede that that year's five-hundred-million-gallon production mandate was unattainable, so the agency again vastly lowered the mandate, and the Department of Energy has since acknowledged that none of the original targets is likely ever to be met.

From the start, the cellulosic revolution careened off the tracks. For example, some 70 percent of the cellulosic fuel supply was supposed to come from a single small company, Cello Energy in Alabama.[55] But in 2009, Cello was found guilty in a federal court of civil fraud for lying to investors about how much cellulosic fuel it could produce. The fuel that Cello showed to investors was derived from petroleum not plants.[56] The firm has never come close to producing the seventy million gallons the feds were counting on.

The prospects for biofuels became even dimmer in 2012 when the federal bio-diesel program, which the EPA was supposed to monitor and regulate, exploded in scandal. Regardless of who was at fault here—and there's plenty of blame to go around, spanning two administrations—the victims of this bumbling renewable energy policy are taxpayers and consumers. Some $400 million of federal "investment" is down the drain, wasted on a series of mini-Solyndras. The mandates and production credits have raised the cost of gasoline.

And for what? A 2012 report from the National Academy of Sciences offered a dire assessment of the biofuels industry, concluding not only that the biofuels target would not be met, but also that they "may be an ineffective policy for reducing global greenhouse gas emissions."[57] Nor have they reduced U.S. reliance on foreign oil. It was all money for nothing.

The Obama administration responded to the manifest failure of biofuels by awarding $510 million to a military biofuels project[58] and lending another $134 million for the construction of a biofuels plant in Kansas that optimists expect to produce twenty-five million gallons of biofuel a year,[59] a miniscule contribution to the federal mandate's goal of 36 billion gallons by 2022.[60] The National Academy of Sciences says it doubts renewable fuel output will come anywhere near the federal requirements.

What About Green Jobs?

Politicians often try to sell these green energy handouts with the promise of additional jobs. In 2006 and 2007, the environmental Left forged an ingenious partnership with organized labor—the so-called blue-green alliance—in which the unions would support the green energy agenda and the construction projects would use union workers. The bargain with the greens turned out to be a catastrophically bad calculation for labor. Far more blue-collar jobs would have been created by fossil fuel projects, whereas the green energy craze has eliminated many of the trucking, coal mining, drilling, welding, pipefitting, electronics, and construction jobs that were the backbone of the industrial unions.

Despite President Obama's promise of five million green jobs over ten years if elected,[61] green energy projects have created hardly a fraction of that. A 2013 study by the Institute for Energy Research found that, for the over $26 billion committed to Department of Energy loan guarantee projects since 2009, only 2298 permanent jobs have been created. In other words, each one of these green jobs cost taxpayers an average of $11.45 million.[62] The amount of waste, moreover, has proved enormous. The Department of Labor's Office of the Inspector General examined a $500 million grant to the Employment and Training Administration to "train and prepare individuals for careers in 'green jobs'."[63] The report found that, out of a target of 80,000 participants, only 8,035 of those trained had found jobs, and only 1,033 had retained employment for more than six months. In other words, only one in ten participants found employment whatsoever, and only one in eighty found long-term employment. Such failure rates make America's inner city schools look like high performers.

The green jobs track record is even more dismal if adjusted to account for the deceptively broad definition of green jobs the Obama administration uses to juice the numbers. A report by the House Committee on Oversight and Government Reform found that "the metric of a 'green job' is nothing more than a propaganda tool designed to provide legitimacy to a pre-determined outcome that benefits a political ideology rather than the economy or the environment."[64] EPA regulators, university ecology professors, school bus drivers, bike-repair shop clerks, and even the Washington lobbyists who lassoed federal green loan guarantees count as "green" employees. The Oversight Committee estimates (charitably) that $157,000 was expended for every person trained through the Department of Labor and permanently placed in a job.[65] Yes, it can be less costly to send a young adult to Princeton for four years than to put one through a six-month federal training program.

EUROPE'S ENERGY FOLLY
Energy Poverty and "Dramatic Deindustrialization"

"A Blunder with Ugly Consequences"

We don't have to imagine what it would be like if we dramatically cut our fossil fuel production and use here in America. Europe has already moved forward in doing just that, and the results have been painful for European Union businesses and workers. As a result of higher prices, much of Europe is now backing off their decarbonization plans as a means of economic survival. We would be wise to learn from their mistakes.

The European Union set ambitious (that is, impossible) targets for the reduction of carbon emissions. To facilitate such reductions, the EU established a carbon emissions trading system, which has been ineffective and rife with corruption.[1] As the *Financial Times* put it, "Europe made the wrong bet on renewables."[2]

Those who believe that industrialized countries can, within a few decades, move from complete dependence on fossil fuels to reliance on wind and solar power need to look closely at the debacle in Germany and the United Kingdom, home of Europe's most radical green energy policies. Pursuing the goal of virtually eliminating fossil fuels within three decades, these two prosperous, educated countries have embarked on the first energy regression in human history.

The leaders of these countries boast of their green success, vaguely admitting the need for some "adjustment" going forward, but the economic damage and human suffering are impossible to conceal. Major European and American newspapers and periodicals have called Germany's radical rush to renewables "environmental lunacy," "a blunder with ugly consequences," "a green energy basket case," "a false bet," "a systematic industrial massacre," and "a suicide wish."[3]

German and British consumers now face electric rates two to three times the average American retail rate, while industries flee to countries with affordable electricity. The German Association of Energy Consumers estimates that hundreds of thousands of families, no longer able to pay their electric bills, are reverting to wood-burning stoves and meager illumination.[4] However well-meaning, the green crusade has become a threat to the foundations of human health and welfare.

Green energy policies are a gamble that renewables can supplant fossil fuels without energy scarcity, economic decline, physical suffering, or increased geopolitical vulnerability. The German and British green mandates have demonstrated that wind and solar energy are incapable of performing the tasks that fossil fuels have easily handled on a vast scale in modern industrial economies.

Germany's Energy Revolution: Money Grows on Trees

Germany's self-imposed green energy goals—40 percent renewables by 2030 and the virtual elimination of fossil fuels by 2050—are the most extreme in Europe, based on a gross miscalculation of the cost of renewable subsidies and the engineering complexity of integrating large volumes of uncontrollable renewable power. Not only has this policy inflicted heavy losses on both renewable and conventional power companies, but coal-fired electric generation has *increased*, and along with it carbon dioxide emissions.[5]

Germany's *Energiewende*—"energy transformation"—began in 2000 with subsidies for renewable electric generation and continued in 2011 with the decision to close all nuclear power plants by 2020, a hasty response to the nuclear disaster following Japan's Fukushima earthquake that will deprive Germany of 25 percent of its reliable electricity, which is also emissions-free.

The escalating costs of Germany's energy transformation have far exceeded the original projections. German taxpayers paid over $30 billion for renewable subsidies in 2014. The former minister of the environment Peter Altmaier estimates that system-wide costs could approach $1 trillion by 2022.[6]

The rising price of electricity is taking a heavy toll on the energy-intensive industries for which Germany is famous. In 2014, the *Financial Times* reported that Germany had incurred a net export loss of $67.6 billion because of high energy costs.[7] Energy intensive industries are relocating to countries like the United States, with its low natural gas prices.

A Wealth Transfer from the Poor to the Rich

The costs of most green policies hit low- and middle-income families disproportionately; the wealthy don't notice the extra digit or two on their energy bills. By design, Germany's lofty *Energiewende* protects industry and spares wealthy homeowners, while the average consumer bears the brunt of the cost through high electric rates and renewable levies.[8]

The German plan subsidizes homeowners' installation of solar panels, usually provided at a substantial discount or even free, and then subsidizes the sale of any excess household generation to the electric grid at a guaranteed price. Renters, however, who represent a much larger share of families in Germany than in the United States and tend to have lower incomes than owners, are not eligible for these benefits, which they

underwrite with their green taxes.[9] Dr. Benny Peiser of London's Global
Warming Policy Foundation testified to the U.S. Senate "that hundreds of
billions are being paid by ordinary families…in what is one of the biggest
wealth transfers from the poor to the rich in modern European history."[10]
Forcing the poor to subsidize green energy for the rich is a step back from
the progress that accompanied industrialization and made the modern
middle class.

While most public officials in Germany stick to their story of a successful energy revolution, evidence of a "fatal blunder" mounts from the
insiders responsible for carrying out the energy transformation. "Development and Integration of Renewable Energy: Lessons Learned from
Germany," a report prepared by the Swiss consulting firm FAA Financial
Advisory, makes for sobering reading: "Over the last decade, well-
intentioned policymakers in Germany and other European countries
created renewable energy policies with generous subsidies that have
slowly revealed themselves to be unsustainable, resulting in profound,
unintended consequences for all industry stakeholders."[11]

The problems with Germany's energy transformation go beyond its
reverse–Robin Hood economic effects. It is increasing the use of coal and
wood and the very carbon dioxide emissions the project was supposed
to eliminate. How did this folly come about?

The designers of Germany's energy revolution overlooked some basic
engineering realities about electricity. Modern systems of electric power
have achieved phenomenal precision, efficiency, and reliability through
the integrated operations of conventional power plants, electric grids,
and transmission networks. As a former control engineer for Scotland's
electric grid put it, "There are two essential facts to understand about
electrical power. It cannot be stored on any appreciable scale and it cannot be spilled. As a consequence, power must be produced as required
instantaneously; any deviation affects system frequency…that sustain
generation output."[12]

Modern systems of electric power are built around "dispatchable"—
or controllable—sources of electric generation such as coal, natural gas,
and nuclear, which can deliver precisely the amount of electricity needed

at the moment, meeting changing demand on the electric grid. Germany now gives priority to electricity generated from renewables, regardless of price or reliability. Weather rather than economics determines which energy source will send electric current down the lines, distorting energy markets. Whenever weather conditions permit wind or solar generation, that green electricity gets on the electric grid, while all conventional generators "stand down," so to speak. Price, safety, and supply—the historical criteria for dispatch to the grid—go by the wayside.

The stability of an electric grid requires the instantaneous balancing of demand with dispatchable generation and the maintenance of stable voltage throughout the transmission system. Putting uncontrollable renewable power on the grid whenever available requires a totally different engineering system. Germany made a national policy decision to flood "unprecedented, extensive, intermittent and uncontrollable forms of generation supply onto this unforgiving beast of a grid system."[13] In other words, the inherent intermittency and variability of wind and sunshine confound the engineering and economic foundation of modern electric power *because the green energy sources cannot be controlled.* Conventional electric generation by coal, natural gas, and nuclear fuels provides a continuous, steady-state flow of electricity that can be ramped up or down to meet demand. Fossil fuels and engineering controls have achieved an energy system that meets human needs. When wind and sunshine are the energy fuels, human demand has to adapt to whatever the variable renewables produce.

Wind and clouds constantly fluctuate, but the electric grid must be kept in constant balance in order to keep demand and electric current in balance. When it appears that the balance is weakening, grid operators can intervene to re-establish balance if they anticipate the need early enough and act promptly and correctly. Otherwise, the electric grid can collapse. In 2002, the operator of the German electric grid had to take exceptional measures to correct grid instability in only two instances. In 2013 after aggressive deployment of renewable generation, the instances of grid instability requiring intervention to avoid brown-outs rose to 1,213 instances.[14] See Figure 9.1 on the following page.

Europe is finding out that it is nearly impossible to estimate the share of electric generation that wind and sunshine will provide. As Germany and Britain attempt to put more and more renewably generated power on the grid, it appears that twice as much generating capacity is necessary as a back-up source of power to deal with the variability of weather.

FIGURE 9.1

Germany: Interventions to Stabilize Electric Grid

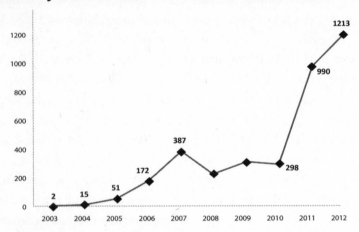

Source: Tennet, Grid and Transmission Systems Operator In "Development and Integration of Renewable Energy: Lessons Learned from Germany," Hans Poser et al, Finadvice .

An Inconvenient Truth:
Green Energy Is Parasitic on Coal

The problem of back-up—or redundant power, as the engineers call it—is the fatal flaw in the future of renewable power under current systems. Imagine that your car had two fuel tanks, and you had to fill them both. One tankful of gas would be burned in your primary engine. The other tankful would be simultaneously burned in an auxiliary engine, an engine that doesn't power your vehicle but is there in case your primary engine falters. You might waste the gas in the auxiliary tank, or you might have to use it sporadically and thus inefficiently. A car that got twenty miles per gallon would now get ten miles per gallon.

This is how the back-up for renewable power generation works. The back-up must come from controllable and reliable conventional sources of electric generation—coal and natural gas. Imagine winning World War II or resisting an increasingly bold Russia with an electric system that requires twice the energy needed for the task. But it gets absurdly worse.

The generous subsidies and dispatch priority given to renewables have made coal and natural gas power plants unprofitable. Remember that Germany imports most of its natural gas from Russia at two to three times the U.S. price. And many coal- and natural gas–fired power plants in Germany have had to close because they cannot compete with the green subsidies. To avoid black-outs, Germany now has to subsidize coal plants to get them back on line. Coal—the vilified fuel that the green scheme was designed to eliminate—becomes necessary to keep the lights on. Although German families and industries have spent hundreds of billions to support the energy transformation, emissions of carbon dioxide are rising not falling.

Negawatts: The Seller as Buyer

Germany's green energy scheme rewards mass deployment rather than reliability, efficiency, and affordability.[15] One of its strangest flaws is negative pricing, or "negawatts"—sellers paying buyers to purchase their product—an absurdity that results from the generation of electricity by wind or solar plants when it is not needed (e.g., in the middle of the night) or when the grid cannot handle it. Wind operators pay the grid to accept their electric power, although not needed, so the generator can get the subsidy. Because the generous tariff is earned only when wind or solar is actually generating power, renewable generators apparently can still make a profit when they sell negawatts—or more precisely when they pay the buyer to take what the buyer does not need or want. So much for the efficiency of a free market.

Most of the record-setting levels of renewable generation that Germany trumpets depend on negative pricing. On May 11, 2014, Germany reported that renewably generated electric power met 75 percent of the country's demand for electricity on one day. That sounds like amazing progress, but the rest of the story is more sobering. Most of that 75 percent rapidly became negawatts that Germany paid other countries to accept because the German grid could not handle it.[16] Paradoxically this is happening even though the cost of electricity is very high in Germany.

Whether a result of the designers' energy illiteracy, wishful thinking, or ideological zeal, green schemes on the scale of Germany's have been counter-productive and economically unsustainable. Rather than modifying the green goals and redesigning the system, it appears Germany is masking the problem by offering more and more subsidies.

The Cradle of Industrialized Civilization Goes Dark

Britain may not be far behind Germany when it comes to green woes. The Climate Change Act of 2008 commits the United Kingdom, over time, to renewable electric power on a scale comparable to Germany's. British electric prices have accordingly risen to levels around twice those of U.S. rates, inducing German-style energy poverty. Before the British took their vow of carbon chastity, the power supply was never a problem, but as the renewable mandates devoured what had been a privatized, competitive electric market, electricity became scarce. In 2013, over thirty thousand winter deaths were attributed to energy poverty—an increase of more than 30 percent from the previous year.[17] Citizens of the most prosperous and advanced countries in the world are freezing to death at home because of their government's ideological commitment to generating power with windmills.

Energy scarcity in Great Britain and Germany is the result of a deliberate choice to dismantle a well-functioning system of modern electric power and replace it with a system that is more expensive, uncontrollable, and inadequate.

Conventional gas- and coal-fired plants have shut down in Britain— as in Germany, Spain, and other countries—because renewable subsidies make them unprofitable. Overly optimistic estimates of the amount of electric demand that wind and solar could meet, as well as escalating costs and delays, have eroded Britain's reserve power supply, also known as capacity margin.[18]

For the first time since World War II, British subjects face the prospect of wintertime blackouts and power rationing. But instead of adopting pragmatic policies to reduce costs and increase the electric power supply, their government is telling them to learn to do without. Officials have urged the populace to schedule laundry and work according to wind conditions and cloud cover.[19] The electorate, of course, will put up with only so much cold and inconvenience, so government has to resort to ever more elaborate subsidy schemes to prop up an insupportable system—paying major industries to reduce hours of operation, for example, and paying small business to use diesel generators. And Britain will soon, like Germany, have to subsidize coal plants to come back on line.

Back to the Forest

The European energy regression continues on an increasingly incoherent path. Spain's early renewable programs, focused on solar power, suffered a major reversal in the brutal recession that began in 2008, but the confidence of the anti-carbon zealots is undiminished. Denmark, ideally situated for the generation of off-shore wind power, insists it can reach a zero-carbon electrical system in the not so distant future, but the Danes depend on nuclear power from Sweden and hydroelectric power from Norway to back up of their variable wind power system.[20]

The dirty little secret of Europe's renewable programs is that the fuel most prevalently burned in its cutting-edge green energy system is wood—the pre-industrial fuel that limited man's economic horizons before the Industrial Revolution. Around 50 percent of the renewable energy used in European countries to meet the EU's goal of 20 percent renewables by 2020 is wood. Trees, woody sticks, and sawdust are now given the distinguished name "biomass" among renewable energy sources, and the sometime tree-huggers are now tree-burners. Even in Germany, home of the most aggressive wind and solar programs, wood accounts for 38 percent of renewables deployed.[21] Poland, perhaps more savvy about the economic pitfalls of wind and solar power, uses wood to achieve 90 percent of its EU renewables obligation.

As a result of the EU's extremely generous subsidy for biomass and a wholly political decision to declare wood a "carbon-neutral" fuel, a new-old firewood industry is thriving. On the basis of simplistic assumptions, the EU decided that the carbon released when a tree is burned can be completely offset by planting another tree. Burn a tree and plant a tree and you are carbon-neutral. The EU will even give you a tidy subsidy for burning a tree!

More serious analyses demonstrate that burning wood emits at least 40 percent more carbon dioxide than burning coal,[22] yet the energy density of wood is less than half that of coal, and the power density of coal is hundreds to thousands of times higher than wood's. The huge rise in economic productivity that was the distinguishing achievement of the Industrial Revolution hinged on the switch from the diffuse, weak energy in wood to the far denser energy in coal. The deforestation that results from using wood as a fuel eliminates an important function of trees as "carbon sinks," absorbing perhaps 15 percent of man-made carbon dioxide emissions.[23]

In an article subtitled "Energy Lunacy in Europe," *The Economist* noted in 2013 that wood made it to the EU's green energy list because it is the only fuel by which European countries can hope to meet (on paper) the EU goal of 20 percent renewables by 2020. Wood also avoids the fatal intermittency of wind and solar generation. Existing coal-fired power plants can be reconfigured to use coal and wood or to burn all wood, but don't bet on reducing emissions of carbon dioxide.

To understand this lunacy, follow the money. Big government's idea of market mechanisms to reduce carbon includes many payoffs but nothing resembling a free exchange in a free market. The EU established generous subsidies for "biomass" (wood), independent of market prices and on top of profits.

Drax, one of Europe's leading electric generators, plans to retrofit three plants to burn wood. CF Partners, the largest carbon trading firm in Europe, estimates that Drax could receive €550 million per year in biomass subsidies after 2016, substantially higher than Drax's pre-tax profit in 2012 of €190 million. Does anyone wonder why Europe still struggles with economic growth?

In response to subsidies and high electric prices, more households are buying wood-burning stoves for heating and cooking. Germans purchased four hundred thousand wood stoves in 2011.[24]

Deforested in the long pre-industrial era, when wood was the only heating fuel, Europe now turns to imports from Canada and the southeastern United States to meet the renewed demand for wood. A new U.S. industry has emerged, producing tidy wood pellets (usually wrapped in fossil-fueled plastic packets) for easy export to the Old World. Global trade in the pellets could rise from ten to sixty million tons by 2020 according to the optimistic European Pellet Council.[25] Burning wood for fuel has driven its price so high that European sawmills, paper companies, and furniture manufacturers are struggling to stay in business.

Save the World: Burn Wood

Europe is now burning more coal and wood in order to supplant fossil fuels with wind and solar. Will this absurdity ever reach a tipping point? The European Parliament and some member countries have sounded the alarm on these counterproductive and damaging programs, and public sentiment seems to be turning. A poll of Germans in 2014 found that 73 percent question the *Energiewende*, while 24 percent support the programs.[26] The costs and the failures of the renewable initiatives are now undeniable but the Church of Climate Change is not yet interested in a change of dogma.

Consider an interview of the German minister of the environment, Barbara Hendricks, with CNN in late 2014.[27] Although a study commissioned by the government recommends that Germany eliminate the main subsidies for renewables, Hendricks declared *Energiewende* an environmental and economic success, benefiting the average citizen and allowing Germany to make it through the global recession "relatively unscathed." Germany is on track, she says, to meet its goal of reducing carbon dioxide emissions by 40 percent. One has to admire her optimism, since carbon dioxide emissions have been rising and Germany plans to bring on line ten more coal-fired plants as necessary backups. And remember that the lion's share of the reductions in emissions claimed by Germany and eastern European countries are attributable to EU carbon credits awarded not for using more wind but for closing decrepit and dirty industrial facilities left over from Soviet communism.

It is difficult to determine what Germany has achieved in the area of renewable energy, so numerous are the accounting tricks available for masking failure. Hendricks claims that renewables now meet almost 30 percent of demand. Most official number crunchers, such as the IEA, arrive at a lower figure. The Germans' number may be padded by including the generation sold by negative pricing to other countries when a surge of uncontrollable wind overwhelms the German power grid.[28]

After investing billions of taxpayer euros in the most radical green plan ever undertaken, the German people are left with ballooning subsidies, spiraling electric bills, energy market collapse, industrial flight to other countries, dependence on Russia's natural gas, energy poverty, and the necessity of increasing coal-fired plants and unavoidably rising emissions of carbon dioxide.

Yet in Germany and other European countries, politicians seem incapable of admitting a mistake. So much money has been spent, so many political careers are at risk, and so much professional integrity and national prestige are at stake that the Europeans are not backing down. Instead, they would like to make *their* pain and suffering *our* pain and suffering with a global treaty on climate change. But remember that each country's "commitment" to a specific amount of carbon cuts in the Paris agreement is a pledge that is not binding. Indeed, this weakening of the EU's earlier insistence on enforceable commitments is a major reason why the Paris agreement is far weaker than the key players had expected. In the face of the mounting damage from Germany's and Britain's ambitious green schemes, the EU transformed renewable mandates into softer targets and goals.[29] The increasing share of renewables intended remains ambitious, but it appears that each country's effort to avert climate change will be voluntary.

The green energy fad has cost the Eurozone its competitiveness over the last decade. The process of force-feeding industry and households green energy has increased utility costs and in some cases crippled manufacturing production. In August 2014, the *Wall Street Journal* called the German renewable energy push the wrong gamble: "[M]any companies, economists and even Germany's neighbors worry that the enormous cost to replace a currently working system will undermine the country's industrial base and weigh on the entire European economy.... Average electricity prices for companies have jumped 60% over the past five years because of costs passed along as part of government subsidies of renewable energy producers."[30]

Many European nations thought that the rest of the world would follow their lead when they went all-in for renewable energy, observes Daniel Yergin, an international energy expert. That has not happened.[31] In fact, some countries have learned their lesson more quickly than Europe. In the mid-2000s, Australia imposed a carbon tax that was supposed to save the planet from rising oceans with no harm to the national economy, but in early 2015, citing lost jobs and higher production costs, Australia repealed the tax.[32] The prime minister, Tony Abbott, admitted that the policy was a disaster for family incomes—especially those of the poor.[33] A government spokesman also declared what seems obvious: "Getting rid of the carbon tax meant that household electricity bills have been reduced, and it makes us more internationally competitive."[34] Australia had hoped that decarbonizing its economy would bring a cascade of new investment and green jobs. It never happened. Instead, the plunge in oil and natural gas prices undermined the economic viability of wind and solar power in Australia.

Germany, France, Spain, and most other European nations have learned this same lesson the hard way. The United States would be better off learning it the easy way. Abundant, affordable, controllable, reliable, and versatile energy is the sine qua non of modern prosperous countries with upward mobility. As Islamist terrorism spreads, the Middle East roils, and Putin brandishes a fist, the last thing that freedom-loving countries need is self-imposed energy scarcity.

DEATH BY REGULATORY ASPHYXIATION
The Bogus Environmental Case against Fossil Fuels

Environmental conditions in the United States have dramatically improved over the past thirty years, and the transition to concentrated fossil fuels from wood and other sources of energy from living nature is part of the reason. Yet the Environmental Protection Agency would have you believe that we face a planetary disaster unless its unprecedented "anti-carbon" agenda is implemented. In fact, the United States has reduced the carbon intensity of the economy without mandates because of highly efficient industrial processes.[1] Still dependent on fossil fuels for 80 percent of energy consumed, the United States is actually reducing emissions of carbon dioxide more successfully than many countries that have imposed carbon reduction mandates.[2] In March 2016, the EIA announced that energy-related emissions of carbon dioxide had decreased 12 percent from 2007–2015, and 2015's emissions were the lowest level since 1994.[3]

Nevertheless, the EPA is grossly misleading the public about carbon dioxide emissions and about genuine threats to the environment and human health. Americans deserve the truth from their government about risks to their health, but under the Obama administration the EPA has become a mouthpiece for ideological propaganda.

Consider the following two propositions:

One of the largest public policy success stories in the past 50 years is the dramatic improvement of our nation's air quality.[4]

We are at the point in many areas of this country when on a hot summer day, the best advice is don't go outside. Don't breathe the air. It might kill you.[5]

Mountains of data from thousands of air-quality monitors across the country confirm the first statement, from the *Almanac of American Environmental Trends*, and refute the second, from the Environmental Protection Agency. Between 1990 and 2010, EPA's own data show a 59 percent

FIGURE 10.1

Comparison of Crime Rate, Welfare, and Air Pollution, 1970–2007

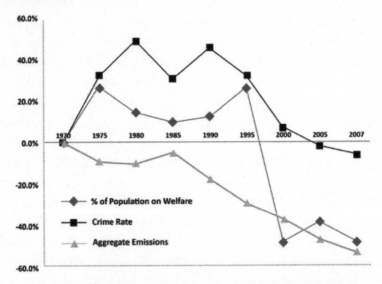

Source: Steve Hayward, *2011 Almanac of Environmental Trends* (Apr. 2011); FBI Uniform Crime Reports, U.S. Department of Health and Human Services, EPA.

reduction in total emissions from the six major pollutants regulated under federal law. Improved air quality should be considered a major public policy success story, as shown in Figure 10.1.

It may be punishable heresy to the dogmatic warmists, but fossil fuels in general and human-induced carbon emissions in particular have improved human health, ecological vigor, and the biological diversity of the natural world.

Mankind's Carbon Footprint Shrinks Mankind's Physical Footprint

Fossil fuels, whose density and efficiency far exceed those of renewable energy fuels, have reduced the size of man's footprint on the earth, while technology has greatly reduced polluting emissions from the combustion of fossil fuels. Our greatest encroachments on the natural world have always accompanied our pursuit of food, fuel, and raw materials—clearing land for crops and pasture, harvesting wood for fuel and building material, mining minerals and the expansion of urban and industrial facilities.[6] The high concentration of energy in fossil fuels has limited man's interference with the surface of the earth. Renewable energy systems based on wind, solar, and biomass, requiring huge tracts of lands and massive amounts of material, reverse this trend.[7]

This powerful benefit of fossil fuels has been entirely ignored over the past four decades. "Carbon footprint," vaguely defined and variously used, refers to the amount of fossil fuel energy consumed per person. Invoked on food containers, clothing labels, and a host of consumer products, this catchphrase is deceptive. Burning petroleum in your car uses less energy, encumbers less land, and emits less carbon dioxide than burning a biofuel like corn ethanol.[8] Although a likely candidate for the most politically incorrect statement of the year, we submit that man's carbon footprint shrinks his physical footprint on the earth.

Replacing fossil fuel–based electric generation with wind and solar generation would require massive amounts of land and the destruction of natural habitats in return for less energy efficiency. On average, one megawatt of the installed capacity of onshore wind delivers less than a third of the electricity of one megawatt of natural gas, coal, or nuclear. So if you need one hundred megawatts from wind, you need three hundred megawatts of installed wind capacity. Green power on a large scale requires building more and more power plants. It also requires reliable fossil-fueled backup generation when wind and solar generation wobble—a necessity to keep the grid stable. Wind and sunshine may be free, but the many indirect costs of concentrating the diffuse and variable flows from these energy sources drives the cost per unit of electricity far higher than fossil fuel generation. Without generous subsidies, renewables literally can't keep the lights on.

The so-called green energy revolution requires encroaching on more and more land and using more and more material. Upon a closer look, green energy is not really clean at all. According to Jess Ausubel, an average wind system uses 460 metric tons of steel and 870 cubic meters of concrete per megawatt. In contrast, a natural gas combined cycle plant uses about three metric tons of steel and twenty-seven cubic meters of concrete.[9]

As we saw earlier, Germany's energy transformation is now requiring construction of ten new coal plants just to keep the electric grid, now overwhelmed with variable wind power, from meltdown.[10] And green transportation fuels, like corn ethanol and soybean biodiesel, lay claim to fertile cropland needed to feed the world's population. If the biofuel mandates persist, millions of acres of additional land will have to be cleared and planted with crops to meet basic global food demand.[11]

Since the late 1960s, the environmental Left has vilified fossil fuels for their potentially harmful—but reversible—effects on air and water quality. Recall that global cropland would have to increase by 150 percent without fertilizers and other carbon-rich contributions.[12] One and half billion hectares of the surface of the earth is now devoted to cropland. Without the productivity achieved through fertilizers derived from natural gas, pesticides, and other modern agricultural machinery dependent on fossil fuels, the amount of land devoted to cropland would be as much as 3.8 billion hectares—enlarging the human footprint almost three-fold.[13]

Consider how the internal combustion engine that powers our vehicles shrank man's energy footprint. Horsepower of the oats-eating, four-hooved variety was a large part of the energy mix in the United States and Europe well into the twentieth century. Replacing that animal power with fossil fuel–driven mechanical power conferred tremendous environmental benefits of the most palpable kind. Mechanized transport in urban areas cleaned the streets and improved sanitation. Horses used to compete with human beings for food energy. It took lots of oats, hay, and pasture land to feed millions of horses. Almost 30 percent of the U.S. crop harvest in 1910 was devoted to feeding 27.5 million horses.[14] Had animal power not been replaced by fossil fuels, the amount of cropland necessary to feed a population now more than three times larger than in 1910 would have required massive land clearing.

Wind, solar, and biofuel systems use thousands of more acres of land than coal, natural gas, or nuclear power plants. In spite of billions of dollars in federal subsidies over several years, solar installations generate a mere two-tenths of 1 percent of America's electric power.[15] For solar to meet total U.S. electric demand, ten thousand square miles would have to be given over to solar panels.[16] Ivanpah, which occupies seven times more land than the average coal plant yet will generate less than one-fourth the electric power, is a good example of the spectacular inefficiency of solar power.

Consider these numbers. In 2010 fossil fuels accounted for 13,600 gigawatts of primary energy while renewables accounted for 130 gigawatts of energy. In other words, renewables contributed only 0.9 percent of commercial energy but claimed at least three hundred thousand square kilometers of land. The entire fossil fuel system (extraction, processing, transport, electric generation and transmission of electricity) claimed only eighty to ninety thousand square kilometers.[17] Forget wind and solar and consider biofuels alone. In 2010, ethanol made from corn or sugar cane amounted to only 1.5 percent of global crude oil production but occupied 260,000 square kilometers of land, accounting for more than

2 percent of our fertile farmland. Recall the contrast in power densities that we explained in Chapter 4: fossil fuels have a power density of 150 170 W/m² while renewables have a power density of 0.05 percent W/m². There are many different ways to calculate the physical footprint of a power plant, and it is easy to make the mistake of comparing apples with oranges, but however you measure it, wind, solar power, and biofuels require far more land than fossil fuel energy systems.

Wind and solar farms also destroy wildlife habitats and kill birds, including endangered species. The U.S. Fish and Wildlife Service, charged with protecting these threatened birds, appears to look the other way when it comes to wind and solar farms. Wind turbines kill between two hundred thousand and four hundred thousand birds each year in the United States.[18] A single wind farm in California, at Altamont Pass, kills approximately nine thousand birds every year, including fifty-five to ninety-four golden eagles.[19]

Fossil fuels have been particularly kind to trees, the dominant source of heat energy until the Industrial Revolution. Growing the timber needed to replace the coal burned in England in 1850 would have required 150 percent of England's land mass.[20]

The current green energy plans, like Germany's, Britain's, and EPA's, assume that renewable energy will be able to displace carbon dioxide emissions by over 80 percent before 2050, yet actual implementation of these plans reveals how little electric power is gained from even the largest wind and solar installations. Wind and solar promoters still claim that a given wind farm will power, for example, 150,000 homes. They talking about "name plate capacity" or "installed capacity," however, a measure of how much electric power the facility could generate if running at maximum-engineered capacity. But wind is inherently intermittent and will never generate electricity around the clock.

The important number is the "capacity factor" (also known as "load factor"). The national average capacity factor for onshore wind generation is approximately 20 to 30 percent of the nameplate capacity. That figure, actually, is quite optimistic, with little historical data to back it up. Although clear data about the actual performance of wind and solar generating farms are scant, grid operators see capacity factors as low as 10 percent in Britain and Germany. After pouring enormous amounts of money into these projects and seeing electric prices soar, officials are reluctant to admit that wind and solar generating facilities are compromising the reliability of the power system. Not long after England narrowly avoided rolling black outs in early November 2015, the secretary of state for energy and climate change, Amber Rudd, gave a speech emphasizing that Britain could no longer pursue renewable energy "at any cost" and that "energy security must be the number one priority."[21] The operators of the Texas electric grid have long rated the capacity factor of their wind generators at only 8 to 12 percent, because the wind rarely blows during the long summers' peak demand.[22] Without much historical data about the actual performance of wind installations, the estimates of capacity factor remain murky.

Nevertheless, it is unquestionable, as Google's green engineers found out, that assembling the land, hardware, and infrastructure required for heavy reliance on wind and solar power "would be [a construction project] like nothing ever attempted by the human race."[23] Such an insight has apparently convinced Bill Gates to shift from investments in new renewable power plants under existing technologies to investments in breakthrough research on storage technologies and other energy alternatives.[24] And it appears that Google has ceased financing the Ivanpah solar plant for similar reasons.[25]

A "Regulatory Spree Unprecedented in U.S. History"[26]

Any discussion of energy and the environment sooner or later comes around to the Environmental Protection Agency, established by President Nixon's executive order in 1970 to protect human health and the environment, now one of the most powerful, unrestrained, and politicized agencies of the federal government. Circumventing Congress, the EPA recently issued the most far-reaching regulation of its forty-five year history. Adopted in the fall of 2015, this rule—dubbed the "Clean Power Plan"—grossly exceeds the regulatory authority that Congress delegated to EPA in law. Look no further than Europe for the likely outcome of EPA's grand plan. This rule would put our country on the path that Germany chose with its *Energiewende*, a path that has led to retail electric rates three times the average rate in the U.S.

A hefty majority of the American people regularly rates "clean air" and "clean water" as high priorities—a view we share. For most of its first forty years, the EPA promulgated regulations in a relatively incremental manner, balancing environmental goals, practicability, and economic growth. After decades of improvement, our air is healthier than it has ever been.[27]

For some time, however, the EPA has pursued an environmental agenda that is more radical than most citizens realize, contemptuous of the engineering reality, economic effects, sound science, and human concerns that stand in its way. EPA's convoluted and stringent rules are now forcing businesses to operate like bureaucracies.

Compliance with regulatory dictates increasingly drives business priorities rather than innovation and profitability in a competitive market place. Under President Obama, any remaining restraints on the agency disappeared, and a newly aggressive EPA began issuing edicts unprecedented in number, scope, stringency, and cost. A torrent of major rules and national standards has overwhelmed the nation's businesses, provoking knowledgeable observers to warn of a regulatory "avalanche" or "train wreck." The American people have choked the federal courts trying to defend themselves from these rules, many of them of negligible benefit to public health and unsupported by credible science. The National Academy of Science and some of EPA's own scientific advisory panels have sharply criticized the weak and manipulated science behind much of the Obama-era regulation.[28]

The Clean Power Plan imposes on the entire country a policy to eliminate the use of fossil fuels, a radical energy policy that Congress has repeatedly rejected. Banning coal-fired power plants and shutting down coal mines are the plan's first objectives. Massive construction of new renewable facilities over millions of acres of now open space is assumed.[29] Mandates for biofuels to replace petroleum are well underway, and regulation of methane—the predominant component of natural gas—is in the pipeline. Annual compliance costs of tens of billions of dollars and the prospect of losing at least 10 percent of the nation's electric generating capacity in the near future reveal the extraordinary hubris behind the Clean Air Plan.[30]

The plan is intended to achieve a reduction of carbon dioxide emissions from the electric sector of 32 percent. When this percentage is plugged into the IPCC's models, the rule would reduce predicted warming by 0.02 degree Celsius—an amount that is so minute that it is meaningless. EPA even acknowledges that the rule has no measurable climate benefits and so has offered four alternative grounds to justify destroying the electric power system of the United States.[31] When questioned by Congress, the EPA administrator, Gina McCarthy, admitted that the Clean Power Plan is not about pollution control but is "an investment opportunity for renewables"—and for yet more subsidies, we would add. In other settings she has asserted that the plan would prevent thousands of early deaths and increase "climate justice for communities of color." Her most repeated rationale for the Clean Power Plan is that it is a powerful symbol to help President Obama "lead the world" to a global climate agreement, as he believes he did in Paris in 2015.

To justify on such irrelevant grounds a rule that would, without statutory authority, dismember at colossal cost and waste the highly intricate electrical system of our country is a chilling affront to the rule of law. Shame on Congress as well for allowing the EPA to usurp this law-making authority from the legislative branch.

Carbon Dioxide Is Not a Pollutant

Labeling carbon dioxide a pollutant is one of the climate change lobby's more absurd gestures. President Obama, Secretary of State John Kerry, and the president's scientific advisor John Holdren repeatedly demonize carbon dioxide and carbon as pollutants or "fearsome weapons of mass destruction." In fact, carbon dioxide is a plant nutrient essential for all human, animal, and plant life. Our bodies and blood are made of carbon. How do our national leaders square their public declarations about carbon dioxide with fundamental scientific facts?

Carbon dioxide is an odorless, invisible, harmless, and completely natural gas lacking any characteristic of a pollutant. It does not contaminate or defile as pollutants do. Carbon dioxide in the air we breathe has no adverse health effects, in contrast to carbon monoxide and high concentrations of the genuine pollutants listed in the Clean Air Act, the source of the EPA's authority to regulate air pollutants.

With good reason, EPA has set no health-based limits on the ambient concentration of carbon dioxide. There are in fact no adverse health effects from current carbon dioxide levels of approximately four hundred parts per million. The Occupational Safety and Health Administration does set some advisory levels for prolonged exposure to carbon dioxide in a tightly enclosed space, but they are set at five thousand ppm—more than ten times the current level to which human beings are exposed.[32] The Princeton physicist Will Happer noted in congressional testimony, "We try to keep CO2 levels in our U.S. Navy submarines no higher than 8,000 parts per million, about 20 times current atmospheric levels. Few adverse effects are observed at even higher levels."[33]

The White House claims that reducing carbon dioxide will prevent premature death and disease is a sleight of hand that conflates reducing carbon dioxide with reducing genuine pollution such as high levels of ozone or sulfur dioxide.[34]

Since uncontrolled combustion of fossil fuels releases real pollutants, EPA has decided that eliminating fossil fuels—rather than decreasing their emissions—is necessary to protect health and advance its climate agenda. Such sweeping authority is far beyond what Congress delegated to EPA in law. What EPA now calls "carbon pollution" apparently includes not only carbon dioxide but also the genuine pollutants listed in the Clean Air Act, heavily regulated for forty years under highly precautionary standards. Burning fossil fuels, without emission controls, certainly emits multiple pollutants, but current technology achieves a massive reduction of those pollutants.

On the basis of this tangled logic, EPA also contends that reducing carbon dioxide will reduce asthma.[35] This is impossible. Carbon dioxide is harmless to human health.[36] And recall that asthma rates have risen over the same time period that air pollution has taken a nosedive. Yet EPA is determined to expand this already broad authority far beyond what the law allows to assert federal control over the sources, generation and consumption of energy.

If EPA can control carbon dioxide, EPA can control everything from large industries to individual behavior. And not surprisingly, prevalent climate policies to reduce carbon dioxide all assume heavily centralized control of the production and consumption of energy.

EPA's Pretense of Science

The EPA has gone a long way toward making Al Gore's dream of treating the environment as "the organizing principle of society" a reality. We would wager that a majority of Americans, with us, think improving human well-being is the better principle![37]

Under President Obama, the agency invented a huge pool of new health risks to justify far more stringent regulation of a long list of "pollutants" already regulated over the past forty years.[38] At the heart of this initiative is the pollutant known as fine particulate matter 2.5 microns in diameter (PM 2.5)—about one-twentieth the width of a human hair. You know it as dust.

The air we breathe contains a mix of natural dust and particles that result from human activities, especially farming and combustion. "Because particles are the byproduct of everything we do in an industrial society as well as natural processes like wind, erosion, forest and brush fires, they are everywhere."[39] The EPA does not distinguish between particulate matter from natural sources like dirt roads and particulate matter arising from urban and industrial sources, which may contain hazardous pollutants.

We will spare you a painfully technical analysis of EPA's statistical magic tricks, but suffice it to say that EPA now assigns risks of "early death" to levels of PM 2.5 that approach zero. Former EPA Administrator Lisa Jackson testified to Congress, "Particulate Matter causes premature death. It doesn't make you sick. It is directly causal to you dying sooner than you should."[40] In 2009, EPA apparently decided its job was to eliminate all risk to human life. We call it "going to zero"...zero risk.

EPA is "going to zero" by means of the statistical methodology known as "no safe threshold linear regression analysis."[41] In simple terms, EPA has concluded that no risk is too low to warrant more regulation, regardless of the cost of regulation or the uncertainty of the hazard. By the logic of that zero-risk tolerance policy, no one should drive a car, play a sport, or cross the street.

A more general version of such an approach is known as the absolutist precautionary principle. Applying the no-safe-threshold analysis increased the statistical risk of premature mortality from particulate matter by almost four-fold![42] EPA offers little to no toxicological or medical evidence of the alleged causal connection between PM 2.5 and death. The outdated studies on which EPA relies make small adjustments for reasons of smoking or obesity but otherwise attribute all non-accidental death to PM 2.5—an implausible assumption.

EPA propaganda might have reached its low point in 2011 when Lisa Jackson, with a straight face, told Congress, "If we could reduce particulate matter to levels that are healthy, it would have identical impacts to finding a cure for cancer."[43] A bold claim. In recent years, cancer has caused the deaths of approximately 7.6 million people worldwide. The agency sticks to its weak and outdated epidemiological studies in the face of a substantial body of toxicological and medical science soundly refuting its absurdly hyperbolic claims and has resisted congressional oversight.[44]

Why is EPA going to such lengths? Perhaps because its new target, carbon dioxide, has no effect on human health and is thus outside its regulatory reach under the Clean Air Act. The conventional pollutants that can harm human health have been reduced to such low levels that only contrived science can support new standards as stringent as EPA seeks—stringent enough to kill coal.

The Greatest (Environmental) Story Never Told

You wouldn't know it from listening to the mainstream media or the green activists, but our environmental record over the past half-century is one of dramatic improvement. As John Wayne reminded us, "No one gets out of this alive." Yet life in the United States is far longer, healthier, and safer than ever before. In highly industrialized countries like the United States, the most dangerous risks to human life from contaminated air and water have been virtually eliminated. There are occasional accidents, and always will be, but our environmental record should make us optimistic.

The sharp decline in air pollution since 1970 has coincided with rapid growth in our economy, population, energy use, and vehicle miles traveled. Although EPA regulation under the Clean Air Act played an important role in the environmental transformation, the main drivers were technological advances in emission controls and market-driven efficiencies—innovations fueled by economic growth, abundant energy, and the dynamics of the free market. Emissions began to fall in the 1960s, almost a decade before the Clean Air Act and the establishment of the EPA.

Many people still think that economic growth unavoidably leads to environmental degradation, but the improvements in America's air quality occurred while our gross domestic product increased by 200 percent and the use of fossil fuels more than doubled. We learned to dramatically reduce the polluting emissions from the combustion of fossil fuels and had the money to absorb the cost of the environmental controls. Contrary to the pervasive pessimism, win-win solutions are indeed possible.

In the Clean Air Act, Congress directed the EPA to establish health-based standards for six named "criteria pollutants." Consider the striking decline in the emissions and ambient levels of these pollutants shown in Figure 10.2. From 1980 to 2010, ambient levels of sulfur dioxide declined by 82 percent, airborne lead by 89 percent, carbon monoxide by 82 percent, nitrogen dioxides by 52 percent, ozone by 27 percent, and fine particulate matter (PM 2.5) by 27 percent.[45]

Over the past few decades, tailpipe emissions from our vehicles have been reduced more than 90 percent; while vehicles miles traveled have

FIGURE 10.2

Air Quality Improvement, 1980–2012

	Ambient 1980-2008	Ambient 1980-2010	Emissions 1980-2008	Emissions 1980-2012
Carbon Monoxide (CO)	-79%	-82%	-58%	-65%
Ozone (O₃)*	-25%	-27%	-49%	-50%
Lead (Pb)	-92%	-89%	-96%	-96%
Nitrogen Dioxide (NO₂)	-46%	-52%	-40%	-58%
Particulates (PM₁₀)	-31%	-38%†	-46%	-48%‡
Fine Particulates (PM₂.₅)	-21%	-27%§	-36%	-36%¶
Sulfur Dioxide (SO₂)	-71%	-83%	-56%	-78%

*Emissions measured here are VOCs, a principal ozone precursor
†1985-2010; §1999-2010; ‡1985-2012; ¶1990-2012

Source: U.S. Environmental Protection Agency, "Air Quality Trends" (Jan. 2011); and Steven Hayward, "2013 Air Quality Environmental Almanac Update," Pacific Research Institute (Apr. 2013) 6-7, www.pacificresearch.org.

increased by 180 percent.[46] This is an astonishing success. In the late 1960s, automobiles emitted over 75 grams of carbon monoxide per mile. New vehicles have lowered those emissions by 99.5 percent to 0.04 grams per mile driven.[47]

Reduction of the ozone-producing emissions from cars and trucks is another spectacular success. From the late 1960s to 2012, tailpipe emissions of volatile organic compounds—a key ingredient in ozone formation—have been reduced by 99 percent.[48] In the region around Houston, Texas—the fourth-largest city in the United States and home to the world's largest petro-chemical industrial complex—the number of days in a year that exceeded the federal ozone standard has fallen from a high of 73 days in 1995 to 14 days in 2012. And the overwhelming majority of the population of Houston lives in areas below the standard.

Most of the innovative emission control technologies that have cleared our skies came from private business. Without any new regulations, further improvement will continue with turnover of vehicles and equipment. As the late journalist Warren Brookes said, the "learning curve" is green. New means cleaner.[49] We should now turn to localized environmental problems instead of over-regulating a handful of pollutants.

In addition to the six criteria pollutants, the Clean Air Act identifies 187 hazardous or toxic pollutants that are to be regulated.[50] The EPA's

Toxic Release Inventory documents a 65 percent reduction of these pollutants since 1988. Mercury emissions in the United States have also declined by approximately 60 to 70 percent, accounting for less than 2 percent of the global deposition affecting ambient levels in the United States.[51] Natural sources of mercury dwarf man-made sources. Volcanoes, sub-sea vents, geysers, and other natural sources release between nine thousand and ten thousand tons of mercury per year. Coal-fired power plants in the United States annually emit less than thirty tons mercury, while Chinese plants annually emit approximately four hundred tons.

The Centers for Disease Control monitors mercury exposure in women of child-bearing age and young children. At certain levels, mercury can retard brain development in babies in utero and children. CDC's most recent study shows that average blood mercury levels have decreased to levels well below EPA's extremely precautionary limit—a standard of risk at least two times lower than the World Health Organization's and U.S. Food and Drug Administration's.[52] Nonetheless, in 2011 the EPA issued a rule to reduce the remaining emissions of mercury from power plants by 91 percent on a short timetable. With an annual compliance cost of $10 billion, this mercury rule is the most costly regulation in EPA's history, but the benefits, by the agency's own admission, are less than negligible. The direct benefits from reducing mercury amount to 0.004 percent of claimed benefits. That means $6 million in benefits and $10 billion in costs.[53]

In a rare ruling questioning regulatory costs, the U.S. Supreme Court didn't buy EPA's shell game, remanding the rule in 2015.[54] But it was too late for the coal industry. The mercury rule had already led to the closure of 411 coal-fired electric generating units.[55] A recent study by McKinsey and Company concludes that the coal industry is bankrupt, without the $45 billion to fund liabilities for debt, employee pensions, and mining reclamation.[56] Since 2012, twenty-seven coal mining companies have filed for bankruptcy protection. Production of coal in West Virginia fell by forty-five percent from 2011 to 2015. From 2009 through 2015, over three hundred coal mines in West Virginia were shuttered at a cost of 9,733 jobs.[57]

Coal production and coal-fired electric generation face an existential regulatory threat, only because EPA decided to impose carbon standards

Carbon Capture and Storage (CCS) Technology

A technology called carbon capture and storage (or sequestration) has long bounced around as the ultimate solution to rising levels of man-made carbon dioxide. Engineers had the idea that carbon dioxide released in the combustion of fossil fuels could be captured and permanently stored underground. While theoretically possible, CCS remains infeasible in commercial operations at scale, and the cost is exorbitant.

The federal government has devoted billions of dollars of taxpayer money to pilot CCS projects, almost all of which have been abandoned because of spiraling costs and technological dead ends. In February 2015, President Obama pulled the plug on Future Gen 2.0, a second iteration of an earlier project abandoned for the same reasons.[58]

An unresolved obstacle to carbon capture is what electric engineers call "parasitic load." Current technology for capturing carbon dioxide consumes 30 to 60 percent of the electricity that the power plant was designed to generate. So much electricity is consumed in the process of generating electricity that there is little to sell.

This is yet another example of green policy mechanisms that are net energy losers. The economic productivity that began in the Industrial Revolution and accelerated in the twentieth century was fueled by achieving more output per unit of energy input. CCS, like ethanol, wind, and solar, reversed that ratio.

The single remaining pilot CCS project, in Mississippi, is estimated to cost $6.6 billion.[59] American Electric Power's comparable new coal plant in Arkansas incorporates state-of-the-art emission controls for genuine pollutants that matter to human health, but the plant will not try to capture carbon dioxide. The efficiency of this plant keeps its emissions of carbon dioxide 25 percent lower than that those of older coal plants. The cost of construction of the AEP plant is $3 billion.

infeasible for coal. Instead of relying on specious predictions of warming temperatures a century from now, EPA might consider the human cost not of carbon emissions but of low-carbon policies.

Why is good news on the environmental front not recognized as important? New coal plants emit 90 percent less sulfur dioxide than plants built in the 1940s.[60] Since 1973, coal-fired electric generation in the United States has increased by 123 percent, while emissions of particulate matter, sulfur dioxide, and nitrogen oxides have decreased by 90 percent per unit of electricity.[61] The adverse environmental effects associated with fossil fuels can be reversed and have already been arrested. While our government is orchestrating a regulatory campaign to kill coal, China, India, and other developing countries are building many coal-fired power plants. Not long after the British government announced plans to close all coal plants by 2023, the *Times* reported that 2,400 new coal plants were under construction or planned in developing countries. At the end of 2015, China and India were building 665 new coal stations, with plans to build an additional 665 plants.[62]

Because of EPA dictates and low natural gas prices, coal is no longer the dominant fuel for electric generation, but it remains a mainstay, reliably and affordably meeting demand around the clock Even John Kerry admitted that, given the increasing emissions in developing countries, the *total elimination* of U.S. emissions would have no climatic benefits. The EPA's lawless war on coal, waged purely for symbolic value and ideological gratification, risks the reliability of our national system of electric power.

Energy policies of such national consequence must be determined by the elected representatives accountable to the people, not federal bureaucrats. If they aren't, this country no longer operates as a constitutional democracy.

The fossil fuels themselves expedited the development of the technologies that have so dramatically reduced the pollution associated with fossil fuels, technologies that require considerable amounts of energy to operate. If energy were not abundant and affordable, use of these technologies would be limited. Additionally, the ever-increasing efficiency made possible by fossil fuel–generated prosperity has allowed businesses and consumers to absorb the steep cost of comprehensive environmental controls now used in prosperous countries.

Power plants and industries have invested hundreds of billions of dollars to reduce genuine air pollution and prevent water contamination, but EPA's new regulation of carbon dioxide may force the closure of those very facilities. The agency is threatening our ability to absorb the high cost of protecting the environment with its extreme standards. By conjuring new health risks at implausibly low levels and exponentially higher costs, the current EPA has radically altered the equation. But, cost matters and matters to human health. Far more epidemiological studies find a stronger correlation between unemployment or low income and premature death than the microscopic correlations between health and fine particulate matter.[63]

The Real Green: Carbon Dioxide Enriches Plant Growth

Why capture and permanently store underground the man-made carbon dioxide emissions that already enrich plant life? Higher carbon dioxide levels increase photosynthetic productivity, tolerance of drought, and moisture retention in plants and trees. Satellite images show that the slightly higher levels of atmospheric carbon dioxide are already "greening" the earth, especially in arid regions.[64]

The historical geology of the earth shows that atmospheric levels of carbon dioxide have been far higher in earlier geological eras when plant life flourished.[65] For some reason, the IPCC science disregards the substantial body of science in paleoclimatology (also known as historical geology). According to agronomical studies, optimum plant growth occurs at three to four times the present ambient concentration of carbon dioxide.[66] Natural carbon dioxide does not operate any differently than anthropogenic carbon dioxide.

The many benefits of carbon dioxide, of course, do not diminish questions about the heat trapping, or "greenhouse," properties of this gas. As a matter of basic physics, rising levels of carbon dioxide could increase temperatures. The extent to which the natural drivers of our climate are "sensitive" to—that is, overpowered by—anthropogenic carbon dioxide remains a key assumption of the IPCC models, but it has not been verified by facts on the ground. Observational evidence from NASA's balloons and satellites gathered for over twenty-five years conflicts with the models' predictions of warming temperatures. The models run much hotter than the measured observations of NASA's satellites and balloons, the most sophisticated, objective instruments. This indicates that the earth's climatic system is not as sensitive to man-made emissions of carbon dioxide as assumed by the IPCC. See Figure 4.6.[67]

How EPA Took Control of the Chemical Basis of Life: Carbon

Congress several times considered and rejected giving EPA the authority to regulate carbon dioxide. In the summer of 2009, the U.S. House passed the American Clean Energy and Security bill, a massive measure intended to reduce greenhouse gases through a dozen new regulatory programs, including an elaborate system of cap and trade. The bill failed in the Senate, but later that year, in what remains an unparalleled seizure of regulatory authority, EPA issued an "endangerment finding" that carbon dioxide is a pollutant under the Clean Air Act.[68]

In the six years since the endangerment finding, the country has become accustomed to EPA's assertion of regulatory authority over carbon dioxide. The vast expansion of this agency's coercive power is evident in its own analysis of its first regulation of carbon dioxide emissions from large industrial sources. In the proposed rule, EPA acknowledged that the number of industrial facilities under its jurisdiction would increase from around twelve thousand to six million![69] Hospitals, schools, hotels, apartment complexes, office buildings, and small business would now be subject to the EPA's top-down, inflexible, soviet-style diktat under its grotesquely distorted interpretation of the Clean Air Act.[70]

An odd Supreme Court opinion in 2007 set the stage for EPA's self-promotion from environmental regulator to free-wheeling energy master of the country. In *Massachusetts v. EPA*, twelve states challenged EPA for failure to regulate greenhouse gases as pollutants. A five-member majority of the Court found that carbon dioxide "fit well" within the Clean Air Act's extremely broad definition of air pollutant. The ruling, however, did not compel the agency to regulate carbon dioxide as most media and commentators still assert. Although the majority opinion assumed pervasive opinion about man-made global warming, the Court held that EPA's current justification for not regulating carbon dioxide was inadequate. In short, the Court told EPA to make a more robust case against regulating carbon dioxide or proceed to regulate.

The Clean Air Act defines an air pollutant as "any air pollution agent or combination of such agents, including any physical, chemical, biological, radioactive…substance or matter which is emitted into or otherwise enters the ambient air."[71] Interpreted in isolation, this definition could include anything in the air, including a frisbee—a point made by one of the dissenting justices.

How the U.S. Supreme Court could view carbon dioxide as a pollutant that defiles the air and overlook the life-sustaining value of carbon dioxide is hard to explain. Most insiders on both sides of the aisle agree that the heavy-handed Clean Air Act is ill suited to control this ubiquitous gas. Congress alone, with a president of similar mind, could resolve the impasse with a brief amendment to the act clarifying that the gas of life in our cosmos—carbon dioxide—is not a pollutant under the Clean Air Act. Policy as consequential to modern civilization as "decarbonizing" is surely the provenance of our elected representatives and not EPA's employees.

Environmental Improvements: A Luxury for the Developing World

Environmental quality remains an unaffordable luxury for much of the developing world. According to the World Bank, the most polluted cities are in developing countries, not in prosperous countries consuming huge volumes of fossil fuels.[72] Consider China.

On January 13, 2013, Beijing, had a monitored level of fine particulate matter of 886 micrograms per cubic meter. The U.S. standard for the same pollutant is an average annual level of twelve micrograms per cubic meter.[73] This makes China's level ninety times higher than the average level in the United States and seventy times higher than the highest ambient concentration ever measured in this country. Monitored readings at 650 U.S. sites showed that a mean ambient concentration of fine particulate matter of only ten micrograms per cubic meter.[74] In the World Health Organization's list of the world's eighty-nine cities most polluted by sulfur dioxide, consider that Guiyang, China—the first city on the list—has sulfur dioxide levels forty-five times higher than Los Angeles—the last city on the list.[75]

Environmental protection has taken a back seat to rapid economic development in countries like China, where provision of basic electrical service to a huge population has been the major priority. The many pollution control technologies developed and used in the United States could transform China's air quality as they did ours. Whether the Chinese communist government is willing to spend the billions of dollars required to achieve healthy air quality remains to be seen. China, as we have seen, is certainly not shuttering coal-fired power plants.

Affordable electricity has improved human welfare in the twentieth more than any other technology. Yet as Matt Ridley reminds us, two billion people in the world have never seen an electric switch.[76] Policies now asserted by the World Bank, the International Monetary Fund, and the U.S. government limit or prohibit financing for affordable fossil fuel–fired electric generation in developing countries. This elite green perspective cruelly denies the world's poorest families basic light, heat, and cooling, on which health and well-being depend. The greatest environmental killers in the world are cook stove smoke, contaminated water, and uncontrolled sewage. The elimination of indoor pollution, the provision of clean water, and the safe disposal of waste require treatment systems running on…electric power.

Less Harm from Extreme Weather

Global warming alarmists and politicized federal agencies tell us that the weather is becoming more extreme, as President Obama did in his 2013 State of the Union address: "Heat waves, droughts, wildfires, floods—all are now more frequent and more intense. We can choose to believe that Superstorm Sandy, and the most severe drought in decades, and the worst wildfires some states have ever seen were all just a freak coincidence. Or we can choose to believe in the overwhelming judgment of science—and act before it's too late."[77] By repeating this nonsense, the president is contradicting the conclusions of the official climate science, which he insists we must accept. The IPCC's Fifth Assessment Report concludes that there is no meaningful evidence that hurricanes, tropical storms, drought, floods, or tornados are more extreme or frequent than in the past.[78] Judith Curry, the former head of the School of Earth and Atmospheric Sciences at Georgia Tech, likewise told Congress that "most types of weather extremes were worse in the 1930s and even in the 1950s than in the current climate, while the weather was overall more benign in the 1970s. This sense that extreme weather events are now more frequent and intense is symptomatic of 'weather amnesia' prior to 1970."[79] Yet some developing countries are demanding "climate reparations" and "climate justice" from developed countries like the United States to pay for the extreme weather damage they incurred allegedly as a result of our country's carbon dioxide emissions.

Whatever weather may arise, human societies have become less vulnerable to destructive weather. Rapid response to natural disasters depends on fossil fuels for air cargo, diesel generators, helicopters, trucks, and bulldozers. The many lightweight but strong synthetic materials derived from fossil fuels also save lives in disasters.[80] Once helpless before the weather, man can now mitigate the damage to human society from the extreme weather events that are inevitable. As Indur Goklany writes, "Despite much more complete reporting of such [weather] events and associated casualties, aggregate mortality declined by 93 percent since the 1920s."[81]

Droughts long accounted for the greatest loss of life among weather-related disasters but no longer. In the not too distant past, prolonged drought or flooding could destroy an entire annual harvest in remote human communities or for a larger portion of the population in developing countries. "Specifically, deaths from droughts were reduced by 99.98 percent since the 1920s because thanks to fossil fuels, the food and agricultural system produced more food and improved its ability to transport and distribute this food rapidly and in large quantities."[82] Americans living in well-insulated homes are largely immune to the vagaries of weather that so dominated pre-industrial societies.

Energy Poverty and Environmental Degradation

In 2015, acute energy poverty still affected the perhaps three billion of the 7.2 billion members of the human race.[83] According to the World Outlook 2011 of the International Energy Agency (IEA), 2.7 billion people depend on energy from woody sticks, wood, crop residues, and animal dung for their essential household energy needs for heat and cooking.[84] Perhaps 1.3 billion persons in this group lack access to electricity, and almost two billion of them live in rural areas in Asia. Indoor household pollution from burning wood or woody residues is a major health problem in many developing countries. Without effective ventilation, burning biomass in close quarters is associated with many life-threatening diseases, including chronic bronchitis, pulmonary tuberculosis, and lung cancer. The United Nations Foundation finds that cook stove smoke kills four million people per year.[85]

In *Fires, Fuel & the Fate of 3 Billion*, Gautami Yadama chronicles the stories of families whose lives revolve around the daily search for the material to fuel their crude stoves. "In rural India, countless numbers of women and children walk for hours each day to secure fuelwood or resort to burning crop residues, charcoal, and animal dung...[to] keep their homes and their families alive."[86]

Such an acute lack of subsistence energy damages the environment, local economies, and human health. "Energy access has become the dividing line between the haves and the have-nots," writes Yadama, "and on one side of the line are those destined to lives of devastating poverty."[87] Access to the simplest of modern electric systems would transform these lives.

Persons relying on indoor cook stoves without basic stovepipes do indeed have a carbon pollution problem. But it is a problem of carbon monoxide, not carbon dioxide. The British government might warn the recipients of its subsidies for wood-burning stoves under the Renewable Heat Initiative of the difference between carbon monoxide—a potential killer—and carbon dioxide—the gas of life.

From "Satanic Mills" to "Green and Pleasant Land"

Charles Dickens offered a graphic description of environmental squalor in industrializing London of the mid-nineteenth century in *The Old Curiosity Shop*: "A long suburb of red brick houses...where coal-dust and factory smoke darkened the shrinking leaves, ... and where the struggling vegetation sickened and sank under the hot breath of the kiln and furnace, making them by its presence seem yet more blighting and unwholesome than in the town itself.... [T]hey came by slow degrees upon a cheerless region, where not a blade of grass was seen to grow; where not a bud put forth its promise in the spring; where nothing green could live but on the surface of the stagnant pools...."[88]

Whether this scene is amplified by poetic license or is an accurate description of extreme environmental degradation, such conditions are rare to nonexistent in mature industrialized democracies today.

Economic growth, technological change and high energy consumption are distinguishing characteristics of industrialization. Many powerful Malthusian voices still maintain that growth, technology, and hydrocarbon energy are inimical to environmental quality and will inexorably lead to some planetary catastrophe. The recent encyclical on the environment by Pope Francis represents an especially doctrinaire version of such pessimism, asserting that modern industrialization has so mistreated the environment that the earth is now "an immense pile of filth."[89] That is more likely to be the case if wind and solar facilities are built on millions of acres across our countryside.

There is no doubt that environmental degradation occurred during the first stages of the transition from low-growth agrarian economies to industrialized economies as occurs now in China. History also shows that prosperity and continued technological innovation eventually reversed the environmental deterioration. And this is especially the case in democratic nations with market-based economies and personal freedom. Countries that structurally enshrine economic liberty under the rule of clear and limited laws also achieve environmental quality.[90]

China and India now offer the most glaring example of rapidly industrializing countries with high levels of real air pollution. The governments of these countries now express commitment to reducing pollution, and they have the advantage of adopting established technologies. Time will tell whether authoritarian regimes will be willing to marshal the innovation, finance, and commitment to societal welfare necessary for substantial environmental improvements.

Democratic societies, legally obliged to protect the health and welfare of every citizen, have engendered environmental sensitivity throughout private businesses. Most Western nations have enacted complex and enforceable laws to protect air and water quality. Russia, however, is a different story, appearing to be far more devoted to enlarging its military than improving air and water quality for the Russian people. Sale of oil and natural gas accounted for over 50 percent of Russia's budget revenue and 68 percent of total exports in 2013.[91]

Countries that nationalize major industries and denied basic human rights in liberty and property rarely put a premium on environmental protection needed to protect human health. The environmental contrasts between Pyongyang and Seoul—the capitals of North and South Korea respectively—are telling. The same stark contrast can be seen on the international border between El Paso, Texas, and Juarez, Mexico. Prosperity is not the enemy of genuine environmental quality. Prosperity and abundant energy make continual improvements in environmental quality possible.

A DECLARATION OF ENERGY INDEPENDENCE
America's $50 Trillion Opportunity

Several years ago Steve Moore attended a climate change conference in Aspen, Colorado. Do-gooder millionaire and billionaire environmentalists, arriving in their private jets, were whisked from the airport in stretch limousines to the four-star hotel, where ostentatious display of wealth was the order of the day.

Apparently billionaires are allowed to leave gigantic carbon footprints as they pontificate about the evils of global warming. When challenged, these greens of great wealth craft excuses about how their lifestyles are "carbon neutral" thanks to purchasing carbon offsets. They sound like the scions of wealthy families who avoided the Civil War draft by paying a poor man to fight in their place.

When it comes to climate change, the greens are a "do as I say and not do as I do" movement. Reducing energy use and living with less—that's the sacrifice that the masses must make to save the planet, but not the elites. The climate change lobby favors policies that severely disrupt other people's lives, mostly the poor and politically weak, not their own.

Contrast this green elitism with the reality that nearly one billion people on the planet lack access to reliable electricity. It's astonishing that in the second decade of the twenty-first century electric power is still unavailable to about one-seventh of the world's population. Many of those living in energy poverty reside in Africa. Since electricity is the ignition switch to higher living standards, making energy more accessible and affordable is arguably the most important and achievable way to alleviate global poverty. Of course increasing food production, fighting disease, and improving access to education are also precursors to eliminating economic deprivation, but those are dependent on cheap energy as well.

To fully appreciate this dependence on electric power, consider what happens here at home when a young person can't find an outlet to recharge his iPhone or laptop computer or Gameboy. I've seen frantic teenagers nearly have a nervous breakdown if their cell phones die and they can't instantly recharge them.

South Korea has universal electricity, and its cities and even its remote towns are lighted up like a Christmas tree at night. North Korea, where children and families suffer severe malnutrition and even starvation, and where lives are dreary and short, is dark at night, except for the cities where the wealthy political class live. It is a near certainty that the North Koreans are not worried about the temperature of the planet in 2100.

Electricity use is highly correlated with growth. Wealthy countries like the United States use a lot of electricity. Countries that are desperately poor use almost none. Which way does the causality run? Wealth causes energy use, to be sure. But energy use also builds wealth. These are self-reinforcing and circular relationships.

Let us take, for example, internet access and "broadband" development. As Senator Richard Durbin of Illinois put it during a congressional hearing in 2007,

> [B]roadband access is not a luxury item but a necessity to compete in the twenty-first century. Quite simply, businesses,

hospitals, schools, and even communities, regions, and states are better able to compete if they have access to or can offer broadband service.

The statistics in this area are compelling. A 2006 report by the U.S. Department of Commerce shows that broadband access enhances the economic growth and performance of communities. Over the three year study, broadband communities significantly outgrew non-broadband communities in terms of employment, the number of businesses overall, businesses in IT-intensive sectors, and property values....

[M]any of our residents living in rural areas do not have access to high speed internet service. The digital divide remains a reality. We all want to jump onto the Information Superhighway, yet there is no on-ramp in many parts of the country.[1]

This all sounds right on the mark. But broadband depends on electric power. Making energy more expensive in rural and poor areas will reduce their access to broadband. The digital divide will widen.

Now consider the 2015 Paris climate agreement's effect on energy usage and wealth. Paul Driessen, an energy expert at the Committee for a Constructive Tomorrow, has run the numbers, and they are frightening to be sure. Writing about the United States, he warns:

The impacts would be far worse than many news stories and White House press releases suggest. Those sources often say the proposed climate treaty and other actions seek GHG reductions of 80% below predicted 2050 emission levels. The real original Paris treaty target is 80% below *actual 1990 levels*.

That means the world would have to eliminate 96% of the greenhouse gases that all humanity would likely release if we reach world population levels, economic growth and living standards predicted for 2050. The United States would likely have to slash its CO2 and GHG reductions to zero.

Moreover, current 2050 forecasts already assume and incorporate significant energy efficiency, de-carbonization and de-industrialization over the next 35 years. They are not business-as-usual numbers or extrapolations of past trends. Further CO2 reductions beyond those already incorporated into the forecasts would thus be increasingly difficult, expensive, and indeed impossible to achieve.

Slashing fossil energy use that far would thus require decimating economic growth, job creation and preservation, and average per-person incomes. In fact, average world per capita GDP would plummet from a projected $30,600 in 2050 to a miserable $1,200 per year.

Average per capita GDP in 2050 would be less than what Americans had in 1830! Many futuristic technologies would still exist, but only wealthy families and ruling elites could afford them.[2]

That is the effect on the United States, which is already rich. Within the United States, the climate change deal will increase inequality and make our economy less productive.

But the wealth divide between countries is also going to widen even more. For poor countries, which should be using *more*, not less, fossil fuel to power their twenty-first-century economic progress, mandatory energy reduction targets spells a cruel regression. But won't "green energy" replace fossil fuels to produce electric power for poor countries? As we've seen, medieval energy sources like windmills can't come close to doing that.

A theme of this book has been that the war against fossil fuels threatens to pull off one of the greatest wealth transfers from the poor to the rich in history. No matter what reparations the rich nations pay to the poor ones—the Third World says it wants $100 billion of bribe money from the Western nations to dance to their climate change tune—it will never compensate for the damage done by higher energy costs.

America's Growth Deficit

Energy is clearly linked to growth, but why is growth so important? Some on the Left argue that "growth mania" is despoiling the planet and that we all should learn to live in harmony with nature, consuming less of everything. The anti-fossil-fuels crusade in America and around the globe is inspired in part by a philosophical and theological revolt against the pursuit of growth and development. They want a "steady state," not a growth state.

Yet nearly every economic problem that America faces—poverty, the national debt, stagnant middle-class incomes, state and local pension liabilities, an over-stretched military that can't protect us, crumbling infrastructure—can be alleviated through faster economic growth. The economy of the Obama decade has grown at less than 2 percent per year. We should and could be growing at more than twice that pace.

America's growth gap is widening. In the post–Great Recession recovery, the economy has had its worst performance on jobs and incomes and GDP growth of any post-recession period since the 1930s. In constant 2009 dollars, we are $1.7 trillion behind where we should be and more than $2.5 trillion behind the pace of growth under the Reagan expansion.[3] The jobs deficit is even more alarming to many Americans. We are about five million jobs shy of where we should be with faster growth. That deficit is the equivalent of every worker in Michigan losing his job.

America's Energy Abundance

What does any of this have to do with energy? Everything. A pro-growth energy policy is the springboard to rapid growth in economic output and enhancing our competitiveness in global markets. America should pursue a number of measures to enhance economic growth, including a cut in the corporate income tax rate, a flat-rate income tax, regulatory reform, repealing and replacing Obamacare, and free trade. But few policy changes would revive the U.S. economy as quickly and powerfully as a pro-development energy policy.

The United States is strategically positioned to become not merely energy independent by 2020 but the dominant energy force on the planet, a development that would have profound economic implications. We spend roughly $150 billion a year importing about 9.2 million barrels of oil a day[4], or nearly half (48%) of all petroleum and crude products consumed. Just over one-third of these imports come from OPEC, with major consequences for our national interest and security.[5] Of course, Russia is also a beneficiary of our excess demand for oil—meaning that we indirectly fund Russian aggression across the Baltic.[6] We now have an opportunity to erase the gap between our need for oil and our ability to produce it ourselves.

And then, of course, there is the energy component of the war against the Islamic State and other terrorist organizations. One of our most effective economic weapons is America's vast shale oil and gas reserves and our five-hundred-year supply of coal. Every barrel of oil we produce here at home is one less barrel we have to purchase from abroad. We know from intelligence reports that the Islamic State receives as much as half a billion dollars a year from oil. As the U.S. drills for more cheap natural gas, we can export it to Europe and liberate our allies from dependence on Russia for energy. The good news is that there is no economic or geological reason why the United States must ever buy another gallon of oil from those who are trying to kill us. We now have the capacity to achieve real energy independence within five years by pursuing a pro-America energy development strategy.

To achieve this goal, America and most of the rest of the world will rely on fossil fuels for their energy needs for the foreseeable future. Contrary to wild-eyed Malthusian claims to the contrary, oil, natural gas, and coal are abundant in the United States. Figure 11.1 shows how many years' worth we have of each.[7] The shale revolution completely discredits the frightening tales of America running out of oil and gas. We have more fossil fuels than any other nation.

For decades, the Malthusians have controlled our national energy policy. In March 2012, President Obama moaned, "America uses 20 percent of the world's oil, and we've got 2 percent of the world's oil

FIGURE 11.1

Total Recoverable Resources in U.S.

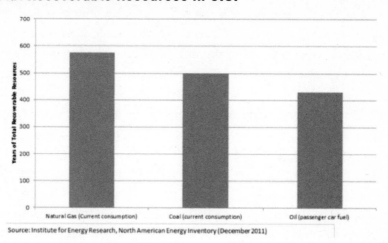

Source: Institute for Energy Research, North American Energy Inventory (December 2011)

reserves. I wasn't a math major, but if you're using 20, you've only got 2, that means you have got to bring in the rest from someplace else."[8] That is complete nonsense. As we have shown, America's reserves of resources are growing every day. In fact, our reserves are at least three times higher than Mr. Obama thought when he made that comment. The Institute for Energy Research points out that America has drilled billions of barrels of domestic oil over the past forty years, but our reserves are much higher today than they were before we started all the drilling. Technology is outpacing depletion. In the mid-2020s, we will have larger recoverable reserves than we have today.

Consider what has happened in less than a decade with oil production. In 2008 the United States produced about five million barrels a day.[9] We hit 8.7 million in 2014[10] and are predicted to hit 10.3 million by 2025. What a refutation of the skeptics who thought America's oil resources were running dry. We are drowning in cheap oil.

No, President Obama, we are not going to run out of oil—at least not any time in the next century. The supply is virtually unlimited. Don't be surprised if in the future we see continued declines in energy costs, the opposite of the trend that was predicted by the limits-to-growth crowd.

The environmental Left's vision for our energy future—the pursuit of an artificial, self-imposed reliance on renewable energy—is entirely wrong. Progressives used to promise a "chicken in every pot and a car in every garage;" now it's a solar panel on every roof and a windmill in every back yard.

There are many problems with this energy strategy. First, in spite of all the subsidies, solar and wind power account for only about 2.5 percent of our energy production today.[11] And even the Energy Information Agency says that the combined marketable and nonmarketable wind and solar energy consumed will account for just 3 percent of all energy consumed in the United States by 2030.[12] The main reason that green energy dreams are quickly fading is that shale oil and gas are crushing so many of the alternative energy sources. The recent drop in oil prices is another nail in the coffin for trendy alternatives. The booming energy source in America and the world isn't solar or wind power, it is natural gas. In Asia, coal has taken off.

A second problem with renewable energy is its exorbitant cost to consumers and taxpayers. We already layer on tens of billions of dollars of subsidies to enhance wind and solar power. The effective per kilowatt subsidy to wind was more than 50 times that of fossil fuels in 2013; and the same average subsidy to solar power was a whopping 345 times the average per unit subsidy for conventional fossil fuels.[13] These sources impose enormous costs on American taxpayers and consumers. If it weren't conveniently hidden from view, there would be a consumer revolt.

Finally, the global war on fossil fuels is a war against progress, prosperity, and the poor. Reliance on inefficient renewable energy will hit the poor hardest, denying opportunity and enhanced living standards to those who need them most. Carbon taxes, cap and trade schemes, regulatory impediments to drilling, and renewable energy standards are all regressive taxes. The policies of "environmental justice" promoted by the Left are robbing the poor, who spend a much larger share of their income on energy than do the rich. The basics of modern human existence—driving our cars, lighting and heating our homes, and producing everything from cereal to televisions to tennis shoes—are all affected by these price hikes.

On the other hand, if the billionaire hedge fund manager and green energy promoter Tom Steyer's utility bill rises by 30 percent, or if he has to pay $5 a gallon for gasoline, he doesn't notice. But for a family living on $30,000 a year, it means keeping the thermostat at sixty-eight degrees in the dead of winter or not buying school supplies.

A 2014 Pew Research Center poll found that only two major voting groups opposed construction of the Keystone XL pipeline: Democrats who make more than $100,000 annually and Democrats with college or advanced degrees—i.e., the elites. They don't need cheap energy and they don't need the jobs.[14]

The chief victims of the war against fossil fuels are the poorest citizens of the poorest nations. Developing countries need cheap energy. Commanding poor countries on the cusp of development to meet "renewable" energy standards, which are not merely inconvenient but prohibitively expensive, defies universal standards of morality. In addition to stunting economic growth, these artificially imposed energy constraints impede the ability of poor nations to enjoy lengthen life expectancy, reduce child death rates, and eradicate disease. Just ask Somalia, Uganda, and Nepal how their ultra-low per capita carbon dioxide emissions are working out for them.[15]

It doesn't have to be this way. The alternative future that we envision for America enhances our security and remains true to our moral values. It makes economic and fiscal sense. It is the way out of our malaise.

A Pro-Growth Energy Strategy

Now let's look at what we could expect if the United States embarked on a pro-energy development economic crusade.

The consultants at IHS have estimated that the 2015 repeal of the 1970s-era ban on exporting American oil over time will provide a $135 billion-a-year boost to energy output in the United States.[16] That means hundreds of thousands more jobs, higher wages, and tens of billions of dollars in additional tax revenues. The average worker in the oil industry earns between $75,000 and $100,000 a year. These are good, often union, jobs.

But that is just step one toward a rational energy policy. If we were to move from an energy-importing nation to an energy-exporting nation, we could nearly double our economic growth rate. Instead of growing at 2 percent we could achieve well over 4 percent growth. As we tap into the full potential of our shale oil and gas, we can become the number-one export nation on the planet. This could easily mean more than $1 trillion a year in oil, gas, and coal exports each year—perhaps exceeding 5 percent of GDP.

The United State government is the most indebted institution in the world—actually in the history of the world. Our debt is now more than $18.5 trillion, and in some recent years we've added more than $1 trillion to that debt. Neither party has a strategy for balancing the budget, let alone reducing the existing debt burden.

How Much Oil Do We Have?

The key to doing so is drilling on public lands. At today's prices, we are sitting on nearly $50 trillion of assets. It is the world's greatest treasure chest. Obama has been determined to keep it in the ground, and his climate change policies make sure drilling doesn't happen.

So far at least 90% of the shale gas and shale oil revolution has happened on private land. But around half of all the land west of the Mississippi is government-owned. How big could the shale boom be if we opened up public land for drilling? It's an exciting question. And the answer is really, *really* big.

A comprehensive survey by the Congressional Research Service in 2010 documented that the United States has the largest endowment of total recoverable proved reserves of hydrocarbon resources in the world.[17] No other country has more of this recoverable oil and natural gas than we do. We have more than Russia, twice as much as China, three times more than Saudi Arabia, and twenty-three times more than Brazil. The United States is also the world's leader in technically recoverable but undiscovered oil and natural gas, with 50 percent more than Saudi Arabia, more than four times that of Brazil, and twelve times that of China.[18] Since then we have discovered even more oil and gas, and what is technologically recoverable keeps growing as the fracking and other drilling technologies improve and get cheaper. We've just scratched the surface—literally and figuratively—of our energy resources in America. The more we use, the more we find.

A 2011 report by the non-profit, non-partisan Institute for Energy Research, "North American Energy Inventory," concludes that the United States sits atop 1.442 trillion barrels of recoverable oil, 2,744 trillion cubic feet of recoverable natural gas, and 486 billion short tons of recoverable coal.[19]

Offshore oil and gas reserves are also extremely large but unfortunately largely unavailable for production. At the time of the last Department of the Interior Offshore Oil and Gas National Assessment in 2011, just over seventeen billion barrels of oil had been produced from the federal offshore,[20] and more than twenty billion barrels of already discovered oil reserves were available for production.[21] Further, the assessment estimated that exploration and production activities in the federal offshore would, in the mean case, eventually produce an additional ninety billion barrels of currently undiscovered and technically recoverable oil[22]—assuming the offshore lands containing this oil are reasonably made available for leasing and production.

Similarly, the National Assessment estimated that just over 173 trillion cubic feet of natural gas have been produced from the federal offshore, and that more than seventy-two trillion cubic feet of already discovered natural gas is available to be produced.[23] Further, the National Assessment estimated that exploration and production activities in the federal offshore would, in the mean case, eventually produce an additional 405 trillion cubic feet of currently undiscovered and technically recoverable natural gas—assuming the offshore lands containing the natural gas are reasonably made available for leasing and production.[24] These two figures combine to an expected potential future production from the federal offshore of 477 trillion cubic feet of conventional natural gas.

So what's the problem?

Contrary to their experiences on state and private lands, our oil and gas producers have been severely hampered in their exploration and production efforts on federal lands because the Obama administration has become increasingly bureaucratic and restrictive. Permitting a well with state regulators might take a few days to a month. The same well on federal lands may take a year or longer. Jack Coleman, formerly an energy expert at the U.S. Department of the Interior, testified to the House Subcommittee on Energy and Power, "A litany of actions by the Department of the Interior have unreasonably, and frequently unlawfully, restricted energy leasing, exploration and production on federal lands, both onshore and offshore."[25]

Consider the many federal restrictions on drilling listed by Mr. Coleman in his testimony:

- Removal of the Atlantic Ocean, Pacific Ocean, Eastern Gulf of Mexico, and Alaska Beaufort Sea from consideration for oil and gas leasing until 2017 at the earliest.
- A decision to send commercial oil shale regulations back through the rulemaking process despite the fact that these regulations were finalized after months of extensive and open public comment, including the reports and recommendations of an 11-member statutorily-mandated task force made up of federal, state and local officials. A failure to move forward with energy projects in Alaska, both onshore and offshore, that exposes the Trans-Alaska Pipeline System to risk of shutdown.
- Placing of severely restrictive and expensive conditions of approval on permits—long after the lessee has made major investments in the lease.

- Failure to properly and expeditiously implement many of the energy law reforms enacted by Congress as part of the Energy Policy Act of 2005, including the NEPA categorical exclusions provision and the oil shale and tar sands commercial leasing program.
- Continued failure to comply with statutory permitting deadlines for exploration plans in the outer Continental Shelf.

These restrictions, along with our current energy and environmental policies, will keep most of our energy resources from being exploited. As Mr. Coleman put it, "Our national energy resources located on federal onshore and offshore lands are locked up in a deep freezer, with many padlocks on it. Each new unnecessary regulatory restraint is a new padlock on that freezer—keeping energy prices high."

So how do we reverse course? The Set America Free Act of 2005[26] established a national policy of ensuring that Canada, Mexico, and the United States are energy self-sufficient by 2025. For a host of economic and national security reasons, this goal of energy self-sufficiency is prudent. Some of the findings of the House of Representatives reveal the staggering scope of the potential resources of the countries of North America, and so we quote from the report at some length:[27]

- North American countries have the resource base and technical ability to increase production of oil by at least 15 Mmbbl/d by 2025 and 20 Mmbbl/d by 2030 even before increases in coal liquifaction, biofuels, gas-to-liquids, and other methods of creating liquid substitutes for crude oil and crude oil products.
- The United States oil shale resource base (2 trillion barrels of oil in place out of 2.6 trillion in the world) [is] believed to be capable of eventually producing 10 Mmbbl/d for more than 100 years.

- The Canadian Alberta oil sands resource base (1.7 trillion barrels of oil in place), [could] eventually produc[e] 10 Mmbbl/d for more than 100 years.
- [We have] 60 billion barrels [of oil] potentially producible with advanced CO_2 enhanced oil recovery technology.
- The United States oil sands resource base [has] 54 billion barrels of oil in place.
- The Arctic National Wildlife Refuge Coastal Plain area (ANWR) [has] a mean technically recoverable resource of more than 10 billion barrels of oil.
- The National Petroleum Reserve-Alaska (NPR-A) [has] a mean technically recoverable resource of 9.3 billion barrels of oil.
- The 12–18 billion barrels of oil [could] be producible in the Canadian Atlantic offshore.

The House Report concludes:

Economists have found that while OPEC is an important source of oil price increases, the United States government is also partly to blame because overly burdensome government regulations on domestic energy exploration, production, and sales have supported OPEC's monopoly power and restricted competition from American energy companies, in addition to making expansive highly prospective areas off-limits to leasing and production.

Our $50 Trillion Treasure Chest

What do these giant oil and gas resources potentially mean for the United States? They mean 4 percent economic growth or more. Millions of new jobs are possible. Wages will rise. We simply need to declare a national commitment to American energy independence. These energy resources are wholly owned by the American people.

Achieving American energy self-sufficiency will generate enough money in royalties and corporate income taxes to pay off much of the national debt without any other tax revenues. But these vast resources will never pay off any of the national debt if they are not made available for leasing, drilling, and production.

According to an analysis by Coleman, all of the oil and gas resources under federal lands and offshore that could be recovered with existing technologies amount to at least $1.5-trillion-worth of barrels over the next twenty years. At the current price of $35 a barrel, this would increase GDP by $50 trillion over two decades.

Ladies and gentlemen: America has won the lottery. We have hit the jackpot. We have found a $50-trillion treasure lying under our feet. The income tax and royalty payments to the federal government would be $3–4 trillion over twenty years.

Such revenues would radically improve our grim fiscal situation, which now includes tens of trillions of dollars of deficits and unfunded liabilities in the decades to come. To try to raise the money to pay these bills by hiking taxes would require crippling tax rates of 50, 60, or even 70 percent.

The story gets even better, because the numbers cited above are highly conservative; they may vastly underestimate how much the government and taxpayers could profit from our energy resources. They "do not include natural gas hydrates which we should be able to commercially produced in the near future. More than 99% of America's 300,000 trillion cubic feet of natural gas hydrates are located in the deepwater federal offshore." Coleman estimates that

> if even only 1% of this resource is eventually producible, it would add 3,200 trillion cubic feet of natural gas. Production of this 1%, or 3,200 trillion cubic feet, of our natural gas hydrate resources would generate approximately $3 trillion in royalties and about $4.5 trillion in corporate income tax on this production from the lessees, for a total of approximately $7.5 trillion.[28]

Finally, these numbers don't include the eight hundred billion barrels of western oil shale. An estimated 70 percent of this or more than half a trillion barrels are estimated to be producible from high density deposits of oil shale on federal lands. Federal royalties on this production are estimated to total $3.214 trillion, with federal corporate income taxes totaling $7.546 trillion, for total federal revenues of $10.76 trillion from production of federal high-density oil shale deposits.

So now we arrive at an upper-bound estimate for the value to the government of our fossil fuel oil and gas resources. Totaling all of the production from onshore and offshore federal lands comes to at least $10 trillion and as much as $20 trillion, which is more than our national debt.

Even if the world eases away from fossil fuels over the decades to come, as the EIA recently reiterated, the United States and the world will rely on oil, natural gas, and coal for the vast majority of their energy resources for at least the next twenty years. This means that the American people still have enough time to reap the vast bounty of fossil fuels that God has bestowed upon us, if we get started now.

What to Do with All That Money: A Proposal

So what should be done with the bounty from all this drilling? Here is what we propose.

The revenues should be shared for high-priority public purposes. For every dollar raised in oil revenues, twenty cents should go to the state from which the resource was produced. Another forty cents should pay off our national debt. Another twenty cents should go to pay for a tax reform package. And the final twenty cents should go to repair and modernize America's infrastructure, including the building of vital pipelines.

We call this a win-win-win-win-win proposal. This could be the most extraordinary public-private partnership in American history and the most transformative act of government since the Louisiana Purchase. It is certainly on the magnitude of the Apollo project that landed a man on the moon.

The upside from producing American energy—both from an economic and national security standpoint—is almost incalculable. Yet the American people have not seen a results-oriented national energy program designed to achieve American energy self-sufficiency, and then large volumes to export to the world.

Voters understand that the United States has abundant oil, gas, and coal resources, and they do not believe that their government is doing all that it can to produce the energy necessary to power the country and provide for our energy, economic, and national security. Imagine the folly if Saudi Arabia had decided not to drill for its resources forty years ago.

Energy is the lifeblood of a nation's economy. If energy is abundant and reasonably priced, the economy will prosper. Some interests have created an illusion that somehow energy will just appear whenever we want it. As Confucius is reputed to have said, "If a man takes no thought about what is distant, he will find sorrow near at hand." Energy sources take many years to develop—they cannot be "turned on" like a light switch. For decades, our government has ignored the challenge of developing energy supplies for the future.

Like every other nation, we should be developing our own oil and natural gas resources. This is a simple matter of economics. Would we rather have the hundreds of thousands of new high-paying oil and gas production jobs in the United States, where the investment will turn over in our economy and build it on a broad base, or would we rather send the production investment and oil purchase dollars to other countries to build the economy and create jobs there? There's nothing wrong with purchasing and importing foreign oil, but there's a big problem when we're forced to do so because we're prevented from producing our own.

So what are the steps necessary to create this prosperous and energy rich future for America? The first was taken, finally, at the end of 2015, which is to allow the exporting of American oil and natural gas. Here are the others:

1. Allow drilling on federal lands. More than 90 percent of all drilling during the Obama years has been on private lands.
2. Build a national network of pipelines across the country.
3. Allow the building of refineries and LNG terminals in the United States. It has been almost forty years since a major new refinery opened in the United States, even though the population has nearly doubled since the mid-1970s and our energy production has doubled as well.[29] Environmental laws that make refineries prohibitively expensive, if they can be built at all, are mostly to blame. LNG terminals are necessary for exporting our natural gas.
4. Rein in the out-of-control EPA. The agency has an agenda to put the coal industry out of business and to destroy the natural gas and oil industries, and it is succeeding. Environmental rules have to be shown to be cost-effective, meaning that the cost to the economy of complying with the rules is justified on the basis of the environmental benefits—and measured honestly. Few if any of Obama's anti-fossil-fuel regulations come close to meeting this test.
5. Build nuclear power plants and allow twenty-first-century micro-nuclear reactors to be used for energy production.
6. End renewable energy standards in the states and at the federal level. The Manhattan Institute has documented that these standards add to the cost of electricity production, gouging consumers and discouraging fossil fuel development.[30]
7. End all subsidies for all forms of energy. The Left complains about taxpayer subsidies for oil and gas. To the extent they exist they should be ended. But the cost of wind and solar energy grants, loans, loan guarantees, and so on is in the tens of billions of dollars. The effective per kilowatt subsidy to wind was more than fifty times that

of fossil fuels in 2013, and the same average subsidy to solar power was a whopping 345 times the average per unit subsidy for conventional fossil fuels.[31]

8. Shut down the U.S. Department of Energy and let the free market work.

If we get this right, America will get rich, and we—not Saudi Arabia or Russia or OPEC—will be the future energy capital of the world.

ACKNOWLEDGMENTS

We would like to thank the many people whose enthusiastic support made this book possible.

During the year that we devoted to writing *Fueling Freedom*, our spouses, family, close friends, and colleagues—and Kathleen's many dogs—rarely received the attention from us they deserved. Our spouses, in particular, went above and beyond exemplary forbearance.

We also salute our employers for their extraordinary support. The encouragement of Kathleen's colleagues at the Texas Public Policy Foundation in Austin and Steve's at The Heritage Foundation in Washington kept us pushing ahead on the project when no end was in sight.

We are humbly grateful for the encouragement we received from Brooke Rollins, president of TPPF. This book would have been impossible without her support and belief in the project. We especially want to thank Leigh Thompson, a policy analyst and attorney at TPPF, for her frequent help, and we are grateful to Nancy Druart, a friend and graphics designer, who worked so patiently to keep our text and graphics neat and tidy. We also salute two extraordinarily capable interns—Bill Brady and Megan Ingram—for their cheerful help on countless details.

We also recognize Bill Murchison, a colleague for more than twenty-five years and a masterly writer, for his wise suggestions and deft edits to our first drafts.

At Heritage, the help of Timothy Doescher, Joel Griffith, and David Allen with our research was indispensable.

The fine minds and great souls whose wide-ranging work has inspired and informed this book are too numerous to list within this brief space. We encourage readers to peruse the recommendations at the end of the book for further reading. They are a rich source of eye-opening facts and insight about energy—information you won't find in the media's superficial treatment of climate policies and energy.

Some of the many scholars on whom we have relied merit individual recognition. First and foremost, we salute the late, great free-market economist Julian Simon (1932–1998) for his effective and timeless critique of Neo-Malthusian pessimism about the fate of humanity uncontrolled by the self-appointed elites. Simon's understanding of energy as the "master resource" capable of transforming all other natural resources into useful goods and services is crucial, and his insight that imaginative human beings free to create are the "ultimate resource" is a central theme of our book. Simon's work goes against the grain of fashionable thought, but it is historically validated and increasingly important as the number of would-be "planetary managers" grows. Simon was Steve's mentor, and we wish he had lived to see the shale energy revolution, a surprise to most energy experts but exactly the kind of transformative innovation that he predicted.

A couple of years ago, Kathleen was inspired by Dr. Indur Goklany's well-researched and provocatively titled monograph "Humanity Unbound: How Fossil Fuels Saved Humanity from Nature and Nature from Humanity," which introduced her to the startling historical connection between increased use of fossil fuels and dramatic improvements in human well-being. Steered by Goklany's paper to a dozen books and twice as many academic papers, she eventually published her own paper, "Fossil Fuels: The Moral Case," in 2014. When Steve read that paper, he thought it extended the message of a book he had co-authored with Julian Simon, *It's Getting Better All the Time* (2000). We decided that a book-length treatment of the clash between the shale revolution and the unjustified, futile, and increasingly damaging climate crusade was urgently needed.

In marshalling the facts of economic history and energy, we have drawn upon the work of the highly-regarded masters Angus Maddison (1926–2010) and Vaclav Smil. One of the founders of the field of macroeconomic history, Maddison compiled worlds of data to calculate income per capita, gross output, population, and other economic variables extending over millennia. His *The World Economy: A Millennial Perspective* and *The World Economy: Historical Statistics* document the unprecedented rate of human advances and modern economic growth ignited in the Industrial Revolution. Vaclav Smil, although not well known among the general public, was among *Foreign Policy*'s top one hundred global thinkers of 2010. As precise as he is prolific, Smil has written more than thirty books on the many-splendored phenomenon known as energy, offering essential data and analytical tools to assess energy and environmental policies.

E. A. Wrigley's economic history of the Industrial Revolution also plays an important role in this book. Dr. Wrigley persuasively argues that the kind of energy available in fossil fuels was a necessary condition for the economic growth spawned by the Industrial Revolution. In four books and many academic papers, Wrigley has helped answer the question why that economic growth has never stopped—unless the Great Recession that began in late 2007 is not an interlude but the beginning of an extended downturn. Let's hope not.

To fortify our optimism about the future, we turn to the engaging English polymath the fifth Viscount Ridley, also known as Matt Ridley, whose *Rational Optimist* (2010) makes a persuasive and spirited case for the value of fossil fuels in a future of increasing prosperity across the world.

The superb Institute for Energy Research also served as an encyclopedia of the energy revolution. Special thanks to IER's CEO and founder, Robert Bradley Jr., and to Tom Pyle and Dan Kish.

In conclusion, we heartily thank Regnery Publishing for taking on our book. Our editors, Tom Spence and Maria Ruhl, were extraordinarily helpful and patient and a delight to work with. Aware of Regnery's long and distinguished history of publishing the work of the leading lights in the conservative movement, we are honored to be among their authors.

RECOMMENDED READING

Daron Aceemoglu and James Robinson, *Why Nations Fail* (Crown Publishing Group, 2012).

Paul Adelman, *"The Genie Out of the Bottle"* (MA: The MIT Press, 1995).

Patrick Allitt, *A Climate of Crisis*: *America in the Age of Environmentalism* (Penguin Press, 2014).

Kendall Ambio, *Constraints On The World Economy*. (Publisher?,1994).

Tim Ball, *The Deliberate Corruption of Climate Science* (Stairway Press, 2014).

Larry Bell, *Climate of Corruption* (Greenleaf Book Group Press, 2011).

Derek Birkett, *When Will the Lights Go Out*: *Britain's Looming Energy Crisis* (Stacy International, 2010).

BP Statistical Review of World Energy (2014).

Robert L. Bradley Jr., *Capitalism at Work*: *Business, Government, and Energy* (M&M Scrivener Press, 2008).

Robert L. Bradley Jr., E*dison to Enron: Energy Markets and Political Strategies* (Wiley-Scrivener, 2011).

Robert L. Bradley Jr. and Richard W. Fulmer, *Energy: The Master Resource* (Kendall Hunt Publishing, 2004).

Arthur C. Brooks, *The Conservative Heart* (HarperCollins Broadside Books, 2015).

Lester Brown, *The Great Transition: Shifting from Fossil Fuels to Solar and Wind Energy* (W.W. Norton & Company, 2015).

Richard Brown, *Economic Revolutions in Britain 1750–1850* (Cambridge University Press, 1992).

Robert Bryce, Power Hungry: *The Myths of Green Energy and the Real Fuels of the Future* (Public Affairs, 2010).

Robert Bryce, *Gusher of Lies: The Dangerous Delusion of Energy Independence* (Public Affairs, 2008).

Pascal Bruckner, *The Fanaticism of the Apocalypse: Save the Earth, Punish Human Beings* (1st Ed., France Grasser & Fasquelle, 2011) (Eng. Ed., Polity Press, 2014).

Carlo M. Cipolla, *Before the Industrial Revolution: European Society and Economy 1000–1700* (W.W. Norton & Company, 1980).

Gregory Clark, *A Farewell to Alms* (Princeton University Press, 2007).

Angelo M. Codevilla, *The Ruling Class* (Beaufort Books, 2010).

Fred Cottrell, *Energy and Society* (Authorhouse, 1955) (Revised ed. 2009).

Earl Cook, *Man, Energy and Society* (W. H. Freeman & Company (1976).

Rupert Darwall, *The Age of Global Warming: A History* (Quartet Books Limited, 2013).

Paul Davies, *The Cosmic Jackpot: Why Our Universe Is Just Right for Life*, Houghton Mifflin Harcourt (2007).

Paul Davies, *The Goldilock's Enigma: Why is the Universe Just Right for Life?* (Penguin, 2006).

Pierre Desrochers and Hiroko Shimizu, *The Locavore's Delemma: In Praise of the 10,000 Mile Diet* (Public Affairs, 2012).

Gregg Easterbrook, *A Moment on the Earth: The Coming Age of Environmental Optimism* (Penguin Books Ltd., 1995).

Paul Ehrlich, *The Population Bomb* (Buccaneer Books, 1970).

John Etherington, *The Wind Farm Scam* Stacey (International, 2009).

Brian Fagan, *The Great Warming: Climate Change and the Rise and Fall of Civilizations* (Bloomsbury Press, 2008).

Brian Fagan, *The Little Ice Age: How Climate Made History 1300–1850* (Basic Books, 2000).

Brian Fagan, *The Long Summer: How Climate Changed Civilization* (Basic Books, 2004).

Richard Feynman, *Six Easy Pieces: Essentials of Physics Explained by Its Most Brilliant Teacher* (Basic Books, 1994).

Richard Feynman, *Surely You're Joking, Mr. Feynman* (W.W. Norton & Company, 1985).

Roger Fouquet, *Heat, Power and Light: Revolutions in Energy Services* (Edward Elgar Publishing, 2010).

Robert W. Foegel, *The Fourth Great Awakening and the Future of Egalitarianism* (Univ of Chicago Press, 2002).

Milton Friedman, *Capitalism and Freedom* (University of Chicago Press, 1962).

George Gilder, *Knowledge and Power* (Regnery Publishing, 2013).

George Gilder, *Wealth and Poverty* (Regnery Publishing, 1981).

Peter C. Glover and Michael J. Economides, *Energy and Climate Wars: How Naïve Politicians, Green Ideologues, and Media Elites are Undermining the Truth About Energy and Climate* (Bloomsbury Academic, 2010).

Indur Goklany, *The Improving State of the World* (Cato Institute, 2007).

Russell Gold, *The Boom: How Fracking Ignited the American Energy Revolution and Changed the World* (Simon & Schuster, 2014).

Al Gore, *An Inconvenient Truth: The Crisis of Global Warming* (Viking, 2006).

Steven F. Hayward, *Almanac of Environmental Trends* (Pacific Research Institute, 2011).

Steven F. Hayward, *The Age of Reagan: The Fall of the Old Liberal Order 1964–1980* (Three Rivers Press, 2001).

Steven F. Hayward, *The Age of Reagan: The Conservative Counter-revolution 1980–1989* (Crown Forum, 2009).

Friedrich Hayek, *The Road to Serfdom* (University of Chicago Press, 1944).

Friedrich Hayek, *The Fatal Conceit: The Errors of Socialism* (University of Chicago Press, 1988).

Leon Hesser, *The Man Who Fed The* World (Durbin Publishing Co., 2006).

Christopher Horner: *Power Grab: How Obama's Green Policies Will Steal Your Freedom and Bankrupt America* (Regnery Publishing Inc., 2010).

Christopher Horner, *Red Hot Lies: How Global Warming Alarmists Use Threats, Fraud and Deception to Keep You Misinformed* (Regnery Publishing Inc., 2008).

Peter W. Huber and Mark P. Mills, *The Bottomless Well: The Twilight of Fuel, the Virtue of Waste, and Why We Will Never Run Out of Energy* (Basic Books, 2007).

Craig D. Idso and Sherwood B. Idso, *The Many Benefits of Atmospheric CO2 Enrichment* (Vales Lake Publishing, 2011).

Paul Johnson, *Modern Times: The World from the Twenties to the Nineties* (Harper Collins, 1983).

Astrid Kander, Paolo Malanima and Paul Warde, *Power to the People: Energy in Europe over the Last Five Centuries* (Princeton University Press, 2013).

Alexander King and Bertrand Schneider, *The First Global Revolution: A Report of the Council of the Club of Rome* (Pantheon Books, 1991).

Thomas Kuhn, *The Structure of Scientific Revolutions* (University of Chicago Press, 1962).

David S. Landes, *The Prometheus Unbound* (Cambridge University Press, 2nd Ed. 2003),

David S. Landes, *The Wealth and Poverty of Nations: Why Some Are So Rich and Some So Poor*, (W.W. Norton & Company, 1998).

Author? *Environmental Stewardship in the Judeo-Christian Tradition* (Acton Institute, 2007).

Ezra Levant, *Ethical Oil: The Case for Canada's Oil Sands* (McClelland & Stewart, 2010).

Mario Vargas Llosa, Vernon Smith and John Mackey, *The Morality of Capitalism* (Jameson Books Inc., 2011).

Bjorn Lomborg, *Cool It: The Skeptical Environmentalist's Guide to Global Warming* (Vintage, 2007).

Charles MacKay, *Extraordinary Popular Delusions and the Madness of Crowds* (Wordsworth Edition Ltd., 1841).

Angus Maddison, *The World Economy: A Millennial Perspective* (Paris: OCED, 2001).

Angus Maddison, *Growth and Interaction in the World Economy* (AEI Press, 2005).

Angus Maddison, *Contours of the World Economy 1–2030 AD: Essays in Macro-Economic History* (Oxford University Press, 2007).

Deirdre McCloskey, *Bourgeois Dignity: Why Economics Can't Explain in the Modern World* (University of Chicago Press, 2010).

Donella H. Meadows, Dennis L. Meadows, Jorgen Randers, William W. Behrens III, *Limits to Growth: A Report for the Club of Rome's Project on the Predicament of Mankind* (Universe Books, 1972).

Stephen Moore and Julian Simon, *It's Getting Better All the Time: 100 Greatest Trends of the Last 100 Years* (Cato Institute, 2000).

Alan Moran, *Climate Change: The Facts* (Institute of Public Affairs, 1st Ed. 2015) (Stockade Books, 2015).

Joel Moykr, *The Lever of Riches: Technological Creativity and Economic Progress* (Oxford University Press, 1990).

Joel Moykr, *The Enlightened Economy: An Economic History 1700–1850* (Yale University Press, 2009).

Patrick Albert Moore, *Confessions of Greenpeace Dropout: The Making of a Sensible Environmentalist* (Beatty Street Publishing Inc., 2010).

Michael Novak, *The Spirit of Democratic Capitalism* (Touchstone, 1982).

Francis O'Gorman, editor, *Cambridge Companion to Victorian Culture* (Cambridge University Press, 2010).

Ian Plummer, *Heaven and Earth: Global Warming the Missing Science* (Connor Court Publishing, 2009).

Kenneth Pomeranz, *The Great Divergence* (Princeton University Press, 2000).

Karl Popper, *The Logic of Scientific Discovery* (Routledge, 1934).

Matt Ridley, *The Rational Optimist* (Harper Perennial, 2010).

Paul Sabin, *The Bet: Paul Ehrlich, Julian Simon, and Our Gamble over Earth's Future* (Yale University Press, 2013).

Nicolas-Théodore de Saussure, *Recherches chimiques sur la végétation* (1804).

Julian L. Simon, *The Ultimate Resource 2* (Princeton University Press, 1996).

Julian L. Simon, *The State of Humanity* (Wiley-Blackwell, 1996).

Julian L. Simon, *Hoodwinking the Nation* (Transaction Publishers, 2006).

Julian L. Simon, *A Life Against the Grain: The Autobiography of an Unconventional Economist* (Transaction Publishers, 2003).

David Schoenbrod, *Saving Our Environment from Washington* (Yale University Press, 2005).

S. Fred Singer and Dennis T. Avery, *Unstoppable Global Warming: Every 1,500 Years* (Rowman & Littlefield, 2007).

Robert A. Sirico, *Defending the Free Market: The Moral Case for a Free Economy* (Regnery Publishing, 2012).

Vaclav Smil, *Energy Transitions: History, Requirements, Prospects* (Praeger, 2010).

Vaclav Smil, *Energy at the Crossroads* (MIT Press, 2003).

Vaclav Smil, *Energy in Nature and Society: General Energetics of Complex Systems* (MIT Press, 2007).

Vaclav Smil, *Energy: A Beginner's Guide* (Oneworld Publications, 2006).

Vaclav Smil, *Energy Myths and Realities* (AEI Press, 2010).

Vaclav Smil, *Enriching the Earth: Fritz Haber, Carl Bosch, and the Transformation of World Food Production* (The MIT Press, 2009).

Vaclav Smil, *Power Density: A Key to Understanding Energy Sources and Uses* (MIT Press, 2015).

Crosbie Smith, *The Science of Energy: A Cultural History of Energy Physics in Victorian Britain* (University of Chicago Press, 1998).

Lawrence Solomon, *The Deniers: The World-Renowned Scientists Who Stood up Against Global Warming Hysteria* (Richard Vigilante Books, 2008).

Thomas Sowell, A Conflict of Visions: Ideological Origins of Political Struggle (Basic Books, 2007).

Roy Spencer, *Climate Confusion* (Encounter Books, 2008).

Roy Spencer, *The Great Global Warming Blunder* (Encounter Books, 2010).

William Tucker, *Terrestial Energy: How Nuclear Energy Will Lead the Green Revolution and End America's Energy Odyssey* (Bartley Press, 2008).

Fritz Vahrenholt and Sebastian Luning, *The Neglected Sun* (Stacey International, 2013).

Alfred North Whitehead, *Science and the Modern World* (Macmillan Company, 1925) (Free Press Paperback 1st Ed., 1967).

Martin Wolf, *Why Globalization Works*, Yale University Press (New Haven, 2004).

E.A. Wrigley, *Energy and the English Industrial Revolution* (Cambridge University Press, 2010).

E. A. Wrigley, *Continuity, Chance and Change: The Character of the Industrial Revolution in England* (Cambridge University Press, 1988).

E.A. Wrigley *Poverty, Progress and Population* (Cambridge University Press, 2004).

E. A. Wrigley, *The Path to Sustained Growth: England's Transition from an Organic Economy to an Industrial Revolution* (Cambridge University Press, 2016).

Daniel Yergin, *The Quest: Energy, Security, and the Remaking of the Modern World* (Penquin Press, 2011).

Robert Zubrin, *Merchants of Despair* (New Atlantis Books, Encounter Books, 2013).

Robert Zubrin, *Energy Victory: Ending the War on Terror by Breaking Free of Oil* (Prometheus Books, 2009).

Gregory Zuckerman, *The Frackers* (Portfolio/Penguin, 2013).

NOTES

Chapter 1

1. Source: Updated from Indur Goklany, "Have Increases in Population, Affluence and Technology Worsened Human and Environmental Well-being?," *Electronic Journal of Sustainable Development* 1, no. 3 (2009); based on Angus Maddison, *Statistics on World Population, GDP and Per Capita GDP, 1–2008 AD*, University of Groningen, 2010, http://www.ggdc.net/MADDISON/Historical_Statistics/vertical-file_02-2010.xls; World Bank, *World Development Indicators 2011*, http://databank.worldbank.org/; T. A. Boden, G. Marland, and R. J. Andres, *Global, Regional, and National Fossil-Fuel CO2 Emissions*, Carbon Dioxide Information Analysis Center, U.S. Department of Energy, Oak Ridge, TN, 2011, http://cdiac.ornl.gov/trends/emis/overview_2008.html.
2. Friedrich Hayek, *The Road to Serfdom* (Chicago: University of Chicago Press, 1994). Originally published 1944.

3. Matt Ridley, *The Rational Optimist: How Prosperity Evolves* (New York: HarperCollins, 2010), 13–14.

4. The pioneering work in this field was done by Angus Maddison (1926–2010), a British economist who studied quantitative macroeconomic history, including the measurement and analysis of economic growth and development. The historical data compiled by Maddison on income per capita, population, life expectancy and demographic factors are used throughout the world.

5. Thomas Hobbes, *Leviathan*, Richard Turk, ed. (Cambridge: Cambridge University Press, 1991 (1651)), 89. Hobbes, of course, was referring to the condition of humanity in a theoretical state of nature, but his famous phrase accurately describes preindustrial living conditions for the average person.

6. Carlo Cipolla, *Before the Industrial Revolution: European Society and Economy 1000–1700*, 3rd ed. (New York: W. W. Norton & Company, 1993).

7. Goklany, *Humanity Unbound*, 8.

8. Ibid., McCloskey, 49.

9. Vaclav Smil, *Energy at the Crossroads: Global Perspectives and Uncertainties* (MIT Press, 2003, MIT Press paperback edition, 2005), 65.

10. Ibid.; See also Angus Maddison, *Monitoring the World Economy 1820–1992* (Paris: OECD, 2006).

11. Michael Kelly, "Technology Introductions in the Context of Decarbonization," *Global Warming Policy Foundation*, Note 7, (London, 2012).

12. Ibid., McCloskey, 50.

13. Robert Fogel, *The Fourth Great Awakening and the Future of Egalitarianism* (Chicago: University of Chicago Press, 2002), 37.

14. Ibid., 266.

15. Matt Ridley, *The Rational Optimist: How Prosperity Evolves* (HarperCollins, 2010), 214.

16. Stephen Moore, *Washington Times* A Times, November 8, 2015.

17. "Secretary Jewell Launches Comprehensive Review of Federal Coal Program," U.S. Department of the Interior, January 15, 2016, https://www.doi.gov/pressreleases/secretary-jewell-launches-comprehensive-review-federal-coal-program.

18. Laurence Tribe, "The Clean Power Plan Is Unconstitutional," *Wall Street Journal*, December 22, 2015.

19. Barak Obama, Speech to the UN General Assembly, September 28, 2015.

20. Paul Johnson, "The Nonsense of Global Warming," *Forbes*, September 18, 2008.

21. Vaclav Klaus, "Environmentalism and Other Challenges of the Current Era," Speech to CATO Institute, March 9, 2007.

22. Charles Krauthammer, "On the New Socialism," *Washington Post*, December 11, 2009.

23. Rupert Darwall, *The Age of Global Warming: A History* (London: Quartet Books Limited, 2013).

24. Robert Zubrin, *Merchants of Despair: Radical Environmentalists, Criminal Pseudo-Scientists and the Fatal Cult of Antihumanism* (New York: New Atlantis, Encounter Books, 2012, 2013).

25. "Paris Climate of Conformity," *Wall Street Journal*, December 13, 2015.

26. Julian Simon, *The Ultimate Resource 2* (Princeton University Press, 1996), 345.

27. Robert L. Bradley Jr., *Capitalism at Work: Business Government and Energy* (M & M Scrivner Press, Salem, Mass., 1009).

28. Ibid.

29. Gabriele Steinhauser et al., "Climate Deal Leaves Hard Decisions to Countries," *Wall Street Journal*, December 14, 2015.

30. Annie Gowen, "India's Huge Need for Electricity Is a Problem for the Planet," *Washington Post*, November 6, 2015.

31. Michael Bastach, "UN Climate Chief: Communism Is Best to Fight Global Warming," Daily Caller, January 15, 2014.

32. Christiana Figueres, United Nations Regional Information Center for Western Europe, (February 3, 2015).

33. Bjorn Lomborg, *The Skeptical Environmentalist* (Cambridge University Press, 2001).

34. Established in 1968, the Club of Rome is a group of former officials, political leaders, UN bureaucrats, economists, diplomats, and business leaders who love government and are wary about capitalist growth, democracy, and nation-states. The club's self-description—"a group of world citizens sharing a common concern for humanity"—is misleading. A line from its 1974 book *Mankind at the Turning Point* provides some perspective on the club's concern for humanity: "The earth has cancer and the cancer is man."

35. Donella H. Meadows et al., *The Limits to Growth: A Report for the Club of Rome's Project on the Predicament of Mankind* (New York: Universe Books, 1972).

36. Alexander King and Bertrand Schneider, *The First Global Revolution: A Report by the Council of the Club of Rome* (New York: Pantheon, 1991).

37. Paul Ehrlich, "An Ecologists Perspective on Nuclear Power," Public Issues Report of the Federation of American Scientists, May–June 1978.

38. Darwall, ibid.

39. Peter W. Huber and Mark P Mills, *The Bottomless Well: The Twilight of Fuel, the Virtue of Waste and Why We Will Never Run Out of Energy* (New York: Basic Books, 2005), xix.

Chapter 2

1. The current global majors, or the "Super Majors" as they often are called—BP, Chevron, ExxonMobil, Royal Dutch Shell, Total SA, and Conoco Phillips—emerged in the late 1990s through mergers.

2. Russel Gold, "U.S. Rises to No. 1 Energy Producer," *Wall Street Journal*, October 3, 2013.

3. EIA, Petroleum and Other Liquids: U.S. Imports from OPEC Countries of Crude Oil and Petroleum Products, January 2015.

4. Ben Lefebvre, "U.S. Refiner Exports Hit High," *Wall Street Journal*, October 9, 2013.

5. "Shale Gas: Reshaping the U.S. Chemicals Industry," Price Waterhouse Cooper for American Chemical Council, October 2012.

6. IHIS Inc., "America's new Energy Future: The Unconventional Oil and Natural Gas Revolution and the U.S. Economy-State Economic Contributions," Prepared for the American Petroleum Institute and American Chemical Council, December 19, 2012.

7. EIA U.S. Coal Reserves, December 16, 2013, http://www.eia.gov/coal/reserves/; EIA, International te and Monthly Energy Review, November 2014, http://www.eia.gov/totalenergy/data/monthly/pdf/sec6_3.pdf.

8. Oil sand is a thick, dense source of petroleum naturally occurring in a mixture of sand, water, clay, and bitumen. Oil sand, like shale oil, is regarded as one of several "unconventional" sources of petroleum that have boomed over the last decade. Also like shale oil, the existence of the oil sands has long been known, but innovative technologies and processes have only recently made extraction feasible at a large commercial scale. Oil sands exist in several countries but Canada's Athabasca field in Alberta holds the largest deposit in the world. The Keystone pipeline was designed, for the most part, to move Canadian oil sand to refineries on the U.S. Gulf Coast.

9. Ezra Levant, *Ethical Oil: The Case for Canada's Oil Sands* (McClelland & Schuster, 2010).

10. "Changing Crude Oil Markets: Allowing Exports Could Reduce Consumer Fuel Prices," U.S. Government Accountability Office, September 30, 2014; see also: Bordof, Jason, "Navigating the U.S. Oil Export Ban." Columbia University Center on Global Energy, January 16, 2015.

11. Russell Gold, *The Boom: How Fracking Ignited the American Energy Revolution and Changed the World* (Simon & Schuster, 2015), 129.

12. Ibid., 54.

13. Fred Lawrence, "The Imperishable Permian Basin: Growing at 90," MasterResource blog May 17, 2013.

14. "Oil Legend Jim Henry and the Fathers of the Wolfberry," *Midland Reporter Telegram*, July 27, 2014; Corey Paul and taped telephone interview with Jim Henry August 25, 2015.

15. EIA, *Drilling Productivity Report*, August 2015.

16. EIA, *Drilling Productivity Report*, Permian Region, August 2015.

17. "OPEC Clout Hits New Low," *Wall Street Journal*, June 1, 2015; see also Bassam Fattou, Oxford Institute for Energy, "Current Oil Market Dynamics and the Role of OPEC," January 15, 2015.

18. "OPEC's Pricing Leverage Is Weakening," *Wall Street Journal*, March 31, 2015.

19. IHS, "US Position in Global Oil Supply Growth," EIA.gov/conference/2013.

20. Summer Said and Ahmed Al Omran, "Domestic Thirst for Oil Drives Saudi Pumps," *Wall Street Journal*, July 3, 2015, Sec. C.

21. Mark P. Mills, "Shale 2.0: Technology and the Coming Big-Data Revolution in America's Shale Oil Fields," Manhattan Institute, May 2015.

22. Stephen Moore, "How North Dakota Became Saudi Arabia: Harold Hamm, Discover of the Bakken Fields of the Northern Great Plains on America's Oil Future and Why OPEC's Days Are Numbered," *Wall Street Journal*, October 1, 2011.

23. EIA Today in Energy: North Dakota and Texas Now Provide Nearly Half of U.S. Crude Oil. July 1, 2014. Also Today in Energy; Five States and the Gulf of Mexico Produce More Than 80% of U.S. Crude Oil. March 31, 2014.

24. Congressional Research Service, U.S. Crude Oil and Natural Gas Production in Federal and Non-Federal Areas, April 10, 2014, http://energycommerce.house.gov/sites/republicans.energycommerce.house.gov/files/20140410CRS-US-crude-oil-natural-gas-production-federal-non-federal-areas.pdf; Bureau of Ocean Management, Combined Leasing Report, November 3,

2014, http://www.boem.gov/Combined-Leasing-Report-November
-2014/ and Institute for Energy Research, Outer Continental Shelf
Statistics, http://instituteforenergyresearch.org/analysis/outer-shelf-
ocs-statistics/; Bureau of Land Management, http://blm.gov/pgdata/
etc/medialib/blm/wo/MINERALS_REALTY_AND_
RESOURCE_PROTECTION_/energy/oil_gas_statistics/data_sets.
Par.67327.File.dat/table-03.pdf; Bureau of Land Management,
Source: BLM, Table 4, http://www.blm.gov/style/medialib/blm/wo/
MINERALS_REALTY_AND_RESOURCE_PROTECTION_/
energy/oil_gas_statistics/data_sets.Par80157.File.dat/
numberofacresleasedeachyear.pdf

25. Congressional Research Service, Federal Land Ownership:
Overview and Data, February 8, 2012.

26. EIA, Potential Oil Production from the Coastal Plain of the Arctic
National Wildlife Refuge: Updated Assessment, 3.

27. Cameron et al., "Central Arctic Caribou and Petroleum
Development: Distributional, Nutritional, and Reproductive
Implications, 58 ARCTIC 1, March 2005, http://pubs.aina.
ucalgary.ca/arctic/Arctic58-1-1.pdf and Arctic Report Card: Update
for 2011, http://www.arctic.noaa.gov/report11/reindeer.html.

28. EIA, "Potential Oil Production from the Coastal Plain of the Arctic
National Wildlife Refuge: Updated Assessment, 3, http://www.eia.
doe.gov/pub/oil_gas/petroleum/analysis_publications/arctic_
national_wildlife_refuge/html/summary.html and Free Republic,
Top 10 Reasons to Support Development in ANWR, http://
freerepublic.com/focus/f-news/2245453/posts.

29. Task Force on Strategic Unconventional Fuels, Development of
America's Strategic Unconventional Fuels Resources—Initial
Report to the President and the Congress of the United States,
September 2006, p. 5, Task Force on Strategic Unconventional
Fuels, December 2009, http://www.hsdl.org/?view&did=696499
and US Geological Survey, Oil Shale and Nahcolite Resources of
the Piceance Basin, Colorado, October 2010, p. 1, http://pubs.usgs.
gov/dds/dds-069/dds-069-y/.

30. Bureau of Ocean Management, Combined Leasing Report,
     November 3, 2014, http://www.boem.gov/Combined-Leasing-
     Report-November-2014/ and Institute for Energy Research, Outer
     Continental Shelf Statistics, http://instituteforenergyresearch.org/
     analysis/outer-continental-shelf-ocs-statistics/.
31. Bureau of Ocean Energy Management, Regulation and
     Enforcement, Outer Continental Shelf Oil & Gas Assessment,
     2006, http://www.boem.gov/About-BOEM/BOEM-Regions/
     Alaska-Region/Resource-Evaluation/RedNatAssessment.aspx.
32. "Why U.S. Oil Rigs Left the Gulf of Mexico for Brazil," *Forbes*,
     March 23, 2011.
33. Congressional Research Service Report, crs.com/98-993/document.
     php.
34. "Assessment of the Potential Impacts of Hydraulic Fracturing for
     Oil and Gas on Drinking Water Resources," U.S. Environmental
     Protection Agency, Office of Research and Development, June
     2015.
35. Robert L. Bradley Jr., *Capitalism At Work: Business, Government,
     and Energy* (M&M Scrivener Press, 2008), 198.
36. Ibid., 189.
37. Rupert Darwall, *The Age of Global Warming: A History* (Interlink
     Pub Group, 2014).
38. U.S. Energy Information Administration, *Monthly Energy Review*,
     "Table 1.1 Primary Energy Overview" & "Table 7.2a Electricity
     Net Generation: Total (All Sectors)," November 2015, http://www.
     eia.gov/totalenergy/data/monthly/index.cfm.

Chapter 3

1.   "A Tale of Two Oil States," *Wall Street Journal*, May 5, 2013.
2.   Daniel Cusick, "New Power Lines Will Make Texas the World's
     Fifth-Largest Wind Power Producer," E&E Publishing, February
     25, 2014.
3.   George Gilder, "The California Green Debauch," *American
     Spectator*, February 2011, 34–39.

4.   Nick Snow, "Industry Officials Attack Latest Call to Raise Oil and Gas Taxes," *Oil & Gas Journal*, November 7, 2011, http://www.ogj.com/articles/2011/11/industry-officials-attack-latest-call-to-raise-oil-gas-taxes.html.

5.   Mark P. Mills, "Oil, Gas, and Coal Can Prime the Jobs Pump: Which States will Benefit?," *Manhattan Institute for Policy Research*, October 2012, http://www.manhattan-institute.org/pdf/ir_30.pdf.

6.   "Shale Gas: Still a Boon to US manufacturing?," *Price Waterhouse Cooper*, December 2014, https://www.pwc.com/us/en/industrial-products/publications/assets/shale-gas-boosts-us-manufacturing.pdf.

7.   "Shale Gas, Competitiveness and new U.S. Chemical Industry Investment: An Analysis Based on Announced Projects," *From Chemistry to Energy*, American Chemical Council, September 10, 2015.

8.   Ibid.

9.   Bruno Waterfield, "Germany Is a Cautionary Tale of How Energy Policies Can Hurt the Economy," *The Telegraph*, January 16, 2014; see also M. Bastach, "CO2 Emissions Have Increased since 2011 Despite Germany's $140 Billion Green Energy Plan," *Daily Caller*, April 9, 2014.

10.   Rupert Darwall, "Clean Energy's Dirty Secrets," National Review Online, September 23, 2014.

11.   Barack Obama, Speech from the Oval Office, June 15, 2010.

12.   Barack Obama, "Remarks by the President on Energy," University of Miami, Miami, Florida, February 23, 2012, transcript available here http://insider.foxnews.com/2012/02/23/full-text-transcript-of-president-obamas-remarks-on-energy-at-university-of-miami.

13.   EIA Petroleum and Other Liquids: Drilling Productivity Report, December 7, 2015.

14.   Mark P. Mills, "Shale Wars Round Two: Congress Acts on Exports, Russia Capitulates on Price. And OPEC Blinks," *Forbes*, December 12, 2015.

Chapter 4

1. BP Annual Review of Energy, EIA.
2. Ibid.
3. Peter W. Huber and Mark P. Mills, *The Bottomless Well: The Twilight of Fuel, the Virtue of Waste, and Why We Will Never Run Out of Energy* (New York: Basic Books, 2005), 18.
4. David Landes, *The Unbound Prometheus*, (Cambridge Univ. Press 2008 Fourth Printing), 98.
5. Vaclav Smil, *Energy in Nature and Society: General Energetics of Complex Systems* (2007), 266.
6. Mark P. Mills, "The Cloud Begins with Coal: Big Data, Big Networks, Big Infrastructure, and Big Power," Digital Power Group, August 2013. Sponsored in part by National Mining Association and American Coalition for Clean Coal Electricity.
7. Michael Kelly, "Technology Introductions in the Context of Decarbonization: Lessons of Recent History," Global Warming Policy Foundation, London, GWPF Note 7.
8. BP Statistical Review of Energy, June 2015, EIA, IER World Outlook
9. Energy Information Administration, Monthly Energy Review, Table 1.3 Primary Energy Consumption by Source, November 2014, http://www.eia.gov/total/data/monthly/pdf/sec1_7.pdf.
10. Michael J. Kelly, "Technology Introductions in the Context of Decarbonization: Lessons from Recent History," Global Warming Policy Foundation, London, GWPF Note 7.
11. Ibid., 397.
12. Peter W. Huber and Mark P. Mills, *The Bottomless Well: The Twilight of Fuel, the Virtue of Waste, and Why We Will Never Run Out of Energy* (New York: Basic Books, 2005), 14.
13. Bjorn Lomborg, "This Child Does Not Need a Solar Panel," *Wall Street Journal*, October 22, 2015.
14. Caleb S. Rossiter, "Sacrificing Africa for Climate Change," *Wall Street Journal*, May 5, 2014, Sec. A.

15. Robert L. Bradley Jr. and Richard W. Fulmer, *Energy: The Master Resource* (2004), 4.

16. Matt Ridley, *The Rational Optimist* (2010), 231–32.

17. Vaclav Smil, *Power Density: A Key to Understanding Energy Sources and Uses* (MIT Press, May 2015).

18. *Consumer Reports*, "Ethanol as a Fuel Alternative," January 2011.

19. Vaclav Smil, *Energy and Nature in Society* (2007), Table A.8 Energy Flows and Stores at 393.

20. Robert L. Bradley Jr. and Richard W Fulmer, *Energy: The Master Resource* (Kendall/Hunt Publishing, Dubuque, 2004), at 8.

21. Vaclav Smil, "Power Density Primer: Understanding the Spatial Dimension of the Unfolding Transition to Renewable Electricity Generation (Part V-Comparing the Power Densities of Electricity Generation)," May 14, 2010, pdf available at www.masterresource.org.

22. Ibid.

23. Ibid.

24. Ibid., IEEE Spectrum.

25. Robert Bryce, *Power Hungry: The Myths of "Green" Energy and the Real Fuels of the Future* (PublicAffairs: 2010).

26. Ibid. Robert L. Bradley, Jr. and Richard W. Fuller, *Energy: The Master Resource* (2004).

27. Vaclav Smil, "The Limits of Energy Innovation," Project Syndicate, May 13, 2009. Limits of Energy Innovation.

28. Ibid, Vaclav Smil.

29. Ibid IEEE Spectrum.

30. Alan Moran, Ed., *Climate Change: The Facts*, "Chapter 1: The Science and Politics of Climate Change," Ian Plimer (Stockade Books, Institute of Public Affairs, Melbourne, 2015).

31. Richard S. Lindzen, "Climate Science: Is It Currently Designed to Answer Questions," Global Research (September 22, 2014), http://www.globalresearch_ca/climate-science-is-it-currently-designed-to-answer-questions/1630.

32. Christopher Booker, "Climate Change: This Is the Worst Scientific Scandal of Our Generation," *The Telegraph*, November 28, 2009; see also Rupert Darwall, *The Age of Global Warming: A History* (Quartet Books Limited, London, 2013), at 219–33.

33. IPCC 2013, "Summary for Policy Makers," in *Climate Change 2013: The Physical Science Basis. Contribution of Working Group I to Fifth Assessment Report of the Intergovernmental Panel on Climate Change of the United Nations*, T. F. Stocker et al., (Cambridge University Press, 2013).

34. Richard S. Lindzen, "Where Does Catastrophism Come From?," Presentation to Crossroads Summit of the Texas Public Policy Foundation, November 19, 2015.

35. Peter Huber and Mark P. Mills, *The Bottomless Well: The Twilight of Fuel, the Virtue of Waste, and Why We Will Never Run Out of Energy* (2007), at 98–100.

36. Paul Davies, *The Cosmic Jackpot: Why Our Universe Is Just Right for Life*, Houghton Mifflin Company, Boston (2007). First published in Great Britain by Penguin Press, 2009.

37. The Earth Observatory, "The Carbon Cycle." NASA, hppt:earthobservatory.NASA,gov/.

38. BBC-GCSE Physical Education: The Respiratory System: Inhaled and Exhaled Air.

39. Vaclav Smil, *Energy in Nature and Society*, MIT Press, (2008), at 327–30.

40. Ibid, Davies at p. 129.

41. M. Pidwirny, "The Solar Source of the Earth's Energy," *Fundamentals of Physical Geography, 2nd Edition* (2006), http://www.physicalgeography.net/fundamentals/6g.html.

42. Fritz Vahrenholt and Sebastian Luning, *The Neglected Sun* (2013) at 43.

43. Ibid. Vahrenholt at 40–41.

44. "Carbon Dioxide Benefits the World," White Paper of the CO2 Coalition, Will Happer Chairman, www.co2coalition.org.

45. Ibid IPCC 2013:Summary for Policy Makers, at 15.

46. "The Sun," NASA Cosmicopia, helios.gsfc.NASA.gov.

47. Richard P. Feynman, "What is Science," *The Physics Teacher* 7, no. 6, (1968), 313; see also, *Surely You're Joking, Mr. Feynman!* (Norton, 1985).

48. *American Heritage Dictionary* (Houghton Mifflin Company: 2006).

49. Fred Cottrell, *Energy and Society*, Revised ed. 2009 (1955), 32.

50. Vaclav Smil, *Energy: A Beginner's Guide* (2006), 14, 46–52.

51. Ibid., John Christy, *Testimony, December 8, 2015*. Note "The Disappointing Scientific Process," page 10.

52. Ibid.

53. John Horack and Roy Spencer, "Accurate Thermometers in Space: The State of Climate Measurement," *Nature*, October 2, 1997.

54. Michael Bastasch, "UN Climate Chief: Communism Is Best to Fight Global Warming," *Daily Caller*, January 15, 2014; "Biggest Emitter China Best on Climate Figueres Says," Bloomberg, January 14, 2015.

55. *Webster's New World Dictionary of the American Language* (The World Publishing Company: 1970).

56. Lewis Carroll, *Through the Looking Glass, and What Alice Found There* (1871).

57. Donella Meadows et al., *The Limits to Growth: A Report for the Club of Rome's Project on The Predicament of Mankind* (New York: Universe Books, 1972).

Chapter 5

1.   Matt Ridley, *The Rational Optimist* (2010), 245.

2.   Carolyn Dimitri et al., "The 20th Century Transformation of U.S. Agriculture and Farm Policy," *Electronic Information Bulletin 3* (June 2005); and U.S. Department of Commerce, Statistical Abstract of the United States 2011, p. 386.

3.   E. A. Wrigley, *Poverty, Progress, and Population* (Mar. 2004), 76.

4.   Cipolla, *Before the Industrial Revolution*, 276.

5. Vaclav Smil, *Energy in Nature and Society: General Energetics of Complex Systems* (2007) 397, Table A.15 Population and Primary Energy, 1500–2005.

6. Paul Ehrlich, *The Population Bomb* (1970); Lester Brown, *Beyond Malthus* (1999).

7. Julian Simon, *The Ultimate Resource 2* (Princeton University Press: 1996), 578.

8. Thomas Robert Malthus, *An Essay on the Principle of Population* (Anthony Flew, ed., 1970) (1798).

9. Ibid.

10. Malthus, *Essay*, 4.

11. E. A. Wrigley, *Energy and the English Industrial Revolution* (2010), 95.

12. Goklany, "The Pontifical Academies' Broken Moral Compass," The Global Warming Policy Foundation, London (2015).

13. Gregory Clark, *A Farewell to Alms: A Brief Economic History of the World* (2007), 92.

14. "Fossil Energy: A Brief History of Coal Use," U.S. Department of Energy: Fossil Energy, www.fossil.energy.gov.

15. "Coal to Remain Major Global Power Source," Institute for Energy Research, December 21, 2015; see also: http://www.thetimes.co.uk/tto/environment//article4629455.

16. "History of the World Petroleum Industry (Key Dates)"; "Gale Encyclopedia of U.S. History: Petroleum Industry."

17. Cipolla, *Before the Industrial Revolution*, 127.

18. Jon Meacham, *Thomas Jefferson: The Art of Power* (Random House: 2013).

19. Wrigley, *Energy and the English Industrial Revolution*, 91–101.

20. Ibid.

21. Ridley, *The Rational Optimist*, 216.

22. William Jevons, *The Coal Question: An Inquiry Concerning the Progress if the Nation, and the Probable Exhaustion of Our Coal Mines* (A.W. Flux ed., 1965) (1865) 2.

23. Wrigley, *Energy and the English Industrial Revolution*, 239.

24. Cipolla, *Before the Industrial Revolution.*
25. Astrid Kander, Paolo Malanima, and Paul Warde, *Power to the People: Energy in Europe Over the Last Five Centuries* (Princeton University Press: 2013), 7.
26. Ridley, *Rational Optimist,* 214–16.
27. Simon, *The Ultimate Resource 2.*
28. "Neolithic Revolution," *Encyclopedia Britannica.*
29. Smil, *Energy in Nature and Society,* 148.
30. Goklany, *Humanity Unbound,* 10.
31. Ridley, *Rational Optimist,* 214–16.
32. "The Fuel of the Future: Environmental Lunacy in Europe," *Economist,* April 6, 2013.
33. United Nations Foundation: Global Alliance for Clean Cook Stoves (2012).
34. Smil, *Energy in Nature and Society,* 188, 392.
35. Ibid.
36. E. A. Wrigley, *Continuity, Chance and Change: The Character of the Industrial Revolution in England* (New York, Cambridge University Press, 1988), 80.
37. MyLearning.org at http://www.mylearning.org/coal-mining-and-the-victorians/p-2070/.
38. Smil, *Energy in Nature and Society,* 175.
39. Ibid., 158.
40. E. Cook, *Man, Energy, Society* (San Francisco: W. H. Freeman, 1976).
41. Ibid., 231.
42. Smil, *Energy in Nature and Society,* 136.
43. Ridley, *Rational Optimist,* 216.
44. Smil, *Energy in Nature and Society,* 182.
45. Paul Warde, *Energy Consumption in England and Wales* (2007), 123–30.
46. Wrigley, *Continuity, Chance and Change* (New York: Cambridge University Press, 1988), 9.
47. Clark, *Farewell to Alms,* 1.

48. Ibid.
49. Vaclav Smil, *Energy at the Crossroads* (2003), preface.
50. Deirdre McCloskey, "The Great Enrichment," Unpublished Paper, 5, http://www.deirdremccloskey.org/docs/pdf/IndiaPaperMcCloskey .pdf.

Chapter 6

1. E. A. Wrigley, Energy and the English Revolution, p. 235.
2. Astrid Kander, Paolo Malanima and Paul Warde, Power to the People: Energy in Europe Over the Last Five Centuries (Princeton University Press, 2013) 8.
3. Gregory Clark, Farewell to Alms: A Brief Economic History of the World, (Princeton University Press 2007), 193.
4. Vaclav Smil, *Energy in Nature and Society*, MIT Press, 2008, p. 336.
5. David Landes is the author of the comprehensive history of the Industrial Revolution "The Unbound Prometheus" (Cambridge, 1969), now in its fourth printing. Other historians who also acknowledge the necessary role of fossil fuels in the Industrial Revolution are Fred Cottrell, Carlo Cipolla, Paul Warde, Astrid Kander, Paolo Malanima and Martin Wolf.
6. Ibid., 101.
7. Deirdre McCloskey, "The Great Enrichment: Came and Comes Ethics and Rhetoric," University of Illinois at Chicago and Gothenburg University. Unpublished Paper. See also Bourgeois Dignity: Why Economics Can't Explain the Modern World, University of Chicago Press 2010.
8. Ibid., Astrid Kander et al.
9. Landes, p. 9.
10. E. A. Wrigley, *Energy and the English Revolution* (Cambridge University Press, 2010) 17.
11. Wrigley, *Poverty*, 32.
12. Matt Ridley, *The Rational Optimist* (HarperCollins, 2010), 216.
13. Wrigley, *Poverty*, 80.

14. George Gilder, *Knowledge and Power* (Washington: Regnery Publishing, 2013), 57.

15. Indur Goklany.

16. Matt Ridley, *The Rational Optimist*, 232.

17. Angus Maddison, *The World Economy: Historical Statistics* (OECD, Paris, 2003).

18. Indur Goklany, *The Improving State of the World: Why We're Living Longer, Healthier, More Comfortable Lives on a Cleaner Planet* (CATO Institute, Washington D.C. 2007), 20.

19. Deirdre McCloskey, Bourgeois Dignity: Why Economics Can't Explain the Modern World (University of Chicago Press, 2010) 51.

20. Statistics on World Population.

21. Wrigley, *Energy and the English Industrial Revolution* (Cambridge University Press, New York, 2010), 95.

22. Robert L. Bradley Jr. and Richard W. Fulmer, *Energy: The Master Resource* (Kendall/Hunt Publishing, 2004) 197–215. Note this list of three hundred scientific and technological energy advances, especially the many that occurred in the 19th century.

23. Landes, 100.

24. Gregory Clark, 2007, 233.

25. Ibid., 234.

26. Astrid Kander, Paolo Malanima, and Paul Warde, *Power to the People: Energy in Europe over the Last Five Centuries* (Princeton University Press, 2013), 169.

27. Gilder, *Knowledge and Power*, 59.

28. Ibid., p. 60.

29. Vaclav Smil, *General Energetics: Energy in the Biosphere and Civilization* (John Wiley & Sons, 1991), 176.

30. "The Oil Industry: Steady as She Goes," *Economist*, April 20, 2006
.

31. Landes, 98.

32. Wrigley, Energy and the English Revolution, 194.

33. Landes, 102. See also Matt Ridley, 244 for his always lively discussion.

34. Landes, 97.
35. Mark P. Mills, "The Cloud Begins With Coal," (Sponsored by the American Coalition for Clean Coal Energy and the National Mining Association) Digital Power Group, August 2013.
36. Ibid., 10 and 14.
37. Energy Information Administration, Today in Energy: EIA Projects World Energy Consumption Will Increase by 65 percent through 2040.
38. William Jevons, *The Coal Question: An Inquiry Concerning the Progress of the Nation and the Probable Exhaustion of Our Coal Mines* (A. W. Flux, ed., 1965), (1865) 2.
39. Tom Randal, "America Is Winning a Race that It Never Signed Up For," Bloomberg (November 4. 2013). See also EIA U.S. Carbon Dioxide Emissions 2014 (November 23, 2015).
40. Ridley, 218.
41. Wrigley, *Energy*, 208.
42. Clark, 1–3.
43. Clark, 1–3.
44. Goklany, Humanity Unbound, 8.
45. Ridley, 219.
46. Ibid., 218.
47. Wrigley, **Energy**, 60–63, 208.
48. Gilder, *Knowledge and Power*, 57.
49. Fred Cottrell, Energy and Society: The Relation Between Energy, Social Change and Economic Development, (Author/House, Bloomington Indiana, 2009). Revised Edition. First published 1955, McGraw Book Company, New York.
50. Wrigley, *Continuity*, 78.
51. Clark.
52. Kenneth Pomeranz, *The Great Divergence: China, Europe and Making of the World Economy* (Princeton University Press, 2000).
53. International Energy Agency, World Energy Outlook 2012, The World Bank Development Indicators 2012. CIA World Factbook 2012.

54. Practical Action Poor People's Energy Outlook 2013: Energy for Community Services, Rugby UK: Practical Action Publishing.
55. Ibid.
56. Saeed Shah, "Power Outages Hobbles Pakistan's Biggest Exporters," *Wall Street Journal*, November 29, 2013.
57. Guatam N. Yadana, "Fires, Fuels and the Fate of Three Billion: The State of the Energy Impoverished," 2013.
58. B. Sudhakara Reddy and Hippu Salk Kristle Nathan, "Energy Development Strategy of Indian Households-The Missing Half," Indira Ghandi Institute of Development Research, 2012.
59. Patrick McGroarty, "Blackouts Dim South African Power," *Wall Street Journal*, July 3, 2015.
60. Caleb Rossiter, "Sacrificing Africa for Climate Change," *Wall Street Journal*, May 4, 2014.
61. Bjorn Lomborg, "This Child Does Not Need a Solar Panel," *Wall Street Journal*, October 21, 2015.
62. Todd Moss et al., "Balancing Energy Access and Environmental Goals in Development Finance: The Case of the OPIC Carbon Cap," Center for Global Development, April 3, 2014.
63. Indur Goklany, "The Pontifical Academies' Broken Moral Compass," The Global Warming Policy Foundation, London, 2015.
64. Benny Peiser, Ph.D., Testimony to the Committee on Environment and Public Works of the United States Senate, Hearing on the Super Pollutant Act of 2014, Washington, D.C., December 2, 2014.
65. Quoted in Byatt, I. 2008 Climate Change Policies: Challenging the Activists. Institute of Economic affairs.

Chapter 7

1. Vaclav Smil, Enriching the Earth: Fritz Haber, Carl Bosch, and the Transformation of World Food Production (2004), 199.
2. Ibid.
3. "Neolithic Revolution," Encyclopedia Britannica, accessed April 1, 2014.

4.   Indur Goklany, *The Improving State of the World* (2007), 59–64;
     Leon Hesser, *The Man Who Fed The World* (Durbin Publishing
     Co., 2006); Ridley, *The Rational Optimist*, at 143.
5.   Madeline Chambers, "German 'Green Revolution' May Cost 1
     Trillion Euros–Minister," Reuters (Feb. 20, 2013) http://www.
     reuters.com/assets/print?aid=USBRE91J0AV20130220/.
6.   Smil, *Enriching*, at 116.
7.   Erisman, J. W., Sutton, M. A., Galloway, J., Klimont, Z., and
     Winiwarte, W., "How a Century of Ammonia Synthesis Changed
     the World," *Nature Geoscience* (2008), 636–39.
8.   W. M. Stewart, D. W. Dibb, A. E. Johnston, and T. J. Smith, "The
     Contribution of Commercial Fertilizer Nutrients to Food
     Production," *Agronomy Journal* Vol. 97 No. 1 (2005), 1–6.
9.   Smil, Enriching, at 119.
10. Hesser, The Man Who Fed the World; *New York Times* Obituary
     (Sept. 13, 2009).
11. E. Borlaug, The Green Revolution: Peace and Humanity: A Speech
     on the Occasion of the Awarding of the 1970 Nobel Peace Prize in
     Oslo, Norway (December 11, 1970).
12. Norman Borlaug, on World Hunger, 1997. Edited by Anwar Dil.
     San Diego/Islamabad/Lahore: Bookservice International.
13. Indur M. Goklany, *Humanity Unbound: How Fossil Fuels Saved
     Humanity from Nature and Nature from Humanity*, Cato Institute
     (Dec. 2012), footnote 64.
14. Ibid., footnote 41.
15. Ibid., at 10.
16. T. J Blom, W. A. Straver, F. J. Ingratta, Shalin Khosla, and Wayne
     Brown, "Carbon Dioxide in Greenhouses: Fact Sheet," Ministry
     of Agricultural, Food, and Rural Affairs, (Dec. 2012), http://www.
     omafra.gov.on.ca/english/crops/facts/00-077.htm.
17. Craig D. Idso, "The Positive Externalities of Carbon Dioxide:
     Estimating the Monetary Benefits of Rising Atmospheric CO2
     Concentrations on Global Food Production," Center for the Study
     of Carbon Dioxide and Global Change, (Oct. 2013).

18. Strain, B. R. (1978) "Report of the Workshop on Anticipated Plant Responses to Global Carbon Dioxide Enrichment." Department of Botany, Duke University, Durham, N.C.

19. Lemon, E. R. (Ed.), 1983. "CO2 and Plants: The Response of Plants to Rising Levels of Atmospheric Carbon Dioxide," (Westview Press, Boulder, Colo.).

20. Craig D. Idso and Sherwood B. Idso, *The Many Benefits of Atmospheric CO2 Enrichment* (Vales Lake Publishing, Pueblo West, Colo., 2011); Craig D. Idso, "The Debt We Owe to Atmospheric CO2 enrichment."

21. http://www3.epa.gov/climatechange/Downloads/EPAactivities/social-cost-carbon.pdf

22. Idso, "The Positive Externalities of Carbon Dioxide."

23. Food and Agriculture Organization, "2013 FAO Statistics Database: Rome, Italy."

24. E. C. Oerke, "Centenary Review: Crop Losses to Pests," *Journal of Agricultural Science* 144 (2006), 31–43.

25. Jenny Gustavsson, Christel Cederberg, Ulf Sonesson, Robert van Otterdijk, and Alexandre Meybeck, *Global Food Losses and Food Waste* (Rome: FAO, 2011), p. v.

26. Pierre Desrochers and Hiroko Shimizu, "The Locavores' Dilemma," *Public Affairs*, (2012).

27. Rod Dreher, *Crunchy Cons* (New York: Random House, 2006), 62.

28. USDA, "Know Your Farmer, Know Your Food," www.usda.gov/knowyourfarmer.

29. Food and Agriculture Organization, "The State of Food Insecurity in the World: 2011–2013."

30. US DOE Alternative Fuels Data Center http://www.afdc.energy.gov/data/tab/all/data_set/10339

31. Smil, Energy at the Crossroads and USDA Major Uses of Land in the United States, (2002 ERS), 264.

32. "Iowa Ethanol Plants and Production Facilities," Iowa Corn Growers Association, IowaCorn.org.

33. Joseph Fargione et al., Land Clearing and the Biofuel Carbon Debt. 319 *Science* 1235 (2008).

34. Kim, D. & Leigh, J. P. (2010) "Estimating the Effects of Wages on Obesity," *Journal of Occupational and Environmental Medicine*, 52(5), 495–500.

35. "Things Made From Oil That We Use Daily: 144 of 6000 Items," www.ranken-energy.com/products.

36. Grecia R. Matos, "Use of Minerals and Materials in the U.S. From 1900 through 2006," U.S. Geological Survey Fact Sheet 2009–3008.

37. Goklany, *Humanity Unbound*, at 11.

38. Ibid.

Chapter 8

1. Jerry Hirsch, "Elon Musk's Growing Empire Is Fueled By $4.9 Billion in Government Subsidies," *Los Angeles Times*, May 30, 2015, http://www.latimes.com/business/la-fi-hy-musk-subsidies-20150531-story.html.

2. U.S. Energy Information Administration, "Table 1.2 Primary Energy Production by Source," *Monthly Energy Review*, November 24, 2015. https://www.eia.gov/totalenergy/data/monthly/#electricity; U.S. Energy Information Administration, "Table 7.2a Electricity Net Generation: Total (All Sectors)," *Monthly Energy Review*, November 24, 2015, https://www.eia.gov/totalenergy/data/monthly/#electricity.

3. The Honorable Adam Sieminski, "Statement of Adam Sieminski," Testimony before Subcommittee on Energy, Committee on Science, Space and Technology, U.S. House of Representatives, February 13, 2013, https://science.house.gov/legislation/hearings/subcommittee-energy-american-energy-outlook-technology-market-and-policy.

4. The Clean Power Plan, Environmental Protection Agency, August 3, 2015, https://www.whitehouse.gov/the-press-office/2015/08/03/fact-sheet-president-obama-announce-historic-carbon-pollution-standards.

5. U.S. Energy Information Administration, "International Energy Outlook 2013", October 2013, http://www.eia.gov/forecasts/archive/ieo13/.

6. Michael Kelly, "Mitigating C02 Emissions: A Busted Flush," Climate Etc., February 23, 2015, http://judithcurry.com/2015/02/23/mitigating-co2-emissions-a-busted-flush/.

7. U.S. Department of Energy, US Energy Information Administration, Annual Energy Outlook 2015, Page ES-7, http://www.eia.gov/forecasts/aeo/pdf/0383(2015).pdf.

8. http://www.eia.gov/totalenergy/data/monthly/#electricity.

9. Diane Cardwell and Matthew Wald, "A Huge Solar Plant Opens, Facing Doubts About Its Future," New York Times, February 13, 2014, http://www.nytimes.com/2014/02/14/business/energy-environment/a-big-solar-plant-opens-facing-doubts-about-its-future.html?_r=0.

10. U.S. Energy Information Agency, "Monthly Energy Review November 2015," Table 7.2a Electricity Net Generation: Total (All Sectors), November 1, 2015, http://www.eia.gov/totalenergy/data/monthly/index.cfm; U.S. Energy Information Agency, "Monthly Energy Review November 2015," Table 1.2 Primary Energy Production by Source, November 1, 2015. http://www.eia.gov/totalenergy/data/monthly/index.cfm; Department of Energy, Energy Information Administration, "Direct Federal Financial Interventions and Subsidies in Energy in Fiscal Year 2010," Table ES2. Quantified Energy-Specific Subsidies and Support By Type, FY 2010 and 2007, July 2011, https://www.eia.gov/analysis/requests/subsidy/archive/2010/pdf/subsidy.pdf.

11. U.S. Energy Information Administration, "International Energy Outlook 2013", October 2013, http://www.eia.gov/forecasts/archive/ieo13/.

12. International Energy Agency, Energy Technology Perspectives 2015, May 2015, http://www.iea.org/etp/etp2015/.

13. Ibid.

14. The White House, Office of the Press Secretary, "Remarks by the President to the Nation on the BP Oil Spill," June 15, 2010, https://www.whitehouse.gov/the-press-office/remarks-president-nation-bp-oil-spill.

15. Julian Simon, *The Ultimate Resource* (Princeton University Press, 1981).

16. Rob Wile, "Yes, Falling Oil Prices Are Derailing the Future of Renewable Energy," *Fusion*, May 4, 2015, http://fusion.net/story/130014/yes-falling-oil-prices-are-derailing-the-future-of-renewable-energy/.

17. Ibid.

18. Mark P. Mills, "The Clean Power Plan Will Collide with the Incredibly Weird Physics of the Electric Grid," *Forbes*, August 7, 2015, http://www.forbes.com/sites/markpmills/2015/08/07/the-clean-power-plan-will-collide-with-the-incredibly-weird-physics-of-the-electric-grid/.

19. Mark P. Mills, "Tesla Derangement Syndrome," *Forbes*, September 18, 2014, http://www.forbes.com/sites/markpmills/2014/09/18/tesla-derangement-syndrome/.

20. Lewis Page, "Renewable Energy 'Simply Won't Work: Top Google Engineers," *The Register*, November 21, 2014, http://www.theregister.co.uk/2014/11/21/renewable_energy_simply_wont_work_google_renewables_engineers/.

21. "Google's Green PPAs: What, How, and Why," Google, September 17, 2013, page 2, https://static.googleusercontent.com/media/www.google.com/en//green/pdfs/renewable-energy.pdf.

22. "Filling the Solar Sinkhole: Billions of Bucks Have Delivered Too Little Bang," Taxpayer Protection Alliance, February 12, 2015, http://protectingtaxpayers.org/assets/files/solar-report-february-12.pdf.

23. "Direct Federal Financial Interventions and Subsidies in Energy in Fiscal Year 2010," Department of Energy, Energy Information Administration, July 2011, Table ES2, Quantified Energy-Specific

Subsidies and Support By Type, https://www.eia.gov/analysis/requests/subsidy/archive/2010/pdf/subsidy.pdf.

24. "EIA Report: Subsidies Continue to Roll In For Wind and Solar," Institute for Energy Research, March 18, 2015, http://instituteforenergyresearch.org/analysis/eia-subsidy-report-solar-subsidies-increase-389-percent/.

25. "Direct Federal Financial Interventions and Subsidies in Energy in Fiscal Year 2010," Department of Energy, Energy Information Administration, July 2011, Table ES6, Subsidies and Support To Fuels Used Outside of The Electricity Sector, https://www.eia.gov/analysis/requests/subsidy/archive/2010/pdf/subsidy.pdf.

26. "Energy and Taxes: Economic Growth and Fairness,"American Petroleum Institute, September 2015, http://www.americanpetroleuminstitute.com/Policy-and-Issues/Policy-Items/Taxes/Energy-and-Taxes.

27. Molly F. Sherlock and Jeffrey M. Stupak, "Energy Tax Policy: Issues in the 114th Congress," Congressional Research Service, September 4, 2015, p. 13, http://nationalaglawcenter.org/wp-content/uploads/assets/crs/R43206.pdf.

28. Ibid.

29. "DeMint, Lee Bill Would End Corporate Welfare for Energy Companies in Tax Code," Office of U.S. Senator Mike Lee, Press Release, February 2, 2012, http://www.lee.senate.gov/public/index.cfm/press-releases?ID=0f3af655-14ca-428c-b6dd-fc413841fd0e.

30. "Form S-1 Registration Statement," SolarCity Corporation, October 5, 2012, http://www.sec.gov/Archives/edgar/data/1408356/000119312512416770/d229977ds1.htm.

31. Congressman Paul Gosar, U.S. House of Representatives, Letter to Federal Trade Commission Chairwoman Edith Ramirez, December 12, 2014, http://gosar.house.gov/sites/gosar.house.gov/files/Final%20Signed%2012%2012%2014%20letter%20to%20the%20FTC%20regarding%20third-party%20rooftop%20solar%20leases.pdf.

32. Ibid.

33. https://www.solarcity.com/

34. Stephen Lacey, "Sunrun Faces Class Action Lawsuit Over Its Marketing," *Greentech Media*, February 21, 2013, http://www. greentechmedia.com/articles/read/sunrun-class-action-complaint; Kyle Barnett, "$5 Million At Stake in Class Action Lawsuit Claiming Solar Panel Installation Companies Lied About Electricity Cost Savings," *Louisiana Record*, February 12, 2014, http:// louisianarecord.com/stories/510584360-5-million-at-stake-in-class-action-lawsuit-claiming-solar-panel-installation-companies-lied-about-electricity-cost-savings.

35. Ibid.

36. Umair Irfan, "Solar, utility companies clash over changes to net metering," *E&E News*, September 3, 2013, http://www.eenews. net/stories/1059986606.

37. Stephen Moore and Joel Griffith, "How These Green Companies Are Gouging Consumers With The Government's Help," The Heritage Foundation, *Daily Signal*, January 18, 2015, http:// dailysignal.com/2015/01/18/how-these-green-companies-are-gouging-consumers-with-the-governments-help/.

38. Travis Hoium, "How Will Residential Solar Play Out in the U.S.?" *The Motley Fool*, June 16, 2014, http://www.fool.com/investing/general/2014/06/16/how-will-residential-solar-play-out-in-the-us. aspx.

39. "Energy's Loan Guarantee Program," *Washington Post*, September 26, 2011, https://www.washingtonpost.com/business/economy/energys-loan-guarantee-program/2011/09/26/gIQAKDDI0K_graphic.html.

40. Barack Obama, "State of the Union Address," 2011 State of the Union delivered at the Capitol Building, Washington, D.C., January 25, 2011, https://www.whitehouse.gov/the-press-office/2011/01/25/remarks-president-state-union-address.

41. U.S. Department of Energy, News Release, "U.S. Energy Secretary Chu Announces $528 Million Loan for Advanced Vehicle Technology for Fisker Automotive," U.S. Department of Energy,

September 22, 2009, http://energy.gov/articles/us-energy-secretary-chu-announces-528-million-loan-advanced-vehicle-technology-fisker.

42. Dashiell Bennett, "The Real Lesson of Fisker Auto's Failure," *The Wire*, April 24, 2013, http://www.thewire.com/business/2013/04/fisker-automotive-failure/64544/.

43. "Fisker to Romney: We're Not 'A Loser'," Fox News, October 4, 2012, http://www.foxnews.com/leisure/2012/10/04/fisker-to-romney-were-not-loser/.

44. http://securities.stanford.edu/filings-documents/1051/AONE00_02/2014327_r01c_13CV06883.pdf

45. DOE's Loan Program Office, Corporate Quarterly Credit Report (Dec. 12, 2011).

46. Ibid.

47. Deepa Seetharaman and Paul Lienert, "Special Report: Bad Karma: How Fisker Burned Through $1.4 billion on a 'green' car," Reuters, June 17, 2013, http://www.reuters.com/article/us-autos-fisker-specialreport-idUSBRE95G02L20130617.

48. Peter W. Davidson, "An Update on Fisker Automotive and the Energy Department's Loan Portfolio," U.S. Department of Energy, September 17, 2013, http://energy.gov/articles/update-fisker-automotive-and-energy-department-s-loan-portfolio.

49. "Fisker Karma earns a failing grade from Consumer Reports," *Consumer Reports* (Sept. 25, 2012) http://www.consumerreports.org/cro/news/2012/09/fisker-karma-earns-a-failing-grade-from-consumer-reports/index.htm.

50. Alan Ohnsman, "Fisker's Karma 'Full of Flaws,' Consumer Reports Says," *Bloomberg* (Sept. 25, 2012) http://www.bloomberg.com/news/articles/2012-09-25/fisker-s-karma-full-of-flaws-consumer-reports-says.

51. U.S. Department of Energy, Loan Programs Office, "Advanced Technology Vehicles Manufacturing Loan Program Overview 2015," September 2014, http://www.energy.gov/sites/prod/files/2015/02/f19/ATVM_Program_Overview_2015.pdf.

52. Kevin A. Hassett, "Ethanol's A Big Scam, and Bush Has Fallen For It," *American Enterprise Institute*, February 13, 2006, http://www.aei.org/publication/ethanols-a-big-scam-and-bush-has-fallen-for-it/.

53. Matthew L. Wald, "Food vs. Fuel in 2013," *New York Times*, December 24, 2012, http://green.blogs.nytimes.com/2012/12/24/food-vs-fuel-in-2013/?_r=0.

54. Institute for Energy Research, "Government Forces Refiners To Pay Fine For Nonexistent Ethanol," January 12, 2012, http://instituteforenergyresearch.org/analysis/government-forces-refiners-to-pay-fine-for-nonexistent-ethanol/.

55. Institute for Energy Research, "Government Forces Refiners to Pay Fine for Nonexistent Ethanol," January 12, 2012, http://instituteforenergyresearch.org/analysis/government-forces-refiners-to-pay-fine-for-nonexistent-ethanol/.

56. Ibid.

57. National Research Council, National Academy of Sciences, *Renewable Fuel Standard: Potential Economic and Environmental Effects of U.S. Biofuel Policy* (Washington, D.C., 2011), http://www.nap.edu/read/13105/chapter/1.

58. Ucilia Wang, "Obama's $510M Bet To Boost Biofuels for the Military," *Gigaom Research*, August 16, 2011, https://gigaom.com/2011/08/16/obamas-510m-bet-to-boost-biofuels-for-the-military/.

59. Clifford Krauss, "Dual Turning Point for Biofuels," *New York Times*, April 14, 2014, http://www.nytimes.com/2014/04/15/business/energy-environment/dual-turning-point-for-biofuels.html?_r=1.

60. Institute for Energy Research, "National Academy of Sciences: Renewable Fuel Standard Goals Unlikely To Be Met," October 17, 2011, http://instituteforenergyresearch.org/analysis/national-academy-of-sciences-renewable-fuel-standard-goals-unlikely-to-be-met/.

61. Ira Boudway, "The Five Million Green Jobs That Weren't," *Bloomberg Business*, October 11, 2012, http://www.bloomberg. com/bw/articles/2012-10-11/the-5-million-green-jobs-that-werent.

62. Alex Fitzsimmons, "The Department of Energy Committed $11 Million Per Job," Institute for Energy Research, May 8, 2013, http://instituteforenergyresearch.org/analysis/does-11-million-jobs/.

63. U.S. Department of Labor, Office of the Inspector General, Office of Audit, "Recovery Act: Slow Pace Placing Workers Into Jobs Jeopardizes Employment Goals of the Green Jobs Program," Report No. 18-11-004-03-390, https://www.oig.dol.gov/public/ reports/oa/2011/18-11-004-03-390.pdf.

64. Committee on Oversight and Government Reform, U.S. House of Representatives, "How Obama's Green Energy Agenda is Killing Jobs," *Staff Report*, September 22, 2011, http://oversight.house. gov/wp-content/uploads/2012/02/9-22-2011_Staff_Report_ Obamas_Green_Energy_Agenda_Destroys_Jobs.pdf.

65. Ibid.

Chapter 9

1. "ETS, RIP?: The Failure to Reform the EU Carbon Market Will Reverberate Around the World," *Economist* (print edition), April 20, 2013; see also, The European Commission's Emission Trading System," http://ec.europa.eu/clima/publications/.

2. John Gapper, "Cheap Energy Is the New Cheap Labor," *Financial Times*, February 26, 2014.

3. *Economist, Die Zeit, Washington Post, Financial Times, WJS, German Business Journal, Forbes*.

4. "Germany's Energy Poverty: How Electricity Became a Luxury Good," *Der Spiegel*, September 4, 2013.

5. Institute for Energy Research, "Germany's Electric Market Out of Balance," page 3 of 9 (August 22, 2014) http://instituteforenergy research.org/analysis/germanys-electricity-market-balance-must- pay-flexible-back-power/.

6. Ibid, *Der Spiegel*.

7. Jeevan Vasagar, "Germans Told of Billions Lost to Trade Due To Energy Policy," *Financial Times* (February 26, 2014. http://on.ft.com/1cRFiKb 6.

8. Vaclav Smil, "Germany's Energy Goals Backfire," *The American*, Journal of the American Enterprise Institute, February 14, 2014.

9. Ibid.

10. Benny Peiser, Dr., Testimony to the Committee on Environment and Public Works of the United States Senate, Hearing on the Super Pollutants Act of 2014 (S. 2911), December 2, 2014. The Global Warming Policy Foundation.

11. Ibid.

12. Derek Birkett, *When Will the Lights Go Out: Britain's Looming Energy Crisis*, Stacey International, London, (2010).

13. Ibid.

14. Hans Poser et al., "Development and Integration of Renewable Energy: Lessons Learned from Germany," FAA Financial Advisory AG (Fina Advice), p. 44.

15. David Garman and Samuel Thernstrom, "Europe's Renewable Romance Fades," *Wall Street Journal*, July 29, 2013.

16. Kiley Kroh, "Germany Sets New Record, Generating74% Percent of Power Needs from Renewable Energy," Climate Progress, (May13, 2014) Oilprice.com, http://oilprice.com/Alternative-Energy/Renewable-Energy/Germany-Hits-Historic-High-Gets-74-Percent-Of-Energy-From-Renewables.html.

17. Jennifer Rankin and Patrick Butler, "Winter Deaths Rose by Almost a Third in 2012–13" (November 26, 2013) *The Guardian*, http://www.theguardian.com/uk-news/2013/nov/26/winter-deaths-rose-third.

18. Rupert Darwall, "Energy Policy: A Disaster in the Making" IoD Big Picture, (Feb. 24, 2015).

19. Andrew Orlowski, "UK Preps World War 2 Energy Rationing to Keep the Lights On," *Register*, June 10, 2014; see also Kathleen Hartnett White, "Renewable Energy Danger: Wealth Transfer from Poor to Rich" (January 16, 2015) *Investor's Business Daily*, http://

news.investors.com/ibd-editorials-on-the-right/011615-735189-renewable-energy-a-wealth-redistribution-scheme.htm?p=2.

20. Justin Gillis, "A Tricky Transition From Fossil Fuel," *New York Times*, November 10, 2014.

21. "Wood: the Fuel of the Future – Environmental Lunacy in Europe," *Economist*, April 6, 2013.

22. Nathanael Greene and Sasha Lyutse, "Forests Not Fuel: Burning Trees for Energy Increases Carbon Pollution and Destroys Our Forests" (August 2011) Natural Resources Defense Council (NRDC), page 2, https://www.nrdc.org/energy/forestsnotfuel/files/forests-not-fuel.pdf.

23. Peter Lehner, Natural Resources Defense Council, "Burning Trees for Electricity is Actually Dirtier Than Coal," EcoWatch, February 2, 2015, http://ecowatch.com/2015/02/20/burning-trees-electricity-dirtier-than-coal/.

24. Ibid.

25. Ibid.

26. Jurgen Kronig, "Energy Policy in Germany: Big Problems in Europe's Powerhouse," Policy Network, March 27, 2014, http://www.policy-network.net/pno_detail.aspx?ID=4612&title=Energy-policy-in-Germany-Big-problems-in-Europes-powerhouse.

27. Barbara Hendricks, "How Germany Banishes Climate Myths," CNN interview, December 18, 2014, http://www.cnn.com/2014/12/18/opinion/hendricks-germany-climate-change/.

28. Ibid.

29. Gregor Schmitz, "Europe to Ditch Climate Protection Goals," Spiegel Online, January 15, 2014. See also Michael Bastasch, "EU Dismantles Its Climate Commission Amid Economic Struggles," *Daily Caller*, September 12, 2014.

30. Matthew Karnitschnig, "Germany's Expensive Gamble on Renewable Energy," *Wall Street Journal*, August 26, 2014.

31. Jan Hromadko, "Yergin: Germany Must Focus on Cost-Effective Renewable Energy," *Wall Street Journal*, February 26, 2014.

32. Rob Taylor and Rhiannon Hoyle, "Australia Becomes first Developed Nation to Repeal Carbon Tax," *Wall Street Journal*, July 17, 2014.

33. Liberal.org.au, "Scrapping the Carbon Tax and Reducing the Cost of Living," http://www.liberal.org.au/scrapping-carbon-tax-and-reducing-cost-living.

34. Ibid.

Chapter 10

1. Energy Information Administration, "Carbon Intensity of the U.S. Economy 1949–2012, (October 2013).

2. Energy Information Administration, Monthly Energy Review, Tablee 1.3 Primary Energy Consumption by Source, November 2014, http://www.eia.gov/totalenergy/data/monthly/pdf/sec1_7.pdf.

3. "Global Carbon Emissions Set to Reach Record 36 Billion Tons in 2013," Phys.org (Nov. 18, 2013).

4. Steven F. Hayward, *2011 Almanac of Environmental Trends*, Pacific Research Institute Apr. 2011). Data from EPA "Our Nation's Air: Status and Trends through 2010."

5. "Jackson Gets Real," *Politico Morning Energy* (October 24, 2011). EPA Administrator Lisa Jackson's statement in an appearance on "Real Time with Bill Maher," reported by Politico (October 24, 2011).

6. Indur Goklany, "Saving Habitat and Conserving Biodiversity on a Crowded Planet," *BioScience* 48 (1998).

7. World Resources Institute, "Avoiding Bioenergy Competition for Food Crops and Land" (Jan. 2015).

8. Ibid., Liska, A. et al., "Biofuels from Crop Residue Can Reduce Soil Carbon and Increase CO2 Emissions," *Nature Climate Change* (Apr. 20, 2014) http://www.nature.com/nclimate/journal/v4/n5/full/nclimate2187.html.

9. Jesse Ausubel, "Big Green Energy Machines." American Institute of Physics, October/November 2004. Based on an address at

Millennium Technology Prize Symposium, Espoo, Finland (June 14, 2004).

10. "Green Revolution? Germany's Brown Coal Power Hits New High," *Der Spiegel* (Jan. 7, 2014).

11. Searchinger, T. and R. Heimlich, World Resources Institute (WRI), "Avoiding Bioenergy Competition for Food Crops and Land." Working Paper, Installment 9 of "Creating a Sustainable Food Future" (Washington, DC: World Resources Institute, 2015).

12. Indur Goklany, *Humanity Unbound: How Fossil Fuels Saved Humanity from Nature and Nature from Humanity* (Cato Institute: Dec. 2012), 17.

13. Goklany, *Humanity Unbound*, 18.

14. Ibid.

15. "Monthly Energy Review," U.S. Energy Information Association (Feb. 2014) Table 7.2a.

16. Robert Bradley and Richard Fulmer, *Energy: The Master Resource, Kendall/Hunt Publishing Company* (2004) 39. Brown Coal Power Hits New High," *Der Spiegel* (Jan. 7, 2014); Searchinger, T. and R. Heimlich, World Resources Institute (WRI), "Avoiding Bioenergy Competition for Food Crops and Land." Working Paper, Installment 9 of "Creating a Sustainable Food Future" (Washington, DC: World Resources Institute, 2015); Indur Goklany, *Humanity Unbound: How Fossil Fuels Saved Humanity from Nature and Nature from Humanity* (Cato Institute: Dec. 2012) 17; Goklany, *Humanity Unbound*, 18; Ibid.; "Monthly Energy Review," U.S. Energy Information Association (Feb. 2014) Table.

17. Vaclav Smil, *Power Density* (MIT Press: 2015) 208.

18. American Bird Conservancy, http://abcbirds.org/.

19. Ibid.

20. E.A. Wrigley, *Energy and the English Industrial Revolution*, Cambridge University Press (2010), p. 99.

21. Rt. Hon. Amber Rudd, PM, Department of Energy and Climate, Speech to the Institution of Civil Engineers, London (Nov. 18, 2014).

22. Kenneth Pennock, "Simulation of Wind Generation Patterns for the ERCOT Service Area" (May 23, 2012) prepared for ERCOT by AWS Truepower LLC.

23. Lewis Page, "Renewable Energy 'Simply Won't Work': Top Google Engineers," *The Register* (Nov. 21, 2014).

24. Ibid.

25. Matthew Wald, "Google Pulls the Plug on a Renewable Energy Effort," *New York Times* (Nov. 28, 2011).

26. Editorial Board "Boiler Room Politics," *Wall Street Journal*, March 4, 2011.

27. Hayward, *2011 Almanac of Environmental Trends*.

28. Kathleen Hartnett White, "EPA's Approaching Regulatory Avalanche," Texas Public Policy Foundation (Feb. 2012).

29. Mike Nasi, "Impacts of the EPA's Clean Power Plan on Electricity Markets," Balanced Energy for Texas, November 10, 2015. Sources: EPA, Greenhouse Mitigation Measures TSD Final Rule.

30. Federal Electric Reliability Council; North American Electric Reliability Corporation, "2010 Special Reliability Scenario Assessment: Resource Adequacy Impacts of Potential U.S. Environmental Regulations" (Oct. 2010).

31. Stephen Moore and Kathleen White, "EPA's Goofy Green Energy Rules," *Investors' Business Daily* (Nov. 30, 2014).

32. Occupational Health and Safety Administration, "Permissible Exposure Limits for Carbon Dioxide." http://osha/dts/dataCH-225400.html.

33. Will Happer, Cyrus Fogg Brackett, Professor of Physics (emeritus) Princeton University, Testimony to Committee on Environment and Public Works of United States Senate (Feb. 25, 2009).

34. White House, "The Health Impacts of Climate Change on Americans" (June 2014), 1–7.

35. Ibid.

36. Don't mistake carbon monoxide (CO) for carbon dioxide (CO2) as some scientifically illiterate journalists do. CO is a lethal inhalant

that at high enough concentrations, typically within an enclosed space like a garage, can kill you. CO2 amplifies plant growth.

37. Fox News Poll with Anderson Robins Research and Shaw and Company Research (Nov. 15–16, 2015).

38. Kathleen Hartnett White, "EPA's Pretense of Science: Regulating Phantom Risks," Texas Public Policy Foundation (May 2012). See also Anne Smith, Ph.D., "An Evaluation of the PM 2.5 Health Benefits Estimates for Regulatory Impact Analysis of recent Air Regulations," NERA (Dec. 2011); and Anthony (Tony) Cox, Jr., "Reassessing the Human Health Benefits from Clean Air," *Risk Analysis* (Nov. 2011).

39. David Ropeik and George Gray, *Risk: Practical Guide for Deciding What's Really Safe and What's Really Dangerous in the World Around You* (Houghton Mifflin Company: 2002).

40. Testimony of EPA Administrator Lisa Jackson before the United States House of Representatives Committee on Energy and Commerce (Sept. 22, 2011).

41. Cox, Smith, supra note 32.

42. White, "Pretense of Science," 8.

43. Jackson, supra note 34.

44. Chairman Lamar Smith, Committee on Science, Space and Technology of the United States House of Representatives, "Smith Reiterates Demand for NOAA Communications after Allegations Climate Study Was Rushed," Press Release (Nov. 18, 2015).

45. The EPA measures trends in air quality in two ways: emissions and ambient levels. The ambient levels are the key measure of potential health effects because they are a physical measurement (through monitors) of the actual concentration of pollutants in the air to which humans are exposed. Emissions are derived from modeled estimates of the volume of pollutants released into the air by human activities. The same volume of emissions will generate different ambient levels depending on prevailing winds, temperature, humidity, and air pressure; EPA, "Our Nation's Air: Status and Trends." http://www.epa.gov/airtrends/2011/.

46. Hayward, Almanac of Environmental Trends (2011) 350.

47. Ibid., 10.

48. Ibid., 14.

49. Shawn Macomber, "The Man Who Saw Tomorrow," *American Spectator*, July 13, 2007.

50. Hayward, *2011 Almanac of Environmental Trends* (2011) 35.

51. Willie Soon, Ph.D., "A Scientific Reply to Specific Claims and Statements in EPA's Proposed NESHAP Rule, Focusing on Mercury Emission Issues," Science and Public Policy Institute (July 21, 2011).

52. Center for Disease Control and Prevention, National Health and Nutrition Examination Survey NHANES 2011-2012. See alsohttp://www2.epa.gov/sites/production/files/2015-10/documents/biomonitoring_mercury_data_tables.pdf.

53. "National Emission Standards for Hazardous Air Pollutants from Coal and Oil-Fired Electric Utility, Steam Generating Units and Standards of Performance for Fossil-Fuel Fired Electric Utility Industrial-Commercial-Industrial and Small Industrial-Commercial, Institutional Generating Units." 40 CFR Parts 60 and 63. Regulatory Impact Analysis, Federal Register 24976 (May 3 2011).

54. *Michigan v. E.P.A.*, 135 S. Ct. 2699, 2706, 192 L. Ed. 2d 674 (2015).

55. Robert Murray, Chairman, President and CEO of Murray Energy Corporation, Presentation before the Texas Public Policy Foundation, Crossroads Summit, November 19, 2015, Austin, Texas.

56. Ajay Lala et al., "Productivity in Mining Operations: Reversing Downward Trends," McKinsey and Company, May 2015.

57. Paul Tice, "Obama's Appalachian Tragedy," *Wall Street Journal*, November 30, 2015.

58. David Mercer, "FutureGen Carbon Capture Project to Shut Down After DOE Pulls Funding," *Associated Press* (Feb. 4, 2015).

59. Marlo Lewis, "Kemper CCS Project 3 Years Behind and $3.9 Billion Over Budget," GlobalWarming.org.

60. Hayward, *2011 Almanac of Environmental Trends* (2011) 35.

61. EIA, Monthly Energy Review March 2015; U.S. Department of Agriculture, Economic Research Service, December 2014; U.S. EPA, National Air Pollutant Trends & Market Program Database.

62. Ben Webster, "2500 New Coal Plants Will Thwart Any Paris Pledges," *The Times* (*December 2, 2015*). Institute for Energy Research, "Coal to Remain Major Power Source-Particularly in China," Latest Analysis, (December 21, 2015). Andrew Follett, "Chinese Coal Is Wrecking Obama's Global Warming Plan," *Daily Caller* (December 23, 2015).

63. M. Harvey Brenner, "Commentary: Economic Growth is the Basis of Decline of the Mortality Rate in the 20th Century Experience of the United States 1901-2000" Oxford University Press for the International Epidemiological Association (2005).

64. R. J. Donohue et al., "Impact of CO2 Fertilization on Maximum Foliage Cover Across Globe's Warm, Arid Environments," Geophysical Research Letters, Vol. 40 (2013) 3031–3035.

65. Ian Plimmer, *Heaven and Earth: Global Warming the Missing Science*, First published Connor Court Publishing Pty Ltd, Ballan, Victoria, Australia, 2009.

66. Craig D. Idso and Sherwood B. Idso, *The Many Benefits of Atmospheric CO2 Enrichment* (Vales Lake Publishing, Pueblo West, CO, 2011).

67. Ibid.

68. EPA, "Endangerment Cause or Contribute Findings for Greenhouse Gases Under Section 202 of the Clean Air Act," 40 CFR, Chapter 1, Federal Register 66496 (Dec. 15, 2009).

69. Prevention of Significant Deterioration and Title V Greenhouse Gas Tailoring Rule, 75 FR 31514-01.

70. David S. Schoenbrod, *Saving Our Environment from Washington: How Congress Grabs Power, Shirks Responsibility, and Shortchanges the People* (Yale University Press: Mar. 2005).

71. 42 U.S.C.A. § 7602(g) (West).

72. Hayward, *2011 Almanac of Environmental Trends* (2011) 68.

73. Vaclav Smil, "Just How Polluted Is China Anyway?" *The American*, American Enterprise Institute (Jan. 31, 2013).

74. Ibid.

75. Hayward, *2011 Almanac of Environmental Trends* (2011).

76. Ridley, *Rational Optimist*, 233.

77. State of the Union Speech, The White House 2013. https://www.whitehouse.gov/the-press-office/2013/02/12/remarks-president-state-union-address.

78. D. L. Hartman, et al., "Climate Change 2013: The Physical Science Basis, Contribution of Working Group I to the Fifth Assessment Report of the Intergovernmental Panel on Climate Change," (2013) (AR5 Ch.2) at 2.6.3.

79. Judith Curry, Chair of the School of Earth and Atmospheric Sciences, Georgia Institute of Technology, Statement to the Committee on Environment and Public Works, U.S. Senate (Jan. 16, 2014).

80. Indur Goklany, *Humanity Unbound*, 17–18.

81. Indur Goklany, *Wealth and Safety: The Amazing Decline in Deaths from Extreme Weather in an Era of Global Warming, 1900–2010* (2011) 6.

82. Goklany, *Humanity Unbound*, 18.

83. "U.S. EPA: Reducing Black Carbon in South Asia 2012," USEPA, Washington, D.C.

84. "World Energy Outlook, 2011, IEA Paris, France

85. Global Alliance for Clean Cook Stoves, United Nations, www.cleancookstoves.org.

86. Gautam N. Yadama, *Fires, Fuel, and the Fate of 3 Billion: The State of the Energy Impoverished* (Oxford University Press: Oct. 2013).

87. Ibid., foreword.

88. Charles Dickens, *The Old Curiosity Shop* (1841). Wordsworth Classics, 1995, pp. 346–348.

89. Kathleen Hartnett White, "Pope Francis's Poverty and Environment Ideas Will Worsen Both," *The Federalist* (June 25, 2015).

90. James Gwartney et al. "Economic Freedom of the World: Annual Report," The Fraser Institute, 2015. Yale Center for Environmental Law and Policy, "Environmental Performance Index," 2014. Terry Miller and Anthony Kim. *Index of Economic Freedom*, Heritage Foundation and Dow Jones & Company, *2015*.

91. EIA, Today in Energy," Oil and Natural Gas Sales Accounted for 68% of Russia's Total Export Revenues in 2013." Also www.eia.gov/beta/international/russia.

Chapter 11

1. Richard Durbin, April 24, 2007, http://www.durbin.senate.gov/newsroom/press-releases/increasing-broadband-access-to-improve-competitiveness

2. http://www.cfact.org/2015/12/13/reprieve-binding-paris-treaty-now-voluntary-mush/ (emphasis in original).

3. Bureau of Economic Analysis and Joint Economic Committee

4. U.S. Energy Information Administration, Independent Statistics & Analysis http://www.eia.gov/dnav/pet/pet_move_impcus_a2_nus_ep00_im0_mbbl_a.htm.

5. U.S. Energy Information Administration, Independent Statistics & Analysis http://www.eia.gov/dnav/pet/pet_move_impcus_a2_nus_ep00_im0_mbbl_a.htm.

6. U.S. Energy Information Administration, Independent Statistics & Analysis, http://www.eia.gov/dnav/pet/pet_cons_psup_dc_nus_mbbl_a.htm.

7. Institute for Energy Research, North American Energy Inventory, http://instituteforenergyresearch.org/wp-content/uploads/2013/01/Energy-Inventory.pdf.

8. https://www.whitehouse.gov/the-press-office/2012/03/21/remarks-president-energy.

9. U.S. Energy Information Administration. http://www.eia.gov/dnav/pet/hist/LeafHandler.ashx?n=PET&s=MCRFPUS1&f=A.

10. U.S. Energy Information Administration, Analysis & Projections. "U.S. Crude Oil Production to 2025: Updated Projection of Crude

Oil Types," May 28, 2015. http://www.eia.gov/analysis/petroleum/crudetypes/.

11.   U.S. Energy Information Administration, Annual Energy Overview, Table 1.2 Primary Energy Production by Source, 2014 total http://www.eia.gov/totalenergy/data/monthly/pdf/sec1_5.pdf.

12.   U.S. Energy Information Administration, Annual Energy Outlook 2015, http://www.eia.gov/forecasts/aeo/.

13.   Institute for Energy Research, "EIA Report: Subsidies Continue to Roll In For Wind and Solar," March 18, 2015. http://instituteforenergyresearch.org/analysis/eia-subsidy-report-solar-subsidies-increase-389-percent/.

14.   Pew Research Center, "Keystone XL Pipeline Divides Democrats," March 19, 2014. http://www.people-press.org/2014/03/19/keystone-xl-pipeline-divides-democrats/.

15.   The World Bank, World Development Indicators, CO2 emissions (metric tons per capita). http://data.worldbank.org/indicator/EN.ATM.CO2E.PC.

16.   "U.S. Crude Oil Export Decision, IHS Global, Inc., 2014. https://www.ihs.com/info/0514/crude-oil.html.

17.   Gene Whitney, Carl E. Behrens, and Carol Glover. "U.S. Fossil Fuel Resources: Terminology, Reporting, and Summary," Congressional Research Service, November 30, 2010. Report R40872. http://www.epw.senate.gov/public/_cache/files/04212e22-c1b3-41f2-b0ba-0da5eaead952/crs-november2010.pdf.

18.   https://energycommerce.house.gov/sites/republicans.energycommerce.house.gov/files/Hearings/EP/20120328/HHRG-112-IF03-WState-ColemanJ-20120328.pdf.

19.   Institute for Energy Research, North American Energy Inventory, http://instituteforenergyresearch.org/wp-content/uploads/2013/01/Energy-Inventory.pdf.

20.   "Assessment of Undiscovered Technically Recoverable Oil and Gas Resources of the Nation's Outer Continental Shelf, 2011 (Includes 2014 Atlantic Update)," at page 5. U.S. Department of the Interior,

Bureau of Ocean Energy Management, Revised December 2014. http://www.boem.gov/2011-National-Assessment-Factsheet/.

21. "Assessment of Undiscovered Technically Recoverable Oil and Gas Resources of the Nation's Outer Continental Shelf, 2011 (Includes 2014 Atlantic Update)," at page 5. U.S. Department of the Interior, Bureau of Ocean Energy Management, Revised December 2014. http://www.boem.gov/2011-National-Assessment-Factsheet/.

22. "Assessment of Undiscovered Technically Recoverable Oil and Gas Resources of the Nation's Outer Continental Shelf, 2011 (Includes 2014 Atlantic Update)," at page 5. U.S. Department of the Interior, Bureau of Ocean Energy Management, Revised December 2014. http://www.boem.gov/2011-National-Assessment-Factsheet/.

23. "Assessment of Undiscovered Technically Recoverable Oil and Gas Resources of the Nation's Outer Continental Shelf, 2011 (Includes 2014 Atlantic Update)," at page 5. U.S. Department of the Interior, Bureau of Ocean Energy Management, Revised December 2014. http://www.boem.gov/2011-National-Assessment-Factsheet/.

24. "Assessment of Undiscovered Technically Recoverable Oil and Gas Resources of the Nation's Outer Continental Shelf, 2011 (Includes 2014 Atlantic Update)," at page 5. U.S. Department of the Interior, Bureau of Ocean Energy Management, Revised December 2014. http://www.boem.gov/2011-National-Assessment-Factsheet/.

25. Hearing before the Subcommittee on Energy and Power of the Committee on Energy and Commerce, House of Representatives, Serial No. 112-133, March 28, 2012. Page 154. http://www.gpo.gov/fdsys/pkg/CHRG-112hhrg78365/pdf/CHRG-112hhrg78365.pdf.

26. Energy Policy Act of 2005, Sections 1421-1424, Public Law 109-58,August 8, 2005. http://www.gpo.gov/fdsys/pkg/PLAW-109publ58/pdf/PLAW-109publ58.pdf.

27. H.R. 6, 109th Congress, Title XXIII, Section 2302. http://www.gpo.gov/fdsys/pkg/BILLS-109hr6eh/pdf/BILLS-109hr6eh.pdf.

28. Statement of W. Jackson Coleman before the United States Senate Committee on Energy and Natural Resources, May 17, 2011, Page

3. http://www.energy.senate.gov/public/index.cfm/files/serve?File_id=fe36d378-0cef-84cd-3414-75d74e48f39b.

29. http://www.eia.gov/tools/faqs/faq.cfm?id=29&t=6.

30. http://www.manhattan-institute.org/html/eper_10.htm.

31. Institute for Energy Research, "EIA Report: Subsidies Continue to Roll In For Wind and Solar," March 18, 2015. http://instituteforenergyresearch.org/analysis/eia-subsidy-report-solar-subsidies-increase-389-percent/.

INDEX